INTRODUCTION TO ADVERTISING MEDIA

RESEARCH, PLANNING, AND BUYING

INTRODUCTION TO
ADVERTISING
MEDIA

RESEARCH, PLANNING, AND BUYING

JIM SURMANEK

Printed on recyclable paper

NTC Business Books
a division of *NTC Publishing Group* • Lincolnwood, Illinois USA

Library of Congress Cataloging-in-Publication Data

Surmanek, Jim.
    Introduction to advertising media : research, planning, and buying
/ Jim Surmanek.
       p. cm.
   Includes index.
   1. Advertising media planning. I. Title.
HF5826.5.S85 1993
659.1'11—dc20   92-9134
                                             CIP

1994 Printing

Published by NTC Business Books, a division of NTC Publishing Group
4255 West Touhy Avenue
Lincolnwood (Chicago), Illinois 60646-1975, U.S.A.
© 1993 by NTC Publishing Group. All rights reserved.
  4 5 6 7 8 9 0 VP 9 8 7 6 5 4 3 2

*For tolerating being a book widow . . . for
her understanding and constant support . . .
and for being the most important person
in my life, I dedicate this book, with
love, to my wife, Paula.*

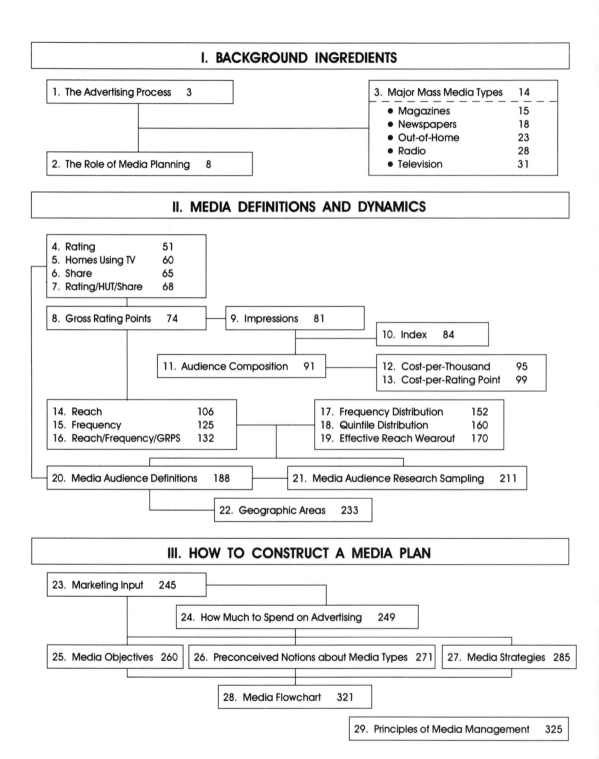

Contents

Acknowledgments

As is usually the case with books like this one, many people directly and indirectly contributed their knowledge, wisdom and support.

I thank my early teachers at Ogilvy & Mather who taught me about advertising and especially how to be a student of this profession. I'm indebted to Jack Hill for hiring me and teaching me the fundamentals and intricacies of media research; to Ken Caffrey, Mike Drexler, and Jules Fine for guiding me through the learning process of media planning; to David Ogilvy for fostering an atmosphere for learning and for being the superb teacher he is.

I thank the many people who took their personal time to gather some facts and figures and who gave me ideas for what to include in this book: Ro Campbell, Sue Gomez, Laura Loveday, Paul Silverman and Lisa Strassman.

I thank Michelle de Castro who labored after hours and on weekends to type my manuscript and who never once objected to the many changes I made as this work unfolded.

I also thank the people who provided me with background material and information about their organizations, and who have allowed me to write about their companies: Kevin Beaumont (Arbitron), Byron Chandler (TAB), Joan Cheramonte (Simmons), Julie Ann Cohn (Donnelley), Jack Dempster (ACT Media), Steven Dyer (A. C. Nielsen), Debbie Ewing (A.C. Nielsen), Julie Goldsmith (Birch/Scarborough), Mark Harris (Gannett), Chuck Levinson (CAB), Bruce MacEvoy (SRI, International), Dan Mahan (NAB), Julie Muer (TDI), Miriam Murphy (RADAR), Solomon Ortasse (Claritas), Bill Shaeffer (Arbitron), Chetah Shah (MRI), Carl Spaulding (Mediaplan, Inc.) and Jacqueline Tobak (Monroe Mendelsohn).

Introduction

What this book is all about

This book is all about selecting media for advertising purposes. Media are mass communication vehicles, like magazines, newspapers, outdoor, radio, and television. This book investigates and summarizes how these media work—how they distribute themselves to people and how people "consume" them.

On the one hand, understanding how an advertising medium works is easy. As you probably know, you can place a commercial in a television program. The people watching that program will see your commercial. On the other hand, the process and dynamics of this simple commercial placement are far more complex. You should know, for example, what the *rating* of the TV program was and what it might be in the future; if it's a *network* or *spot* announcement; what the *coverage* pattern is; what the *demographic profile* of the viewers is; how many commercials you need to place to have *effective reach*; how many commercials can air before there is *wearout*; what the *cost-per-thousand* is vis a vis alternatives, and so on.

All of these questions contain a specialized language (jargon) which is part and parcel of understanding the dynamics of advertising media. This book defines that jargon and other concepts peculiar to advertising media planning.

The entire spectrum of advertising media outlets changes almost daily. There are constantly new magazines being published, new radio stations, and old radio stations that change their format, new television programs, new ways to reach people within television, and new technologies that are having a direct effect not only on the media you know today, but also on the media forms that will be introduced tomorrow.

This book touches on all the major mass media outlets in existence today and how you might go about selecting one or another medium to carry your advertising message. But no book on the subject of media is ever totally current. From the time this manuscript was completed until the publisher printed the first copy, new media forms came on the scene, new media research has been conducted, new evaluation tools have been devised. The *concepts* discussed in this book will generally hold true, but the specifics will always change. To partially overcome changing specifics, most of the explanations, charts, and exhibits are based on hypothetical data rather than real-world numbers.

Much has been written in other books, pamphlets, and advertising industry periodicals by a host of advertising experts about advertising media. There are entire books, for example, on just the radio medium, cable television, direct marketing, advertising strategy, and so on. Digesting that storehouse of literature would be extremely beneficial to anyone desiring to understand the complexities of media planning. This book is not meant to replace that library. Its purpose is to highlight the dynamics of media planning—from the formulation of advertising objectives through the strategic use of media to accomplish goals; from understanding the relationship of one medium to another to comprehending the relationship between various analytical devices used to evaluate media.

How this book can be used

Dealing with the decision-making process in media planning requires a three-dimensional perspective. When choosing a medium you need to know how many different kinds of people consume that medium (width), how many people in total are part of that medium's audience (height), and the period of time it takes to reach those audiences with your advertising message (length). Additionally, many of the concepts and mechanics of media are interrelated and interdependent, thus also forcing a 3-D perspective.

Current physical laws require this book be produced in two dimensions. Further, current publishing formats demand it be written in some form of sequential order—starting at page one ... starting with *something*. This book does that. But it also allows you to start anywhere you wish. It's divided into three sections for your convenience in selecting a topic about which you have most interest. It's also organized within each section in both a sequential order and in terms of interrelationships. The Schematic Table of Contents allows you to pick a specific subject (such as "Reach") and simultaneously see the other concepts which affect that subject (such as "GRPs").

If you are relatively new to advertising media planning, you might best start at page one. If you are somewhat familiar with the many terms and concepts used in media planning, you could start anywhere else, referring to the Glossary or Index whenever you encounter an unfamiliar term. If you are not sure about your level of knowledge, you could turn to those pages in Part II, "Media Definitions and Dynamics," which are entitled Professional Workshop. These pages present a series of questions about each concept or media dynamic. If you are able to easily answer all these questions, you certainly do not need to labor through reading all of Part II.

Lastly, if after studying all that is contained in this book, you need review a particular media formula (e.g., converting CPP to CPM) you could turn to the last several pages, which contain a series of the most commonly used formulas.

PART I

BACKGROUND INGREDIENTS

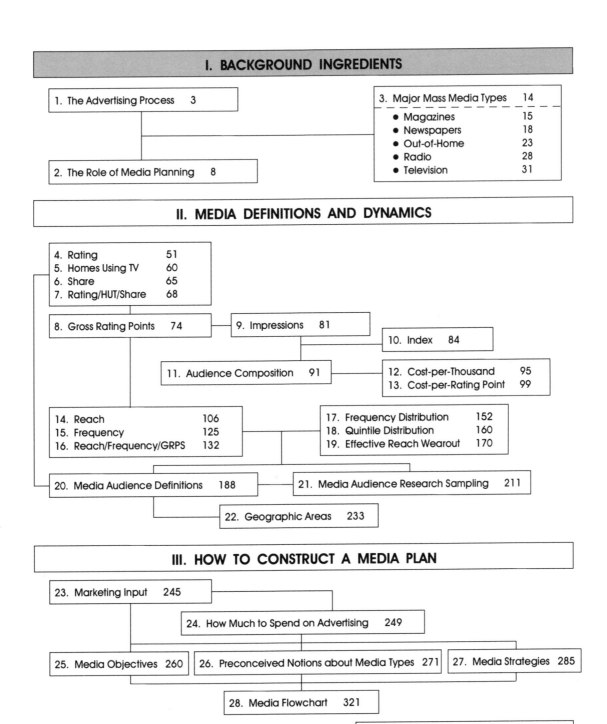

Chapter 1

The Advertising Process

I n this chapter we summarize how advertising fits into the overall marketing effort. We highlight some of the questions advertisers must face *before* advertising is created, such as what is the advertising supposed to accomplish. We also highlight the various types of advertising companies which create and place advertising.

You're eight years old and open up a lemonade stand in front of your home. As a youngster with more experience than reflected by your years, you establish a financial plan to determine your costs, probable revenue, and gross profit. You predict you will sell 50 drinks each week (all on Saturday, the only day you can devote to this effort). You calculate your expenses for this anticipated volume:

- manufacturing: lemons, sugar, water, ice.
- distribution: wood, nails and paint for signage, pitcher, cups.
- labor: your anticipated hourly wage times the number of hours.

Your total expenses divided by total anticipated sales equals a cost of 8 cents per drink. You decide to charge customers 10 cents and thereby seek a 2 cent profit (a healthy 20 percent margin).

Alas, you find you are not selling as many drinks as you expected. Your costs exceed your revenue. You are operating at a loss. What to do?

After some research and analysis you discover the probable cause of low sales volume is lack of consumer awareness that your lemonade stand exists. Not enough people are passing by your stand or coming to it on purpose. You conclude that advertising is necessary and set out to launch an awareness campaign.

You create and produce fliers which you distribute to every home within a reasonable distance of your stand. You place signage at strategic points around the block. Although you invest additional money for this advertising (paper, ink, paint, tape, tacks, labor) you're hopeful that sales volume will increase beyond your original expectations, thereby lowering your proportionate cost per drink back to the 8 cent level.

It turns out you're right. More people come to the stand. Sales are skyrocketing. Demand becomes greater than your supply. You open a second stand, then a third. You start selling franchises to your friends. As your business grows, economy of scale reduces your cost per drink. Your profits soar.

Noting your success, a competitor comes on the scene offering essentially the same product but at a lower cost. Wary of losing business, you lower your prices, which cuts into your profit margin but still allows you to stay in business. Your competitor announces a "two drinks for the price of one" special promotion. You counter with a "free cookie with every drink." They announce a new formula which is sugar-free. You introduce "caffeine-free diet lemonade." Throughout all of this, advertising is a critical ingredient. By making people aware of your product, you generated sales. By letting them know you have a special cookie offer, you kept them coming back for repeat purchases. By announcing a new product formulation, your competitor was able to entice new customers.

Whether it's lemonade or toothpaste, cars or cosmetics, the same marketing/advertising process takes place—from manufacturing to distribution to sales. Just as advertising played a role in the sale of your lemonade, so it does—albeit in a much more complicated arena—with just about all products and services. Advertising takes on the same charge: making people aware and giving them reason to buy.

There have been many research studies suggesting advertising is a critical ingredient in the marketing of a product or service, and that it stands the test of return-on-investment. Advertising does not, however, *guarantee* success. It merely gives a product a better chance of success than it would have if it was not advertised. The chance for success is directly dependent on the quality and effectiveness of the advertising message as well as the breadth, scope, quality, and effectiveness of the media delivery placed behind the advertising message. Unlike the simple effort of producing a flier stating "Cold Lemonade on Sale" and distributing the flier around the neighborhood, advertising requires a disciplined approach that takes into consideration the innumerable questions that arise as part of the advertising process. The answers to these questions mold the advertising plan and provide a road map to guide the journey that leads to creating and placing advertising.

The macro-questions that need answering are basically two:

1. What is the advertising supposed to accomplish?

2. To whom should the advertising be directed?

Within the macro-questions are many micro-questions, each one critically important. Answers to all these questions form the basic advertising strategy that will be followed in creating and placing the advertising. Some of these questions are:

1. *How will the product be positioned to the consumer?* Going back to lemonade, will it be positioned as the best tasting? Most refreshing? Most filling? Best value given the quantity and the cost of the drink? Most healthy? Least expensive? Most glamorous liquid you can drink? Most sociable drink to have and to serve?

2. *What creative execution elements are most effective?* Is a combination of sight, sound, and motion necessary? Is color needed? Is a spokesperson needed—celebrity or person-on-the-street? Must a cents-off coupon be distributed to potential customers? Must the advertising have long copy or can it be as effective with short copy? Must the advertising be large in scope (e.g., longer TV commercials or larger print advertisements)?

3. *How much will be spent on advertising?* What sales might be expected as a result of spending at a level of X versus Y or Z? At what level of expenditure does advertising "pay out"? How much must be spent to deliver what is perceived as a threshold level of advertising messages? What level of expenditure is needed to sustain advertising during a needed period of time?

4. *To whom should the advertising be directed?* Which demographic group of people is most likely to buy this product? What is

their age, individual income, household income, marital status, education level, and occupation? What are their lifestyle characteristics? Is there a secondary or tertiary group of people that should also be addressed? What is the quantity and value of one group versus another?

5. *Where should advertising be directed*? Throughout the United States or only in certain geographic areas? More in some areas than others? How much for each area?

6. *When should advertising be scheduled*? Throughout the year or only during certain seasons or months or weeks? All week or only on certain days? All day or only during certain times of the day?

7. *Which media should be used*? TV? Radio? Magazines? Newspapers? Outdoor posters? Subways? Bus sides? Bus shelters? Kiosks? Walls? Direct mail? Yellow pages? Skywriting? . . .

8. *Which component of the medium should be used*? Within television: broadcast, cable, or both? Within radio: national, regional, or local? Within print media: national, regional, or local? . . .

9. *What specific media placement will be made*? Which TV or radio programs? Which magazines or newspapers? Which sections of magazines? Which sections of newspapers? What are the locations of outdoor posters? Which bus routes? . . .

Most often an advertiser will seek help from advertising professionals to answer these questions and to devise an advertising plan. These professionals are sometimes employees of the advertiser (usually called an *in-house agency*) and sometimes outside professionals. Outside professionals generally are within one or more of the following categories:

1. **Consultant**—a person (or company of people) who directly creates an advertising plan, as well as the advertising and its media execution, or who oversees and coordinates all the elements of the advertising plan which are produced by other advertising suppliers. Consultants can be generalists or specialists and often have working titles such as marketing consultant, advertising consultant, creative consultant, or media consultant.

2. **Creative Boutique**—a company that specializes in the *creation* of advertising: writing and producing television and radio

commercials, print advertisements, etc. The creative boutique usually does not have substantial staffing, if any, for functions outside the specific creative arena such as market research, marketing, strategic planning, media planning, and media buying.

3. **Media Buying Service**—a company that specializes in the *placement* of advertising in various media and often also advises the advertiser on which media to be used to accomplish the advertising objectives. This latter function is generally known as a *media planning* capability.

4. **Advertising Agency**—a company that provides the multiple advertising services needed by the advertiser. Most medium-sized and large advertising agencies are considered "full-service" in that they provide nearly all needed services. Most small and some medium-sized agencies provide many of the needed services, but traditionally do not have a media department for planning and buying media—relying, more often than not, on a media buying service to accomplish these tasks. The services provided by a full-service agency usually encompass, at minimum, the functions shown in the left column of the following chart, and might also provide the services shown in the right column. All of the services shown in the right column are provided by specialty companies, which are either independently operated or owned or affiliated with other advertising companies:

Services Usually Provided by Ad Agencies	Other Services—Provided Either by Full-Service Agencies or Specialty Companies
• Marketing expertise	• Direct Response Advertising
• Market Research	• Sales Promotion
• Strategic Planning	• Sports Marketing
• Creative	• Ethnic Marketing/ Advertising
• Media Research	• Yellow Pages
• Media Planning	• Event Marketing
• Media Buying	• Public Relations

As advertising is a critical ingredient in the marketing process, so media planning is a critical element in the advertising process. Whether the advertiser opts for a consultant, boutique, buying service, advertising agency, specialty company, or any combination of these services, media planning is involved.

Chapter 2

The Role of Media Planning

I n this chapter we discuss the role of media planning and, specifically, the role of the media planner in the advertising process. We examine various points-of-view about what advertising media are and what they are supposed to accomplish. We also explain the thought processes of a media planner in analyzing quantitative and qualitative information about media.

Some might argue that a powerful creative message, brilliantly executed, can produce consumer awareness and stimulate sales. A further argument is that the media vehicles carrying that message are of little or no importance, because the advertising itself is just that good. It can also be safely argued that an ineffective, poorly produced advertising message stands little or no chance of convincing consumers to buy, regardless of the general effectiveness of the selected media in which the advertising appears. Because none of these arguments has ever been proven, they are open to question.

One argument, although not necessarily proven, is logical and stands on safe ground: great creative carried by highly effective media vehicles will probably give a product the best chance of success. The two cannot be separated. You cannot have great creative that leads to product sales unless consumers are exposed to the advertising by seeing it, hearing it, or both, in the media they consume. The extent to which the chosen media deliver the same people as those to whom the advertising message is written is the extent to which the advertising is most effective. Also, advertising has a greater opportunity to be effective when the chosen media reflect the tone, manner, and executional elements of the creative message, by nature of their programming or editorial environment or physical location.

This is not to say that media planning is as simple as choosing a medium that is apparently an extension of the creative message, such as placing a commercial for a food product in the environment of a television program about cooking. This can be, and often should be, a consideration in the media selection process, but it is only one of the many considerations that are part of media planning.

No component of the advertising process can be devised and implemented in a vacuum. Each component must contribute to the others and must be focused on achieving the same overall advertising communication goal. Although the people involved in the advertising process might be expert in one or another discipline (market research, copywriting, art direction, media planning, etc.), all are first and foremost part of a professional advertising force. Although different disciplines might march to different beats at different times, the combined advertising force must operate within the same strategic guidelines and accomplish the same specific advertising objective.

As will be seen in the remainder of this book, media planning requires dealing with a host of variables and phenomena which affect the media forms selected and the extent to which these forms are used. The knowledge and skills of the media planner are often brought to bear on nearly all aspects of the advertising process. There may be either direct or indirect involvement in analyses or in answering the many questions that need answering; and there certainly is a direct contribution in terms of recommending media forms and purchasing the media.

The Role of the Media Planner

On the one hand, media planning is merely a science which requires analysis of *quantitative* information and concludes with a plan of action. One of the simpler analyses for magazines, for example, might follow this path:

- List audience delivery for each magazine.

- List the cost for an advertising insertion.

- Divide the cost by audience delivery to determine the cost efficiency (cost per person delivered).

- Rank the magazines from most cost efficient (lowest cost per person delivered) to least cost efficient.

- Recommend the purchase of magazines according to the rank order shown until no funds remain in the advertising budget.

On the other hand, there is a belief that *qualitative* factors overshadow quantitative information and should, therefore, be the guiding force in media selection. Just a few of the many factors used to decide magazine selection, for example, might be these:

- Editorial environment—does it reflect what is being said in the creative message? Is the environment conducive to reception of the advertising?

- Quality of reproduction—Will your advertisement be reproduced with the highest standards of registration and color?

- Positioning of advertisement—Will your ad be positioned within the pages of the magazine to give it the best opportunity to be read?

- Perceived reaction to the advertisement—Will the reader of a specific magazine take action as a result of seeing your advertisement?

Which point of view leads to the best media plan: decisions based on quantitative analysis, or decisions based on qualitative considerations? The answer lies partly in the expectation of what advertising media are supposed to accomplish, and partly in the definition of the role of what a media planner is supposed to contribute to the advertising plan.

In the advertiser's view, advertising media are devices for delivering audiences (which the advertiser defines as consumers). Consumers may see media as sources of entertainment or information—they are entertained by viewing a movie on TV or informed by reading a newspaper. But advertisers see media as a conduit for communication about their product. From the advertiser's perspective, therefore, a medium's reason-for-being is to put bodies in front of the advertising carried by that medium— to expose advertising to the people who are consuming the medium.

From the media supplier's point of view, media perform both functions. First, to give consumers—their audiences—a reason to consume the medium and second, to give advertisers a reason to place advertising in that medium. No advertising medium can exist and thrive without people wanting to consume it, and none can exist within their current financial framework without paid advertising carried in the medium.*

Media suppliers must first offer an audience to the advertiser: the people viewing their television program or listening to their radio program, or reading their periodical, etc. The quantity and the kinds of people that make up the audience are a result of the programming or editorial offering or the physical location of the medium—not a result of the kind of advertising that is carried by the medium. People do not view a television program because of its advertising. They view it because it fulfills their needs and wants at that particular time (because of what the program is all about—the actors and actresses, the quality of writing and production, etc.). The television programmer strives to fulfill these wants and desires, hoping that people will view the show. If people do view the show, the media supplier has something to sell to the advertiser: audience. Yes, there are media which are partially consumed *because* of the advertising (some fashion magazines, coupon mailings, etc.), but the same general concept of consumer expectation fulfillment is operative.

At this juncture we can conclude that *quantitative* analyses should form the foundation for all media planning because, from the advertiser's point of view or, in part, from the media supplier's view, advertising media deliver audiences via paid insertions into the products they produce: commercials in TV or radio programs, ads in magazines, etc. The role of the media planner is, therefore, to find those media that deliver the people with whom the advertiser wants to communicate. But what of quality and effectiveness?

Let's step back and confirm why media vehicles are used in the first place. Clearly, the most important ingredient in an advertising plan is the advertising. Without the creative product there is no plan. Without a creative message to consumers, there is no advertising. At the hub of the entire advertising process is the creative message. All forces concentrate on and contribute to

---

* Although there are media that do not rely on advertiser support, none is part of an advertiser's considered set and therefore none is pertinent to this exploration of media selection.

the creation and delivery of the advertising. The media planner must, therefore, select the media that not only deliver the "bodies" but also simultaneously fuel the creative message by making sure it is exposed to the consumer in the most effective way possible.

How the consumer might receive the advertising message is critically important. The "how" certainly depends on the creative message itself, but also very much on the mind-set of the consumer at the time he or she is exposed to the advertising. Clearly, a person's state of mind changes throughout the day and over time. This state of mind has a cause-and-effect relationship with the actions a person takes. Some of these actions involve media consumption: which TV program will be viewed, which radio station will be listened to, which magazine article or newspaper section will be read. As you might attest looking at your own media consumption pattern, people sometimes deliberately tune in to a TV program intending to view it or deliberately pick up a magazine to read it, but sometimes not. Sometimes people tune in to TV to fill a room with noise or scan through a magazine to fill a time void. During these various media consumption periods, a person has different degrees of receptivity—both to the media vehicle and to the advertising within that vehicle.

Not all people pay full attention to a TV program or voraciously read every page of a magazine. The mind-set people bring to the media consumption period affects their receptivity to the advertising message. And even if they intend to deliberately consume that medium—that is, pay full attention to it—there are other dynamics that could be at play at a specific time which also might affect their receptivity. For instance, the degree to which they like the TV show, preoccupation with what happened at the office that day, or dinner preparation while viewing TV are all factors that affect receptivity.

There are reams of paper and millions of bytes on computer disks of quantitative data to help the media planner find the right audiences for a specific product. There is also a goodly number of market and media research studies which address the issues of audience receptivity and advertising effectiveness on a *general* basis. Additionally, there are product-specific case histories which can help decide media selection—sometimes published, sometimes proprietary. All of this vast storehouse of information is no more than a guide. It is based on past situations—past performance of the media vehicles. It says nothing of future performance. It is usually based on a sampling of the population, not on the entire population. It reflects media and product performance in a particular competitive environment in a particular economy. It does not purport to predict performance in a changed environment or economy.

Is media planning a science or an art? It is both. The media planner must consider himself or herself a money manager looking for the greatest return on the advertising investment, but he or she must step back and consider the *value* of the media selected to accomplish the advertising task. More often than not, value transcends numbers. A media plan based solely on numbers will produce the lowest cost-per-person or the highest amount of audience delivery, but it will not necessarily produce the most effective advertising effort. *Effectiveness* of the media program, and not necessarily efficiency, is a key criterion in the development and execution of a media program. *Cost-per-results* instead of cost-per-person must be the watchword. The role of the media planner must be to bring together the message and the right audience efficiently and effectively.

Chapter 3

Major Mass Media Types

This chapter introduces the various major mass media forms, and the sub-segments of these media, which are used for advertising. We look at the historical beginnings of each of these media and track their growth into the 1990s. We discuss the kinds of advertising units the media offer for sale to advertisers, such as a full-page advertisement in a magazine or a thirty-second commercial on television.

There is an abundance of media available for advertising—from doorknob hangers to commercials on national TV, and everything in between. In 1990, advertisers spent approximately $130 billion in various media to communicate their advertising message. Table 3.1 lists the proportions of this expenditure by media type

---

TABLE 3.1: U.S. Advertising Volume by Media Type

Mass Media		Other	
Magazines	5%	Direct Mail	19%
Newspapers	25	Yellow Pages	7
Outdoor	1	Other	14
Radio	7	Total:	100%
Television	22		

Source: McCann-Erickson

This book concentrates on those media that are commonly called *mass media*. Conceivably a misnomer, the term "mass media" is nevertheless used because these media characteristically are able to reach a large quantity of people in all markets throughout the United States. Direct mail, yellow pages, and even doorknob hangers can also reach the masses, but these media are generally considered a specialized form of communication for which a different set of analytical tools are needed than those reviewed in this book. Indeed, the subjects of direct mail, et al., are amply covered in other publications.

It should be noted that direct mail is but one vehicle used in *direct response* advertising. The primary differences between direct response advertising (regardless of the media vehicle used) and general mass advertising are these:

- Direct strives for *interaction* with the consumer. It tries to get the consumer to take immediate action as a result of seeing the advertising message—such as calling a 1–800 number or mailing back a response card to the advertiser. General advertising also strives to get consumers to take action, but not in an interactive way. General advertising asks consumers, for example, to buy product X next time they are in a supermarket.

- Direct attempts to sell to *individuals*, identifying to the extent possible the name and address of the prospective consumer. General advertising, again, is directed to the masses, identifying them in broad demographic/lifestyle terms.

Notwithstanding these differences in intent, direct response advertising is often carried in major mass media—magazines, newspapers, out-of-home, radio, and television. The audience delivery dynamics of mass media, therefore, are as important to understand for direct response as they are for general advertising.

Following are general descriptions of the five major mass media types, with specific emphasis on how each is configured for the purposes of advertising.

Magazines

In 1741 there were two magazines published in the United States. Andrew Bradford published the first one, *American Magazine*, which was on sale three days before Benjamin Franklin's *General Magazine*. Although neither publication is available today for advertising, over 11,000 others are. More than 2,000 of these are within the *consumer and farm publications* category, written and distributed for what we can label "the masses." See Table 3.2.

TABLE 3.2:   Number of Magazines

	Total U.S. Periodicals	Consumer & Farm Publications
1970	9,573	1,197
1975	9,657	1,163
1980	10,236	1,456
1985	11,090	1,805
1990	11,092	2,231

Source: Magazine Publishers Association

In recognition of a more affluent and better educated society, as well as magazine publishers' perception of reader interest in special interest or lifestyle editorial focuses, publishers have launched an average of 1.3 new magazines every day for the last several years. Although the majority are short-lived, many continue to be published. Table 3.3 highlights the growth in the number of magazines and their combined circulation as reported by the Audit Bureau of Circulation for the (currently) 541 magazines that are members of this organization.

TABLE 3.3:   Circulation of A.B.C. General & Farm Magazines

	# Magazines or Groups	Circulation (millions)
1970	302	244
1975	325	251
1980	407	286
1985	477	326
1990	541	363

Source: Magazine Association

Consumer magazines are generally classified according to their primary editorial focus—business, entertainment, men, women, general interest, sports, newsweekly, etc. The classification is merely a convenience when planners are considering the types of magazines that might be appropriate for a specific advertising effort. The classification, per se, has nothing to do with the audience size of a publication, or even necessarily the appropriateness of the magazine for a specific ad campaign. Table 3.4 lists the top 20 magazines according to circulation count. Note that circulation varies by magazine, rather than by classification.

TABLE 3.4: Circulation of Top 20 Magazines

	Circulation (millions)		Circulation (millions)
Parade	35.1	Good Housekeeping	5.2
Modern Maturity	22.4	McCall's	5.0
Reader's Digest	16.3	Ladies' Home Journal	5.0
TV Guide	15.6	Woman's Day	4.8
USA Weekend	15.5	Time	4.1
Sunday	15.4	Redbook	3.9
National Geographic	10.2	National Enquirer	3.8
Cable Guide	8.9	Playboy	3.5
Better Homes & Gardens	8.0	Star	3.4
Family Circle	5.4	Sports Illustrated	3.2

Source: Audit Bureau of Circulation

Also notable in this table is the inclusion of *Parade* and *Sunday*, both of which are also referred to as *Sunday Magazines* or *Newspaper Distributed Magazines* or *Syndicated Supplements* or simply *Supps*. In addition to these two national supps are two others (as shown in Table 3.5). All four are centrally published, distributed in metropolitan newspapers, and usually appear within the Sunday edition. Although commonly considered magazines, supps often fall within the classification of newspapers, especially those supps that

TABLE 3.5: Newspaper Distributed Magazines

	# Newspapers Carrying	Circulation (millions)
Parade	338	35.1
Sunday	29	15.4
USA Weekend	308	16.4
Vista	20	.9

are locally edited and published by the major daily newspapers (as discussed in the next section, Newspapers).

Magazine advertising can be purchased nationally, regionally, or locally. The larger national magazines often offer opportunities for purchasing less than national circulation in predetermined geographic areas (for example, the Northeast, or the state of Florida, or the Chicago Metropolitan Area). Additionally many magazines circulate only in defined areas, such as *Sunset* on the West Coast, or various local magazines designated only for specific cities.

Some national magazines also offer demographic editions whereby an advertiser can buy space that runs only in copies directed to particular audiences—doctors, businesspeople, upper income groups, etc.

There are an enormous number of advertising units available in magazines—ranging from a small classified-type ad to full color pages and multiple pages to just about anything you can imagine that can be printed. These advertisements are generally printed by the publisher but can also be preprinted by an outside supplier and inserted into the magazine. You need only thumb through a few issues of several magazines to get a good sense of the wide variety of creative units available in magazines.

Newspapers

Advertising in newspapers goes as far back as newspapers themselves—back to the 1600s. The first ads ran free because the publishers believed they contained information that was a vital part of the news that readers expected from the newspaper. As the centuries rolled by, publishers started charging advertisers for the space their ads occupied. Sales agents were recruited to *sell* advertising space to local advertisers to help defray the cost of publishing and to increase the publishers' profits. These agents then started selling advertising space to "foreign" advertisers in distant cities. "Agencies" sprang up to represent national advertising clients in dealing with local newspaper advertising. With the support from advertising, traveling salesmen put national brands into stores from coast to coast. Some of this advertising began to move out of print and into radio and eventually into television. As the media choices proliferated and products obtained national distribution, agencies expanded their services to their clients by providing "creative" and "media buying" expertise. Today we refer to these agencies as *advertising agencies*.

There are over 6,000 newspapers in the United States that accept advertising. Those with the largest circulation are metropolitan daily newspapers, which may distribute in the morning, evening, all day, and often on Saturday and Sunday. The average metro daily has a Monday-through-Friday daily circulation of 39,000 (higher in morning than in evening editions) and a 73,000 circulation on Sunday. Suburban weeklies, which generally service smaller communities, average 19,000 circulation. Some suburban weeklies publish more frequently than once weekly. The average college newspaper (mostly published once weekly) has a circulation of 5,000. National dailies (*Christian Science Monitor, Investors Daily, USA Today*, and *The Wall Street Journal*) average nearly a million circulation. See Tables 3.6 and 3.7.

TABLE 3.6: Number of Newspapers and Circulation

	# Papers	Circulation (000) Total	Average
Metropolitan Dailies*			
Daily	1,611	62,328	39
Morning	559	41,312	74
Evening	1,084	21,019	19
Sunday	863	62,635	73
Suburban Weeklies**	3,041	37,177	12
College Newspapers**	1,692	7,720	5
National Newspapers	4	3,628	907

* Includes some "all day" papers.
** Published with varying frequencies.
Source: American Newspaper Directory of Community Newspapers; Cass College Newspaper Directory; Editor & Publisher Co.

Newspapers are one of the more geographically flexible media forms. In addition to availabilities in small suburban communities and colleges, a number of the larger metropolitan dailies also offer zoned editions which cover specific smaller areas within the metropolitan area.

Nearly every metro daily (and especially the larger dailies) offers its readers, and therefore advertisers, various sections of the newspaper that concentrate on one or another specific editorial focus. The more popular sections, in addition to main news, are these:

Business, Finance
Entertainment
Fashion
Food
Home
Lifestyle, Women
Science
Sports
TV, Radio
Travel

TABLE 3.7:   Top Ten Metropolitan Daily Newspapers

| | Circulation (000) | |
	Daily	Sunday
Los Angeles Times	1,243	1,576
New York Times	1,209	1,762
Washington Post	839	1,166
Newsday	826	960
Chicago Tribune	741	1,131
New York Post	645	—
Detroit Free Press	622	1,215
San Francisco Chronicle	570	704
Chicago Sun-Times	538	559
Boston Globe	517	798

Source: Audit Bureau of Circulation, March 31, 1991.

Free Standing Insert (FSI) A preprinted advertising message which is inserted into, but not bound into, print media (generally into newspapers).

Many newspapers also carry supplementary material or periodicals, such as **Free Standing Inserts (FSIs)**, Sunday magazines, and comics. FSIs are preprinted inserts of one or more pages which are mostly 100 percent advertising and/or coupon offers.

In addition to the four syndicated supplements discussed in the previous section on magazines are five of the larger dailies which publish their own Sunday supp. Although primarily distributed through newspapers, supps (especially national supps) are commonly considered part of the magazine medium.

Newspaper-published:	Syndicated:
Chicago Tribune Magazine	*Parade*
Los Angeles Times Magazine	*Sunday*
New York Times Magazine	
San Francisco Examiner—Image	*USA Weekend*
The Washington Post Magazine	*Vista*

Broadsheet
Synonymous with a "standard" size newspaper, as compared to a "tabloid" size.

Tabloid A newspaper with pages smaller than the size of the standard "broadsheet" newspaper.

S.A.U. (Standard Advertising Unit) A measurement system for selecting and placing ad sizes in newspapers.

ROP Run-of-Press or Run-of-Paper. A position request to run an advertisement anywhere (unspecified) in the publication. Also commonly used to describe any form of newspaper advertising.

Newspapers are published in one of two sizes. A **broadsheet** paper generally measures 21 inches to 22 1/2 inches high by six columns wide; a **tabloid** is usually about 14 inches deep by five columns wide. A column generally measures 2 1/16 inches wide, with 1/8 inch between columns. A vast array of standardized and customized units are available to the advertiser. Most papers have adopted the **Standard Advertising Unit (SAU)** measurement system both in their advertising cost structure and in placement of advertisements on their pages. For example, as displayed in Exhibit 3.1, a full-page ad in a broadsheet measures 6 columns wide by FD (full depth); a 5 × 18 ad measures five columns wide by 18 inches deep.

Advertisements can be placed in any section of the newspaper. These can be black/white ads or, depending on the policy of the newspaper and the availability, color advertisements. The majority of newspapers offer color—either one color, two color, or full color (in addition to black/white), as shown in Table 3.8. The advertiser can stipulate an **ROP (Run-of-Paper)** ad, which allows the newspaper to place the advertisement on any page, or may request a specific section or specific position within a section. The later two placements usually require a premium price.

TABLE 3.8: Newspaper Color Availability

Metropolitan Areas	Cumulative Percent of Total Circulation Represented by Newspapers Offering Color		
	One Color	Two Colors	Full Color
Top 50	93%	86%	85%
Top 100	95	89	88
Top 200	96	91	89
Total U.S.	90	91	90

Source: Newspaper Advertising Bureau.

EXHIBIT 3.1:   Standard Advertising Unit System

Depth in Inches	1 COL. 2-1/16"	2 COL. 4-1/4"	3 COL. 6-7/16"	4 COL. 8-5/8"	5 COL. 10-13/16"	6 COL. 13"
			◄————————13"————————►			
FD*	1xFD*	2xFD*	3xFD*	4xFD*	5xFD*	6xFD*
18"	1x18	2x18	3x18	4x18	5x18	6x18
15.75"	1x15.75	2x15.75	3x15.75	4x15.75	5x15.75	
14"	1x14	2x14	3x14	4x14	N 5x14	6x14
13"	1x13	2x13	3x13	4x13	5x13	
10.5"	1x10.5	2x10.5	3x10.5	4x10.5	5x10.5	6x10.5
7"	1x7	2x7	3x7	4x7	5x7	6x7
5.25"	1x5.25	2x5.25	3x5.25	4x5.25		
3.5"	1x3.5	2x3.5				
3"	1x3	2x3				
2"	1x2	2x2				
1.5"	1x1.5					
1"	1x1					

Out-of-Home Media

Out-of-Home Media
Those media meant to be consumed only outside of one's home, e.g., outdoor, transit, in-store media.

The **out-of-home media** category encompasses a wide array of different forms, all with one thing in common: consumer exposure to these media occurs outside one's home (and also, for the most part, outside one's place of business). Unlike television, radio, magazines, and newspapers, out-of-home media usually do not provide any form of programming or editorial matter in which to place an advertising message. There are some minor exceptions where, for example, there might be non-advertising matter adjacent to the advertising message (such as a placard next to a clock), but the vast majority of these media units carry only advertising. With apologies to Marshall McLuhan, the medium is the advertising.

Out-of-home media are the second most geographically flexible media form, preceded only by direct mail. They can be purchased almost everywhere in the United States in any configuration of national or local placement, right down to the purchase of one outdoor poster on a specific street corner.

Billboard   In outdoor media, an advertising structure—see *Painted Bulletin*.

Out-of-home media became a commercial entity in the United States in the 1800s, when companies began leasing out space on wooden boards (fences) to post "bills"—hence the term **billboards**. The term *outdoor* is often used interchangeably with *out-of-home* media, but is technically only one of the forms available. The list of out-of-home media that appears in the rest of this section is extensive, but not exhaustive. It does not necessarily include every specific form, nor those currently in a testing mode, nor those which are on the entrepreneur's drawing board.

In-Store Media

These are media vehicles which are designed to reach consumers on-site, primarily in supermarkets, drug stores, convenience stores, and mass merchandise outlets. Following are the major forms currently available, organized by general type:

- Audio Systems. Depending on the system used, transmissions into the store are delivered by satellite or tape. Programming is usually entertainment and music, with one system offering a live disc jockey. Commercials are inserted every four to six minutes. The In-Store Satellite Network (ISN) is currently available in 3,500 stores in 29 markets; P.O.P. Radio is transmitted into 6,500 food stores and 7,900 drug stores.

- Couponing Systems. These are terminals which are used primarily to dispense coupons directly to consumers. The Savings Spot terminal is located near the entrance of stores (approximately 70 stores as of this writing); the Checkout Coupon terminal is located at the checkout counter (now in 3,300 supermarkets in 27 markets).

- Shelf Advertising. ActMedia, Inc. offers Shelftalk, Shelftake-One, Shelftalk RX and Shelftake-One RX. All are advertisements which extend from the store shelf. They are now used in 11,000 grocery stores and 6,000 drug stores.

- Signage. In-store signage is available in multiple forms—some of which are electronic. For example:
  - AisleVision—ads inserted in directories suspended above the aisles. Now available in 8,000 grocery stores in 176 markets.
  - Health Monitor Center—a freestanding machine for measuring blood pressure and pulse rate with a **backlit** advertising message in the unit. Nationwide, 5,200 units are available.
  - INSIGHT Aisle Marker—internally lighted aisle or area information center placed at the center or ends of the aisle.
  - In-Store Advertising—A structure containing a lighted electronic display (LED) which can be changed from a remote location. Now in 39 markets, 6,000 stores.
  - Look Ups—placards placed in convenience stores within a frame and usually on poles, with the placement determined by the advertiser. Available in 7,000 stores.
  - MediaOne—a two-sided backlit advertisement located at the checkout counter in 7,000 stores.
  - Superclocks—an illuminated display with a backlit advertisement next to a large clock. Available in 4,100 stores in 45 markets.

- Shopping Carts. Two major forms are available:
  - Shopping Cart Advertising—these are printed advertisements, in frames, attached to the shopping carts. Available in 8,000 grocery stores in 79 markets.
  - VideoCart—this looks like a small TV monitor hooked to the front of a shopping cart. The monitor shows commercials, price specials and other messages relevant to the cart's position in the store.

Backlit Describes an out-of-home display where the advertising message is printed on translucent plastic and backlit with fluorescent bulbs.

Outdoor

Poster Panel An outdoor advertising structure on which a preprinted advertisement is displayed.

Bleed In print media, to extend the illustration or copy to the edge of a page so there is no white border. In outdoor media, a poster panel that uses the entire available space.

Junior Panel A scaled-down version of a 30-sheet poster.

Sheets A way of designating poster panel size based on the number of pieces of paper originally needed to cover a poster panel area. It used to take 30 sheets to cover the average panel.

30-Sheet Poster A 10' by 22' poster panel.

8-Sheet Poster A 5' by 11' poster panel, also known as a *Junior Panel* because it has the same proportions as, but is smaller than, a 30-sheet poster.

Painted Bulletin (Paint) An outdoor advertising structure on which advertising is either painted directly or preprinted on special vinyl and affixed.

Poster panel—Poster panels can be either free-standing structures or units attached to the sides of buildings. They are offered in various sizes with the most common being 30-sheet (**bleed**— printed to edge of panel—or non-bleed), and *8-sheet* (also called a **junior panel**). The **sheets** refer to the number of pieces of paper originally needed to cover the panel area. At one time, posters were printed in 30 pieces, but with today's larger presses, the 30-sheet poster is usually printed using only 8 to 10 pieces of paper. Posters can be illuminated, offering nighttime visibility, or unlighted.

The advertising area on a **30-sheet poster** measures approximately 9' 7" high by 21' 7" wide. Surrounding this display is white blanking paper which usually resembles a mat used for framing a picture. Bleed posters, with a larger advertising area (10' 5" by 22' 8"), are either printed to the edges of the copy area or they require blanking paper printed to match the background. An **8-sheet poster**, which is printed on three sheets of paper, has the same proportions as a 30-sheet, but is produced in a smaller size: 5' by 11'. Although these junior panels are wider than they are high, some plant operators are beginning to offer *on-end* units to accommodate advertisements that are designed for vertical rather than horizontal presentation.

Painted bulletins—Painted bulletins are also called **paints** because they can accommodate advertising that is physically painted onto the structure, but paint is only one of the reproduction media that can be used for displaying advertising. Bulletins are generally free-standing structures erected alongside major highways, expressways, and tollways or in other high-traffic areas. The standard bulletin measures 14' high by 48' wide but can be larger or smaller. A *super bulletin*, for example, measures 20' by 60'.

The advertising on a bulletin can be reproduced using several techniques: painting directly onto the surface, hand-painting on paper then mounted on the bulletin, lithography, silk-screening, or opaque pvc/vinyl (a plastic material produced in one sheet and affixed to the face of the structure, which can be reproduced using the aforementioned reproduction devices as well as being computer-painted).

Permanent (Display or Bulletin)   An outdoor bulletin at a specific location—that is, the bulletin is not rotated to other locations. See *Rotary Display.*

Rotary Display   An option for purchasing painted bulletins whereby the display face is periodically rotated to new locations, as opposed to a *Permanent Bulletin.*

Bulletins are sold in two ways:

—**Permanent**—advertising remains fixed at one location for the duration of the purchase contract;

—**Rotary**—the display face is physically moved to a new location within the market at stated intervals—usually every 30, 60, or 90 days.

Permanent paints are sold by the individual unit on a one-year basis. Paints are usually given priority placement in a market and therefore generate higher levels of traffic (auto as well as pedestrian). They also have greater visual impact than posters. These advantages, combined with the fact that paints are more costly to produce, result in paints costing significantly more to purchase than posters.

Rotary painted bulletins can be purchased individually or in packages where all locations are changed periodically with no location being used more than once. This type of purchase depends on the availability in a market and/or the advertiser's requirement.

Transit

Transit advertising encompasses multiple media forms which have, as their common thread, a direct relationship with mass transit vehicles or locations. The more commonly used transit units are these:

Bus exteriors—These are displayed on the sides, front, or rear of a bus and come in various sizes (depending on the market). For example: "King" display is 27" by 141" mounted on bus sides; "Headlight" display is approximately 19" by 41"; "Taillight" display is approximately 19" by 68".

Clocks—These are located above platforms and in terminal corridors and accommodate advertising next to one or both sides of the clock. They are backlit.

Diorama   A backlit display often located in airports, bus terminals, and sports arenas.

Dioramas—Dioramas are wall-mounted units similar to 2-sheet posters. They are displayed in transit terminal ticketing areas, baggage claim areas, and the like. Dioramas are backlit. Alternative versions include two or three dioramas connected together, which rotate within a cylinder or three-sided concave, as well as a four-sided, non-rotating version. These alternative forms are located in high-traffic areas of the airport.

Car Card An advertising unit within a transit vehicle, such as a bus.

Interior car cards—Found on the inside of buses, subways and commuter rail vehicles, **car cards** are of various dimensions ranging from 10" by 27" to 32" by 20" depending on the market and the vehicle.

Rail/Subway Posters—These are located on terminal platforms/station stops and are commonly offered in these sizes: 1-sheet (28" by 44"), 2-sheet (44" by 58"), and 3-sheet (40" by 82").

Miscellaneous

There are innumerable other forms of out-of-home media which do not conveniently fit within the general descriptors of the previous three categories. Among these are:

- "Channel One"—Television programming telecasted directly into school rooms, in which a typical TV commercial can be inserted.

- Cinema (Theatre) advertising—Video and/or slides with or without voice delivered on a movie screen, generally prior to the movie being shown.

- College bulletin boards—Structures mounted on corridor walls which contain space for typical college news/information as well as paid advertising.

- "Health Club TV" (or radio)—Television or radio programs telecasted into physical fitness membership clubs, which can accommodate the typical TV or radio commercial.

- Hot-air balloons—These have advertising messages painted or printed onto the balloon.

- Inflatable—Free standing inflatable can be manufactured to represent any reasonable shape or design and can be either placed on the ground or floated with a tether.

- Queue advertising—Television monitors mounted near waiting lines at amusement parks and the like which might carry programming and can include typical TV commercials (e.g., "Primetime Video").

- Restroom displays—Printed advertisements in restrooms, which can be mounted on walls or on the inside of toilet doors.

- "Silent Radio"—This is a structure containing a matrix of light bulbs which are electronically turned on and off to create printed words and/or the illusion of movement. Transmissions of information and advertising messages are sent to each unit via radio waves. The units are generally found in restaurants/ bars, commuter terminals, etc.

- Sky writing—White "smoke-like" messages created against the sky's background by one or more airplanes.

- Telephone enclosures—Backlit panels, affixed to street telephone booths.

- Video walls—A matrix of TV monitors mounted within a shopping mall corridor which can accommodate a wide variety of video formats.

Radio

The oldest radio station in the United States broadcast for the first time out of San Jose, back in 1909. In 1921 it was given the call letters KQW which was changed to KCBS when CBS acquired it in 1949. There are now more than 10,000 radio stations in the United States. The vast majority accept advertising, as the following figures show:

4,932 commercial AM stations
4,155 commercial FM stations
1,374 non-commercial stations

The standard radio commercials are 30-second and 60-second spots, although shorter and longer commercials can be purchased. Purchases can be made on radio networks, in individual markets via "spot" radio, or through a buying system known as an *unwired network*.

Network Radio

Network radio is used to advertise throughout the United States. There is usually no particular attempt by the advertiser to select local markets for either more or less advertising than might be achieved via network in the average market. There are 29 radio networks (or programs)—some affiliated with and/or owned by their television counterparts (e.g., ABC), and some independent. Each network has its own **clearance** by market and by station. The clearance indicates how many local stations carry the network or program, and the percent of United States population in the markets where the network or program is carried. Some of the radio programs are broadcast daily, often throughout the day, while others are broadcast only one day a week or only one time during the day. ABC has five distinct networks as well as a number of programs that air on various stations within one of the five (see Table 3.9).

TABLE 3.9: Network Radio

ABC Networks/Programs	Other Networks
Excell Radio Network	CBS
Galaxy Radio Network	CBS Spectrum
Genesis Radio Network	Keystone Broadcasting Network
Prime Radio Network	Mutual Radio Network
Platinum Radio Network	NBC
Bob Brinker—Moneytalk	Sheridan Broadcasting Network
Bob Kingsley with America's Music Makers	Source
Dr. Dean Edell—Medical Minutes	Talknet
The Dow Jones Report	Unistar Power
The Gordon Williams Business Report	Unistar Super
Mike McClintock—Home Sense	Unistar Ultimate
Paul Harvey	WONE (Westwood One)
Ralph Snodsmith—The Garden Hotline	
Rush Limbaugh	
Tom Snyder	
Tom Snyder Commentaries	
The Wall Street Journal Report	

Spot Radio

Spot Refers to the purchase of TV or radio commercial time on a market-by-market basis as opposed to network (national) purchases. Also commonly used in lieu of "commercial announcement."

Spot refers to a local piece of geography—generally an area encompassing a Metropolitan area, but often extending beyond the metro area boundaries. Spot purchases can be made on any of the over 10,000 commercial radio stations, whether or not they are part of a radio network.

Unwired Networks

Unwired Network Applicable to either radio or TV, the purchase of preselected local stations not connected by wire or satellite, through a sales organization representing the stations.

Spot radio can also be purchased in a pseudo-network grouping of stations known as an **unwired network**. With an unwired purchase the advertiser chooses the markets to receive advertising and the programming format(s) desired, but deals with a sales representative organization representing all the stations to effect the purchase, rather than dealing with each individual market or station. There are two such organizations: Katz Radio Group and Interrep Radio Store.

TABLE 3.10: Radio Programming Formats

| | Percent of Stations | | |
Format	AM	FM	AM/FM
Adult Contemporary	18%	21%	21%
Country	19	19	19
Rock/Contemporary Hit Radio (CHR)	3	21	10
Religious	13	4	9
Golden Oldies	11	4	8
Nostalgia/Big Band	9	1	6
Album Oriented Rock (AOR)	1	9	4
Easy Listening	2	8	4
News/Talk	7	*	4
Variety	1	—	1
Urban Contemporary	2	4	3
Spanish	4	1	2
Soft Contemporary (Light)	1	3	2
Black/Rythm & Blues	2	1	1
New Age/Jazz	1	2	1
Classical	*	2	1
All News	1	—	*

* Less than one percent (rounded).
Source: Radio Advertising Bureau.

Advertisers usually choose networks, unwired networks, or spot radio on the basis of programming format, which defines the kind of audience attracted to a particular radio station. The most common formats are shown in Table 3.10 along with the percent of radio stations in the top 100 markets programming each format.

Dayparts Broadcast time periods (segments), e.g., daytime: 10:00 a.m. to 4:00 p.m.

Purchases are often made on the basis of **dayparts**. Each daypart, on average, attracts different total amounts of audience (e.g., more in *morning drive* than *evening*), and generally a varying demographic group (e.g., adults versus teens). The common radio dayparts are shown in Table 3.11.

TABLE 3.11: Radio Dayparts

Morning drive	6:00 a.m.–10:00 a.m.
Midday	10:00 a.m.–3:00 p.m.
Afternoon drive	3:00 p.m.–7:00 p.m.
Evening	7:00 p.m.–Midnight
Overnight	Midnight–6:00 a.m.

Television

Although advertisers spend only 22 cents out of every dollar for advertising on television, the medium is so highly consumed and "visible" that the average person probably thinks the vast majority of advertising is on TV. For many people it's difficult to think about advertising without thinking about TV. It's also difficult to think of a time when television was not a communications medium. It has, nevertheless, been around for a long time. Technically, television was invented in the 1800s in the form of a perforated rotating disc through which one could scan "moving" pictures. In the early 1900s John Baird developed the first "television set," and in 1927 Philo Fransworth created color television. A few years later Vladimir Zworykin invented an electronic television camera pickup tube. The TV set as we know it today was demonstrated at the 1939 World's Fair in New York.

As an advertising medium, television has grown from the days when it offered a handful of programs, each of which was totally controlled and sponsored by a sole advertiser. Today it offers many programs broadcast throughout the day and night, in which many advertisers place one or more commercial announcements.

There are two basic categories of TV available to advertisers— national and local. The various categories within national and local TV are:

National
—Network broadcast
—Network cable
—Syndication
—Unwired

Local
—Spot TV (broadcast)
—Spot cable
—Unwired

Network Broadcast

Network A broadcast entity that provides programming and sells commercial time in programs telecast nationally via affiliated and/or licensed local stations—e.g., ABC television network, ESPN cable network, Mutual radio network.

O&O A station Owned and Operated by a broadcast network.

A **network** is any group of stations joined to broadcast the same programs—usually simultaneously. There are four networks in operation: ABC, CBS, NBC, and Fox. The local TV stations affiliated with these networks contract to air a certain amount of network programming each week, in return for which they are paid a compensation fee*. Some of these stations (referred to as **O&Os**) are Owned and Operated by the networks. Table 3.12 lists the network-owned and -operated stations.

The reason for the compensation is that the network is placing a program (with commercials in it) on a local station, which therefore preempts the station from airing its own program and selling advertising in that program. This loss of local advertising revenue is somewhat compensated for by the network fees. This arrangement, however, is symbiotic inasmuch as the local station does not have to create or produce local programming to air at the time a network program is airing, and there is a belief that network programs allow the station to attract more viewers than it might with just local programming. This greater attraction could have a rub-off effect on the local station whereby viewers are retained even when local programs air.

The networks can transmit their programming to local stations via telephone lines or satellite, or by sending a videotape. The intent is to air a program simultaneously in all markets, with

---

* Immediately prior to the publishing of this book, compensation agreements between the networks and local stations were under discussion. These talks could lead to local stations no longer being compensated by the networks for carrying network programming.

TABLE 3.12: O&O TV Stations

	ABC	CBS	NBC	FOX
Chicago	WLS	WBBM	WMAQ	WFLD
Dallas	—	—	—	WDAF
Denver	—	—	KCNC	—
Fresno	KFSN	—	—	—
Houston	KTRK	—	—	KRIV
Los Angeles	KABC	KCBS	KNBC	KTTV
Miami	—	WCIX	WTVJ	—
New York	WABC	WCBS	WNBC	WNYW
Philadelphia	WPVI	WCAU	—	—
Raleigh/Durham	WTVD	—	—	—
Salt Lake City	—	—	—	KSTU
San Francisco	KGO	—	—	—
Washington	—	—	WRC	WTTG

---

the exception of compensating for time zone differences for the East and West Coast markets, when possible. For example, a program originating from New York and broadcast at 9:00 p.m. will be seen on local stations as follows:

Time Zone

Eastern	9:00 p.m.
Central	8:00 p.m.
Mountain	7:00 p.m.
Pacific	9:00 p.m.

Live broadcasts, such as a Presidential speech, do not usually have time zone adjustments—that is, if the President spoke at 9:00 p.m. New York time it would be seen at 6:00 p.m. on the West Coast.

When a network program in a local market airs at a different time or on a different day from the original telecast, it is termed a **delayed broadcast** or **DB**. This is quite common, for example, for Alaska and Hawaii.

Delayed Broadcast (DB) The term given to a network TV program that is delayed for airing in a given market at a different time than the time it airs nationally.

Networks can also offer an advertiser "regional" advertising which is accomplished by inserting the advertiser's commercial at one or another "feed" points. For example a 9:00 p.m. program transmitted from New York is essentially videotaped for retransmission in the Pacific time zone three hours later—when it is 9:00 p.m. on the West Coast. At this feed point an advertiser's commercial could be inserted and therefore broadcast only to those living in the Pacific time zone. Regional advertising via network TV is, however, relatively uncommon. It requires that more than one advertiser or more than one brand from the advertiser's stable of brands "pool" to buy the national commercial slot, with each brand or advertiser airing its commercial in a different region.

An advertiser can also insert a different commercial from the one being broadcast nationally in any one or more of the local stations carrying the program. This is done through a mechanical process called a **cut-in** where the national commercial is literally removed (cut) and replaced with the local commercial. The advertiser usually must first have purchased a commercial in the national program to effect a cut-in—advertiser A is not permitted to cut-over a commercial purchased by advertiser B unless A has arranged for this execution with B. Additionally, the network or the local station charges the advertiser for effecting a cut-in. For these reasons cut-ins are also not common practice for national advertisers and are generally done only when absolutely necessary, such as during a consumer or sales test of a product or the testing of an alternative commercial message.

Network programs can usually be classified into one of the following major categories, although commercials can be purchased in any individual program regardless of its classification:

Adventure	News
Children's	Quiz & Audience Participation
Daytime Drama (Soap)	Special
Feature Films	Sports
General Drama	Suspense & Mystery Drama
Information	Variety

Additionally, programs are also classified according to the time of day they air. Exhibit 3.2 displays the standard TV dayparts according to their average timespan (Eastern Standard Time).

Commercials of varying lengths (e.g., 10, 15, 30, or 60 seconds) can be purchased. All network TV commercials air *in-program*, that is, between the absolute beginning and absolute end of the program. For the most part, several commercials from different advertisers

Cut-in   The insertion of a commercial, at the local level, which replaces the nationally purchased (and airing) commercial originally placed in a network broadcast program. Generally used to test media and/or alternative commercial executions.

EXHIBIT 3.2:   Network Television Dayparts

Time	Monday–Friday	Saturday	Sunday
6 A.M. – 9	Early Morning Network		
9 – 10		Children	Information
10 – 1 P.M.	Daytime Network		
1 P.M. – 5		Sports	Sports Public Affairs
6 – 7	Network News	News	News
8 – 11	Primetime	Prime	Prime
12 Midnight – 1 A.M.	Late Night	Late Night	
2 – 6	News		

Pod   A grouping of commercials and nonprogram material in which (usually) more than one advertiser's commercials air. Also referred to as a "commercial interruption" or "commercial break," but airing in-program.

Billboard   In broadcast, free airtime given to an advertiser, usually to one that purchases multiple commercials within a program—i.e., a "sponsor" of the program.

are grouped into what is called a commercial **pod** and air sequentially during a period known as the *commercial break*—of which there are several during the telecast of the average program.

Two types of commercial purchases can be made, and three methods of buying are available:

Types

- Participation—This refers to the purchase of one or more commercials in one or more programs.

- Sponsorship—This usually requires a majority purchase of the announcements available within a program or a program segment. Sponsoring advertisers are generally given one or more **billboards** at the beginning and/or end of the program. Billboards are generally of short duration (e.g., five seconds). They announce program sponsorship to the audience and afford the advertiser free advertising.

Upfront A method for purchasing TV commercial time well in advance of the telecast time of the programs and generally for a protracted period, such as for a one-year schedule. A relatively common practice among many advertisers for the purchase of primetime TV as well as other TV dayparts and entities (e.g., daytime network, cable TV, syndication).

Methods

- Upfront Buy—An **upfront** buy is a purchase of many commercials, negotiated well in advance of air-dates, which encompasses multiple programs airing during a *broadcast year*. The broadcast year starts when the networks premiere new TV shows (the new season) in primetime—generally around mid-September. An upfront advertiser usually negotiates with the networks for quarterly cancellation rights (a quarterly option to cancel a part or all of the commercial inventory purchased), audience delivery guarantees, and various other scheduling/flexibility options.

- Scatter Buy—Unlike an upfront buy, scatter buys are made only for defined periods (say, one quarter) and do not generally include the scheduling/flexibility options of an upfront buy.

- Opportunistic Buy—This is any purchase of any one or more programs, generally made immediately prior to air-date.

Spot Broadcast

As opposed to network buys, spot purchases can be made on any station in any market in just about any program being broadcast, whether national or local. Purchases may range from one market to all U.S. markets, with the specific purchases varying from one market to another. This geographic and local market purchase flexibility is generally the primary reason for purchasing spot versus national TV.

There are approximately 200 distinct TV markets in the United States—200 nonoverlapping geographic areas where the local stations within that market provide programming for the households in that area. Table 3.13 lists the ten biggest markets in the United States (according to TV household population count) and the percent of United States households accounted for by the remaining markets.

TABLE 3.13:   Spot TV Markets

Top 10	% U.S. TV Households
New York	7.7%
Los Angeles	5.4
Chicago	3.4
Philadelphia	3.0
San Francisco/Oakland/San Jose	2.4
Boston	2.3
Dallas/Fort Worth	1.9
Detroit	1.9
Washington, D.C.	1.9
Houston	1.6
Subtotal	31.4
Top 20	45.0
Top 30	54.2
Top 40	61.4
Top 50	67.4
Top 60	72.6
Top 70	76.9
Top 80	80.5
Top 90	83.7
Top 100	86.4
Remainder	13.6
Total U.S.	100.0%

VHF (Very High Frequency) TV channels 2-13.

UHF (Ultra High Frequency) The band added to the VHF band for television transmission—channels 14-83 on a TV set.

Within these 200 markets are 1,093 stations, half of which are **VHF (Very High Frequency**—TV channels 2–13) and half of which are **UHF (Ultra High Frequency**—TV channels 14–83). Stations also fall within one of two categories, regardless of channel numbers:

Affiliate—Those stations affiliated with at least one of the four TV networks (whether or not the station is an O&O), and therefore carry network programs. These are identified to the local viewer during the "station identification" in which, for example, a station will identify itself as "Station XXXX, an ABC-affiliated station."

Independent—those stations not affiliated with a network.

Adjacency A commercial time period that is scheduled immediately preceding or following a scheduled program on the same station in which a spot TV commercial can be placed. Opposite of an in-program placement. Also called a *break position*.

Commercials of varying lengths can be purchased in spot TV. These commercials are usually purchased in packages encompassing one or more dayparts—although one spot could be purchased in one program regardless of daypart designation. Spots can air in locally originated programs, between national programs (called *break positions* or **adjacencies**) and, in some instances, within a national program. Network program positions available for local market sale by the local station are not common and generally occur only when the network has unsold national inventory and turns back a commercial slot to its affiliates for local sale. Local placement in a *syndicated* program, however, is common. This will be discussed later.

Daypart designations are common for all spot TV stations, but not all precisely follow a specific time frame. Table 3.14 displays the most commonly used dayparts with the timings generally used by the average station. Anomalies abound depending on the station's programming practices and its standing as an affiliate or independent.

TABLE 3.14: Spot TV Daypart Timings in the Average Market

Early Morning	Sign-on–9:00 a.m.
Daytime	10:00 a.m.–4:30 p.m.
Early Fringe	4:30 p.m.–7:30 p.m.
Early News	(within Early Fringe)
Prime Access	7:30 p.m.–8:00 p.m.
Prime—Monday–Saturday	8:00 p.m.–11:00 p.m.
—Sunday	7:30 p.m.–11:00 p.m.
Late News—Affiliates	11:00 p.m.–11:30 p.m.
—Independents	Various
Sports	Various
Children	6:00 a.m.–9:00 a.m.;
	3:00 p.m.–5:00 p.m.

As with network TV, there are various types of purchases and several methods used:

Types
- Long-term—similar to a network TV upfront buy, these kinds of purchases are made for a period generally longer than a calendar quarter.

Scatter Purchasing commercial time in broadcast media in many different programs. Also refers to the purchasing of network TV time which is not purchased during an "upfront" media buy.

- Scatter—The most popular way to buy spot TV, **scatter** purchases are made for a specific period of time. For instance, all commercials may be aired within a specified four-week period—known as a "four-week flight."

Methods

- Daypart packages—As previously described, daypart packages specify the time of day in which commercials will air. They may or may not include specific program designations.

- Specific programs—This is simply the purchase of advertising within one or more specific programs, as opposed to a combination of programs within a daypart.

ROS (Run-of-Station) A tactic used in broadcast media whereby commercials are scheduled throughout the day and night at the discretion of the station or network, as opposed to time periods designated by the advertiser.

- Run-of-Station (**ROS**)—This is the purchase of announcements that will air in programs and/or in time periods at the discretion of the TV station. The advertiser in this case gives the local station an expenditure level to achieve and requests the station to place as many commercials as are affordable within that budget.

Syndication Broadcast

Syndication In broadcast media, a program carried on selected stations which may or may not air at the same time in all markets. In newspapers, an independently written column or feature carried by many newspapers (e.g., Dear Abby). In magazines, a centrally written/published section carried by newspapers, generally in the Sunday edition (e.g., *Parade*).

Syndication is a term borrowed from the print publishing field. In print, articles or publications are sold to a number of newspapers or periodicals. For instance, *Parade* magazine is syndicated nationally in newspapers throughout the United States. In television, a syndicated program is sold to local TV stations. The program can be of any type and length and may be a one-time event or a continuing series. When scheduling a continuing program, the local station generally assigns it to the same time slot every time it airs. This makes it easier for the local station to promote the show to the viewing audience, and for advertisers to track viewership. This time slot, however, can vary from one market to another.

The programs can be original creations (never before seen on television) or off-network properties (programs which originally aired on network TV). Unlike network TV, where stations generally air just about all the network fare broadcast, local stations license individual programs from syndicators. Therefore, different

Clearance The broadcast stations carrying a network or syndicated program. This list is usually accompanied by a "coverage" percentage indicating the percent of U.S. TV homes in markets in which the program airs.

syndicated programs have different **clearances** throughout the United States. Table 3.15 shows 20 of the many syndicated properties available, along with the number of stations carrying each program and the resulting percent coverage of United States TV households. You'll note that the number of stations, per se, does not necessarily correspond to the amount of coverage (e.g., "American Gladiators" has fewer stations and higher coverage than "Love Connection").

TABLE 3.15:   A Sampling of Syndicated TV Programs

	Number of Stations Carrying	Percent U.S. TV Household Coverage
American Gladiators	160	91%
Arsenio Hall	206	96
The Cosby Show	210	99
A Current Affair	193	96
Donahue	234	99
Entertainment Tonight	184	96
Family Feud	120	82
Geraldo	162	96
Hard Copy	172	91
Hee Haw	176	90
Jeopardy	219	99
Joan Rivers	115	90
Love Connection	162	90
Oprah Winfrey	224	99
People's Court	178	93
Sally Jessy Raphael	197	96
Siskel & Ebert	201	93
Star Trek	239	98
Wheel of Fortune	223	99
World Wrestling Federation	228	96

Source: A.C. Nielsen

Syndication can be considered a hybrid within the broadcast TV spectrum. It has some of the characteristics of network TV—for instance, it is national in scope—and some of the traits of spot TV —specifically, it can be purchased on a local market basis. An advertiser can purchase commercial time in a syndicated property either on a national basis or on a market-by-market basis as available.

Network Cable

Cable TV Reception of TV signals via cable (wires) rather than from over-the-air (i.e., via a TV antenna).

Cable TV began in the late 1940s as a means of providing a television signal, or an improved signal, to households in areas unable to receive "over-the-air" broadcasts due to mountains or other signal interference. The cable operator built a high antenna designed to receive broadcast signals and then retransmitted these signals to subscribing households via coaxial cable—hence the name "cable TV." Cable TV was originally called Community Antenna Television (CATV).

The number of households subscribing to cable TV did not show any remarkable increases until the 1980s, when an increase in the amount of quality programming made available to subscribers resulted in an influx of new subscribers who did not necessarily need improved reception. Six out of ten homes in the United States now have cable TV, brought to them by over 10,000 individual cable systems. See Table 3.16.

TABLE 3.16:   Growth of Cable TV

	# Subscribing Households (millions)	% U.S. Households with Cable TV	# Cable Systems in U.S.
1991	56.0	60%	10,704
1990	54.9	59	9,612
1985	38.0	45	6,600
1980	15.2	19	4,225
1975	8.6	12	3,506
1970	3.9	7	2,490
1965	1.3	2	1,325
1960	.7	1	640

Source: Cable Advertising Bureau

Basic Cable The offering to subscribers of broadcast and cable TV originated programs as part of a "basic" service agreement in which a subscriber pays a cable TV operator or system a monthly fee. Does not include "pay" services which might be offered by the cable operator.

Pay Cable Programs and/or services provided to basic cable subscribers for an additional fee (e.g., HBO).

Pay-per-View A telecast, usually of a special event, for which subscribers pay a one-time fee to view.

A subscriber pays a monthly fee for **basic cable** service and has the option of paying additional fees for additional programming. There are five categories of basic or pay television fare available to subscribers:

- Broadcast—Everything someone without cable could receive over-the-air.

- Cable origination—Any programming the cable operator wishes to make available to its subscribers.

- Distant signals—programs from TV stations geographically too distant to receive over-the-air.

- Pay—**Pay cable** provides programs which commonly do not contain advertising, for which the subscriber pays an additional monthly fee (e.g., HBO).

- Pay-per-view—**Pay-per-view** offers individual programs for which the subscriber pays a one-time additional fee for each program selected (e.g., a championship boxing match). These are also usually non-commercialized.

Any broadcast program transmitted into a cable household includes the commercial an advertiser purchased in that program from a broadcast network, syndicator, or local TV station. The cable operator is prohibited from deleting that commercial or cutting over it with another commercial (unless specifically directed to do so by the advertiser). Therefore, when an advertiser buys commercial time in a broadcast program the commercial will appear in all homes receiving the program, whether over-the-air or cable.

An advertiser can also purchase commercial time in cable-originated programs. These programs are either local (that is, designed for and transmitted to only one cable operator's subscribers), regionally distributed, or available nationally to any cable operator who wishes to carry that program. Table 3.17 lists the national cable networks and their **circulation**—the number of households that subscribe to the cable services carrying these networks. Table 3.18 lists the regional networks along with their subscriber base.

Circulation In cable TV, the number of households that subscribe to the cable services that carry a given network.

TABLE 3.17: Cable TV Networks

	Number Subscribing Households (millions)
ADC—America's Disability Channel	14.2
A&E—Arts & Entertainment	50.0
BET—Black Entertainment Network	30.5
CMT—Country Music Television	12.0
CNN—Cable News Network	57.5
Comedy TV	15.0
CNBC—Consumer News and Business Channel*	17.0
Court—Courtroom Television Network	TBD
The Discovery Channel	53.2
E!—Entertainment Television	18.0
ESPN—Entertainment and Sports Programming Network	57.8
The Family Channel	52.1
FNN—Financial News Network*	36.0
Galavision (Hispanic)	1.1
Headline News	47.3
The Learning Channel	21.0
Lifetime	50.0
The Monitor Channel	TBD
MTV—Music Television	53.0
TNN—The Nashville Network	52.5
Nickelodeon	53.5
Nostalgia Network	10.0
Prime Network	23.0
Sci-Fi Channel	7.0
Sports Channel America	11.0
TBS—Turner Broadcasting System	57.5
TNT—Turner Network Television	49.0
The Travel Channel	16.0
USA Network	53.7
VH-1—Video Hits One	39.6
The Weather Channel	46.0

*Merged in 1991.
Source: Cable Advertising Bureau

TABLE 3.18: Regional Cable TV Networks

	Number Subscribing Households (thousands)
ASPN—Arizona Sports Programming Network	340
Empire Sports Network	895
Home Sports Entertainment	2,300
HomeTeam Sports	1,900
KBL Sports Network	1,500
Madison Square Garden Network	4,400
News 12 Long Island	650
Pacific Sports Network	1,200
Prime Sports Network:	
Rocky Mountain	780
Intermountain	300
Upper Midwest	100
Prime Ticket	4,200
Prism	475
Pass Sports—Pro-Am Sports System	700
Sports Channel:	
Bay Area	250
Chicago	1,800
Cincinnati	190
Florida	1,100
Los Angeles	150
New England	1,300
New York	1,400
Ohio	750
Philadelphia	1,400
Sports South Network	1,200
Sunshine Network	2,900

Source: Cable Advertising Bureau

As noted by the number of subscribers for each of the networks, not every cable system offers every network to its subscribers. There are a number of reasons why cable operators may not carry all programs:

- Capacity. Some cable operators offer more channels to their subscribers than others, depending on the operator's technological configuration. Table 3.19 displays the percent of total U.S. cable-subscribing households that can view various numbers of channels. The total number of channels required to transmit broadcast TV, national networks, regional networks, and (if desired) locally originated programs can exceed a cable system's physical capacity.

The introduction of new technologies, such as video compression and **fiber optics**, will eventually increase capacity—from the current average of 37 channels per cable system to 150 channels—thereby allowing more systems to carry more networks and/or local programs.

Fiber Optics   Thin glass fibers used for transmitting information —e.g., audio/video from a central source to a person's TV set.

- Choice. An operator may choose not to carry a network because the programming does not fit with the demographic and lifestyle characteristics of the subscribing households.

- Competitive availability. An operator may elect not to carry two or more networks which are deemed very similar to each other.

- Economics. Operators usually pay the networks a licensing fee to carry their programming. These fees vary from one network to another, but all are based on the number of subscribers in the cable system. If these fees cannot be recouped via household subscription costs (or advertising revenue), the operator has a losing proposition.

- Local advertising availability. Many operators sell advertising in the cable programs they transmit—in the locally originated programs or, by agreement, in the network programs. The number of commercials they can sell in network programs is regulated by the networks. Some networks offer more "local avails" than others. The cable operator may opt to carry those networks that offer more local avails, which can be used to generate advertising revenue for the operator.

TABLE 3.19:   Channel Capacity in Cable TV Households

Percent of Subscribers	Number of Channels
24%	54+
66	30–53
7	20–29
3	5–19
100%	

Source: Cable Advertising Bureau

Interconnect   Two or more cable systems which are linked together to air commercials simultaneously (if possible). A "hard" or "true" interconnect is linked by cable or microwave. A "soft" interconnect is a group of systems with an agreement to insert commercials into programs or time periods.

Penetration   The percentage of people (or homes) within a defined universe that are physically able to be exposed to a medium.

As with broadcast TV, commercials of varying lengths can be purchased on cable TV. The purchases can be made on a network basis (via an upfront or scatter buy) or a system-to-system basis.

When an advertiser wishes to purchase multiple systems within a TV market to "cover" the market, it can be accomplished either by dealing with each system, or dealing through an **interconnect**. An interconnect is two or more systems joining together to form a larger combined subscriber base for advertising sales purposes. Table 3.20 lists the top ten interconnects in the United States.

Whether purchasing system by system or through an interconnect, an advertiser can purchase cable TV in the same manner as spot TV. The only difference between spot cable and spot broadcast is one of coverage. Broadcast covers nearly every home within a TV market, while the coverage or **penetration** of cable TV is always less. On average, cable TV has a 60 percent penetration, but this varies substantially by market. Table 3.21 lists cable penetration in each of the top 25 TV markets.

TABLE 3.20:   Top 10 Interconnects

Name	Coverage Area	Number Subscribing Households (000)
New York Interconnect	Greater N.Y. Metro Area	3,346
Urban Contemporary Interconnect	14 Markets nationwide	2,600
Philadelphia Cable Advertising	Philadelphia	1,353
Bay Cable Advertising	San Francisco/Oakland	1,123
Boston Interconnect	Boston	1,100
Greater Chicago Cable Interconnect	Chicago	800
Tampa Bay Interconnect	Tampa	773
Detroit Interconnect	Detroit	765
Time Warner Interconnect	Manhattan, Brooklyn, Queens	725

Source: Cable Advertising Bureau

TABLE 3.21:   Cable TV Penetration in Top 25 Markets

Top 25 Markets Ranked by TV Households	Percent Cable Penetration
New York	57%
Los Angeles	53
Chicago	49
Philadelphia	66
San Francisco/Oakland/San Jose	62
Boston	70
Washington, D.C.	54
Dallas/Fort Worth	46
Detroit	56
Houston	50
Cleveland/Akron	57
Atlanta	55
Tampa/St. Petersburg	60
Seattle	63
Minneapolis/St. Paul	46
Pittsburgh	73
St. Louis	45
Denver	54
Phoenix	47
Sacramento/Stockton	54
Baltimore	50
Hartford/New Haven	80
San Diego	74
Orlando/Daytona Beach/Melbourne	63

Source: Cable Advertising Bureau

Superstations

Superstation An independent TV station whose signal is transmitted throughout the United States via satellite. Technically refers only to WTBS, but is also used for other stations.

There are four TV stations in the United States commonly referred to as **superstations**, although technically this distinction belongs only to WTBS/Atlanta. A superstation transmits its signal locally via normal broadcast and also nationally via satellite, thus allowing people in distant markets to receive the broadcast via cable TV.

WTBS is the only superstation that sells advertising time either in its local coverage area (Atlanta) or nationally (via cable TV). The non-Atlanta purchase is the TBS network, as shown in Table 3.17. The other three superstations (WGN/Chicago, WPIX/New York, WWOR/New York) do not offer a local/national split.

PART II
MEDIA DEFINITIONS AND DYNAMICS

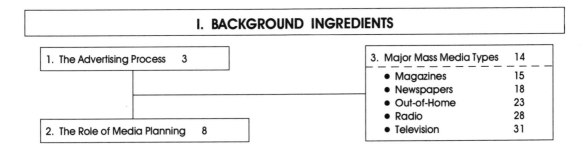
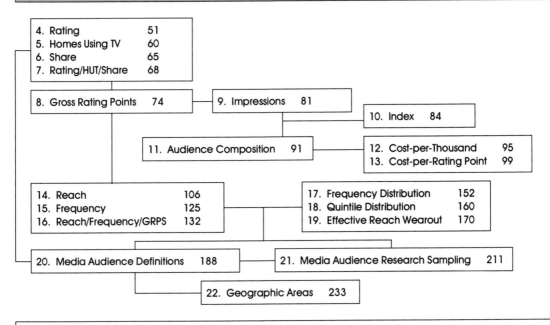
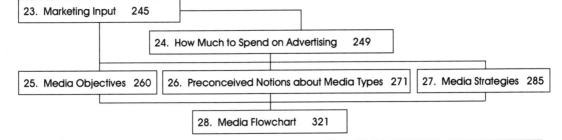

Chapter 4

Rating

I n this chapter we define what a rating is and how it
is calculated. We explain why a rating is one of the
more important media terms and how rating information
is perceived by the media planner and by the media
supplier. Finally, we investigate ancillary factors that
might affect the "quality" of a rating point.

Rating The
percentage of a given
population group
consuming a medium at a
particular moment.
Generally used for
broadcast media, but can
be used for any medium.
One rating point equals
one percent.

You've heard newscasts or read articles that talked about
ratings: The Superbowl got such and such a rating, or a program
was cancelled due to poor ratings, etc. The reference to ratings is a
reference to the quantity of the television audience that viewed
a program. The precise definition is the percentage of individuals
(or homes) exposed to an *advertising medium*. In its simplest form, a
one rating is equivalent to one percent of a given population group.
The definition can apply to many media forms, but is commonly
used for television or radio programs.

How Ratings Are Calculated

Let us assume there are 1,000 adults (age 18 and older) in the
television population (those living in households that have a TV
set) of a given geographic area, which we'll call market X. Let us
also assume they have the capability of viewing any of three TV
programs which are being broadcast at a particular time. Of the 1,000
adults, 300 view program A, 200 view program B, 100 view program
C, and 400 decide to not view at that time. By dividing the number

of viewers of program A by the TV population (300/1000) we obtain a rating of 30 (the percent sign is never used when referring to a rating, even though that's exactly what it is: 30 percent). Likewise, program B has a 20 rating and program C has a 10 rating. Those not viewing any of the programs are obviously not counted as part of the *viewing* audience of any program. See Table 4.1.

TABLE 4.1:   Program Ratings in Market X

	Adults 18+	
	Viewing Audience	Rating
Program A	300	30
Program B	200	20
Program C	100	10
Not viewing	400	—
Total Population	1,000	

The same dynamics apply to calculating a rating for any population base—households, men, women, men 18–34, teens, etc. For example, let us assume your primary target audience (those to whom you want to direct the advertising) is men 18–49, and you also want to apply secondary emphasis to men 50+. You'll therefore want to know the ratings of TV programs for each of these audiences.

Because programs have different appeals to different demographic groups, a program rating for one group could be quite different from the rating for another group. The demographic ratings for the three TV programs in market X in Table 4.2

TABLE 4.2:   Program Ratings in Market X For Different Demographic Groups

	Men 18–49		Men 50+	
	Viewing Audience	Rating	Viewing Audience	Rating
Program A	30	10	40	20
Program B	60	20	60	30
Program C	45	15	20	10
Not Viewing	165	—	80	—
Total Population	300		200	

demonstrate this phenomenon. Program A has greater appeal to men 50+ than to men 18–49, as shown by the 20 rating it delivers to the former group versus the 10 rating to the latter. Program C, on the other hand, has more appeal to men 18–49. You'll note that the ratings for these demographic groups apply to the total population of that group, not to all people in the market.

It is important to note that because a rating is a percentage, it merely indicates the proportion of a population group that is viewing the program; it does not indicate the *number* of people viewing. In the above example, the 10 rating delivered by program A to men 18–49 is equivalent to 30 people; the 10 rating for Program C to men 50+ is equivalent to 20 people.

"Average" Rating

Not all people view an entire TV program or listen for a long period of time to a particular radio station. There's tune-in and tune-out during a program as people switch channels—which has become easier to do with the advent of the remote control device. When media research suppliers estimate a program rating they calculate the *average* rating the program produces for its time duration. A program rating of 20, for example, means that during the average minute of broadcast 20 percent of a population group was tuned in to that program. Commonly, research suppliers provide *Average Quarter Hour* ratings, meaning the average rating that was produced during the average minute of that 15-minute segment.

Commercial Ratings

When we defined *rating*, we emphasized the words *advertising medium* to dispel any misconception that a rating applies to advertising *message* delivery—that is, commercial exposure. Although there is a movement afoot to obtain ratings for commercials, they are currently not available. A rating, therefore, is only an indicator of the percentage of a group of individuals that have the *opportunity* to be exposed to the advertising. The percentage of people who will actually see or hear the commercials can vary substantially, ranging from zero (although this is highly improbable) to 100 percent of the viewing/listening audience. The "commercial rating" that might be obtained is influenced by many factors, including (1) how many people are *paying attention* to the broadcast program in the first place; (2) the relative position of the commercial within a pod of different commercials (first position, middle position, last position); (3) the number of different commercials within the pod; (4) the length of the commercial; (5) the creative effectiveness of the commercial; and (6) the relevance of the commercial message to the viewer's/listener's needs and wants at that particular time.

Importance of Ratings

Rating is the most important broadcast term. Ratings are used extensively by media planners and media buyers to evaluate alternative programs or combinations of programs that can best achieve the advertising goals. As will be seen in later sections of this book, ratings form the foundation from which various other measures (reach and frequency, impressions, effective reach, wearout, etc.) are calculated to determine media selection and scheduling tactics.

Media suppliers (TV and radio networks, local market TV and radio stations) use rating information to assess a program's or station's popularity, and, in part, to determine how much it will charge an advertiser to place a commercial within that program or on that station.

Popularity

The higher a program rating, the more people are watching it. The higher the rating, the greater chance the program will continue to be on-air; conversely, the lower the rating, the greater the chance the program will be cancelled. But the ratings are not considered in isolation from other factors, such as the time of day of broadcast. For example, because more people view TV during 8:00–9:00 *p.m.* than during 8:00–9:00 *a.m.*, a program has a greater opportunity to generate a high rating at night than in the morning. The fact that program A in the morning gets a 5 rating and program B in the evening gets a 20 rating does not necessarily indicate that program A is less popular that program B. In fact, program A might be *relatively* more popular than program B—it might garner a greater proportion of the total audience viewing TV at that particular time than program B does in its time slot. This concept of "relative popularity" is known as *share* and is discussed later.

Commercial Pricing

Media suppliers use ratings as one criterion for establishing the prices they will charge advertisers. Generally, the higher the rating, the greater the cost of advertising time. But the relationship of cost to rating is not necessarily linear: A 10-rated program will not necessarily cost twice as much as a 5-rated program—it could be proportionately more or less.

Among the many factors that influence pricing are these:

1. The size of the rating against various demographic groups

2. The program's share of audience

3. The supplier's cost for producing the program and/or the price paid by the supplier to secure the rights to broadcast the program (e.g., the Superbowl)

4. The laws of supply and demand: the greater the demand by advertisers to advertise in a TV program, the higher the price charged by the supplier

Ratings for Unreported Demographics

Because syndicated rating research does not report on all age ranges in its demographic cells, it is sometimes necessary to calculate a rating for a target group not contained on the rating report. For example, let us assume you need to know the rating of Program A for adults 35–49, but the rating report shows only a 20 rating for adults 18–49 and a 10 rating for adults 18–34. You cannot subtract the 10 rating from the 20 rating and determine that the rating for adults 35–49 is 10. You must go back to the foundation of the ratings and proceed as follows (see also Table 4.3):

1. Determine the population base for the target audience by subtracting the population of the smaller group from the larger group: 3,000 adults 18–49 minus 2,000 adults 18–34 equals 1,000 adults 35–49.

2. Likewise, determine the number of viewers for the target audience: 600 viewers minus 200 viewers equals 400 adult 35–49 viewers.

3. Having the viewers and the population base, you can determine the rating by division: 400 viewers divided by 1,000 population equals a 40 rating.

TABLE 4.3:   Calculating a Rating from Other Ratings

| | | Program A | |
Reported	Population Base	# Viewers	Rating
18–49	3,000	600	20
18–34	2,000	200	10
Calculated			
35–49	1,000	400	40

Note: If you cannot conveniently find the population base in the ratings report, you can calculate it by using the rating and number of viewers, for example, 600 adult 18–49 viewers divided by a 20 rating (use 20 percent or .20) equals 3,000.

As with demographic groups, ratings cannot be averaged across geographic markets. For example, if you are advertising in market X and market Y and need to determine an average rating for program A in both markets combined, you must add the number of people viewing program A in market X and market Y and divide the total number of viewers by the combined population of the two markets. Program A in our example delivers an average 18.5 rating —not a 17.0 rating as might be incorrectly calculated by adding the two ratings (14.0 and 20.0) and dividing by 2. (Note: You see a shift in the way a rating is reported in Table 4.4—for example, instead of "14," "14.0." Although either number could be used [inasmuch as they are identical] it is always best to have consistency of how

---

TABLE 4.4:   Program Ratings by Markets and Groupings

| | Market X | | Market Y | | Total | |
	Population	Rating	Population	Rating	Population	Rating
Program A	70	14.0	300	20.0	370	18.5
Program B	120	24.0	300	20.0	420	21.0
Program C	65	13.0	300	20.0	365	18.3
Not Viewing	245	—	600	—	845	—
Total	500		1,500		2,000	

numbers are reported within charts and tables and media plans so there is no reader confusion. All ratings in this table are therefore shown to the nearest tenth of a percent.)

Ratings for Non-Broadcast Media

Although ratings are a common reference point for TV and radio programs, they can also be applied to other media. While the concept remains the same, the terms vary for different media. Three of the more common terms used for other media follow. They are more fully explained in later sections.

Coverage The percentage of a population group covered by a medium. Commonly used with print media to describe their average issue audience within defined demographic or purchasing groups. Akin to a *rating*.

Circulation In out-of-home media, the number of people passing an advertisement who have an opportunity to see it.

- Magazines: The number of readers of a publication divided by the population base is usually called **coverage**.

- Newspapers: The circulation of a newspaper divided by the population base is commonly referred to as penetration.

- Outdoor: The number of people (not percentage of people) who pass by a given poster or billboard is known as **circulation**. Circulation is combined with a series of other units to result in a *showing*.

A Rating Point Is a Rating Point

There is often discussion as to whether all rating points are equivalent. On one hand, by definition, they are equal. A 1.0 rating in program A is identical to a 1.0 rating in program B—both represent one percent of the population group. On the other hand, they might not be equal for any number of reasons—some of which follow:

1. Program environment might have an effect on audience exposure to a commercial. For example, a commercial that announces a new, improved formula for product X might "play better" in a news environment than in a comedy show—if you assume that the commercial is a kind of news. However, an argument could be made that the comedy environment places people in a more relaxed mood, perhaps more receptive to commercial exposure.

The commercial's creative execution is important to consider. If the tone and manner of the commercial are representative of "hard news," a news program environment might be more compatible. Conversely, if the tone and manner are upbeat and humorous, a comedy show might afford greater compatibility. But this discussion can be turned completely around by arguing that it is more effective to place a hard-news commercial in a comedy show for shock value—to surprise the viewer. The compatibility question comes into play with nearly all media forms. For example:

- Does a full-color advertisement have more impact in a black-and-white editorial format than in a full-color editorial format?
- Will an advertisement about travel get better readership in a travel magazine or in a general editorial magazine?
- Will an ad for a food product get better readership when placed within a food environment, or when placed outside this environment and separate from competitive food ads?
- Will a radio commercial using a lot of music "break through" the commercial clutter if scheduled in an all-talk program, or will it be received better if placed in a music format?

2. As we will see, the size of the program rating affects reach and frequency levels. All things being equal, two 10-rated TV programs will generally not achieve the same reach as one 20-rated program because there will probably be duplication of audience between the two 10-rated shows—some people will view both programs. Extending this argument further, five 20-rated programs will usually accumulate more reach than twenty 5-rated programs.

3. There is some evidence that the higher a TV program rating, the more people think of that program as one of their "favorites" and pay comparatively greater attention to it. More attention to the programming could translate to more attention to the commercials in that program.

4. There is usually more advertiser demand for the most popular, higher-rated programs than for the lower-rated, ostensibly less popular programs. Increased demand always leads to increased prices. Stations and networks generally charge a premium for high-rated programs. The question is whether or not the premium is commensurate with the advertiser's expected return on investment.

5. As will be discussed later in Chapter 21, "Media Audience Research," it has been shown that the higher the rating, the greater the statistical reliability. There is proportionately less risk in higher-rated than in lower-rated programs.

There are no conclusions for this question of rating point equality, only arguments—some of which support the notion that a rating point is a rating point, some of which suggest all rating points are not equal. You might want to mark this section and return to it later, after you have a greater understanding of the various other dynamics that affect consumer exposure to advertising—and then you decide if all rating points are equal.

PROFESSIONAL WORKSHOP

1. TV program A is viewed by 100,000 adults age 18 and older in market X, which has a total population of adults age 18 and older of 1,000,000. What is program A's average rating?

2. This same market has a teen (12–17) population of 100,000. Program A is viewed by 5,000 teens. What is program A's rating among teens?

3. What is the average rating of program A among all people age 12 and older in market X (above)?

4. Program B is broadcast in markets X and Y and receives a 10 and 8 household rating respectively. What is the average rating of program B in both markets combined?

5. Program C has an average quarter rating of 10.0 during its 9:00–9:15 segment, and an 8.0 rating during the second quarter hour. What is program C's average rating during its half-hour telecast?

6. If your commercial airs at 9:10 in program C (above), what is the average rating for your commercial?

7. Magazine A is read by 1 million women in market Z, which has a women's population of 5 million. What is magazine A's rating among women? What is its coverage?

Chapter 5

Homes Using TV: HUT/PUT/PVT/PUR/Cume

I n this chapter we define the term *Homes Using TV* and related terms, and explain how they are calculated. We highlight how this media phenomenon varies according to the demographic group, geographic market, or media form with which you are dealing.

HUT The percentage of Homes Using (tuned in to) TV at a particular time.

Cume (Cumulative) Rating The reach of a radio or TV program or station, as opposed to the "average" rating.

PUR The percentage of People Using Radio at a particular time.

PUT The percentage of People Using TV at a particular time. Identical to *PVT*, People Viewing TV.

Several terms are used to describe the total viewing or listening audience at a given time. Although the terms used by different media research suppliers may vary, all indicate the same concept: how many people or homes are viewing/listening to anything being broadcast at a particular time of day (which can be expressed as a percentage of the population universe or in absolute numbers of people):

- The Arbitron Company refers to **HUT (Homes Using TV)** and PVT (Persons Viewing TV) for television, and to **Cume (Cumulative) Rating** for radio.

- Birch/Scarborough Research Corporation, which studies radio listening, employs the term **PUR (People Using Radio)**.

- Nielsen Media Research, which reports only on television viewing, prefers the term HUT and **PUT (Persons Using TV)**.

Returning to our example of program ratings in market X (previously shown in Table 4.1), let us assume all three programs were broadcast 8:00–8:30 p.m. In total, 600 adults 18+ were viewing TV at that time–60 percent of the population universe. The PUT (or PVT) is therefore 600, or 60 percent (See Table 5.1).

TABLE 5.1:   PUT: Adults 18+—Market X

	8:00–8:30 p.m.	
	# Viewers	**Rating**
Program A	300	30
Program B	200	20
Program C	100	10
PUT	600	60%
Nonviewers	400	—
Total Population	1,000	100%

As ratings can vary by demographic segment, so can PUT levels. Additionally, PUT levels do not necessarily reflect HUT levels. It is therefore important to accurately describe the demographic segment for which you are seeking information or describing your findings. Tables 5.2 and 5.3 show examples of the PUT and HUT variations that can exist at exactly the same time of day.

- The PUT level for adults 18+ at 8:00–8:30 p.m. is 60 percent, compared to a 45 percent PUT for men 18–49.

- Let us assume there are five TV homes, each with four people (one man, one woman, one teenager, one child). Further assume that not all the household members are viewing, and of those who are viewing, there is no consistency from one home to another. As shown in Table 5.3, four of the five TV homes have their set turned on—80 HUT. Of the five men in this population base (one per home) only one is viewing (20 PUT). Of the five women in the population, two are viewing (40 PUT). Using the same math, the PUT for teens is 20; for children, 40; for total people, 30.

TABLE 5.2:   PUT Levels by Demographic Group

	Market X—8:00–8:30 p.m. Rating	
	Adults 18 +	Men 18–49
Program A	30	10
Program B	20	20
Program C	10	15
PUT	60	45
Nonviewers	40	55
Total Population	100%	100%

TABLE 5.3:   PUTS/HUTS—Market X

		8:00–8:30 p.m. People Viewing				
	Homes Viewing	Men	Women	Teens	Children	Total
Home #1	1	1	1	—	—	2
Home #2	1	—	1	—	1	2
Home #3	1	—	—	1	—	1
Home #4	1	—	—	—	1	1
Home #5	—	—	—	—	—	—
Total	4	1	2	1	2	6
Population Base	5	5	5	5	5	20
HUT/PUT	80%	20%	40%	20%	40%	30%

Viewing/listening levels vary by time of day, by day of the week, and by month of the year. They also vary from one geographic area to another. The variations are primarily a function of *when* people are physically able to consume a medium, and *what* they decide to do during these timespans. Let's say you live in Los Angeles and have a nine-to-five office job, and your cousin lives in New York City and works eight to four. At 8:30 a.m. you are physically able to listen to the radio while driving in your car, and you indeed choose to do that. At this same time your cousin is working in the office and either cannot or chooses not to listen to radio. Jump the time-span to evening. You watch TV. Your cousin is working late. Now leapfrog into the weekend. You decide to read a book rather than watch TV. You might be listening to the radio while reading. Your cousin decides to watch TV. In all these examples you and your cousin were sometimes able to watch TV or listen to the radio, sometimes not . . . and you either chose to watch or listen, or chose not to. By expanding these same dynamics to the entire population, we find why viewing/listening levels vary.

Table 5.4 demonstrates the kinds of variations which are generally reported by media research suppliers.

TABLE 5.4:   HUT Variations

By Time of Day (8–11 p.m. PST) (Total U.S.–Annual Average)		By Calendar Quarter (8–11 p.m. PST) (Total U.S.)	
8–9 p.m.	58%	Jan.–Mar.	64%
9–10 p.m.	59	Apr.–Jun.	53
10–11 p.m.	54	Jul.–Sep.	48
		Oct.–Dec.	61
Average 8–11 p.m.	57	Annual Average	57
By Geographic Area (11 p.m.–1 a.m. PST)		**By Market (11 p.m.–1 a.m. PST)**	
Northeast	20%	New York	30%
Central	36	Chicago	42
South	25	Miami	21
West	22	Reno	13

Given that people do not usually consume both TV and radio at the same time, coupled with the *when* and *what* dynamics previously reviewed, we find that the usage levels of television and radio tend to complement each other: Radio listening is at its highest level when TV viewing is at its lowest, and vice-versa, as shown in Exhibit 5.1.

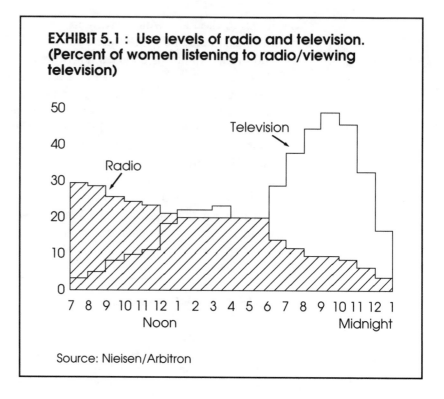

EXHIBIT 5.1 : Use levels of radio and television. (Percent of women listening to radio/viewing television)

Source: Nielsen/Arbitron

PROFESSIONAL WORKSHOP

1. Three programs are available for viewing in market X at 8:00–8:30 p.m. and receive adult 18+ ratings of 20, 15, and 10 respectively. What is the PUT level at this time?

2. For the same configuration listed above, what is the HUT level?

3. There are five radio stations available in market Y, which has 100,000 women age 18 and older. The average station is listened to by 10,000 of these women from 6:00 to 7:00 a.m. What is the PUR level at this time?

Chapter 6

Share

I n this chapter we define what *share* is as it relates to media planning, how it is calculated, and how it is intertwined with *HUT*.

Share "Share of audience" is the percentage of HUT (or PUT, PUR, PVT) tuned to a particular program or station. "Share of market" is the percentage of total category volume (dollars, units, etc.) accounted for by a brand. "Share of voice" is the percentage of advertising impressions generated by all brands in a category accounted for by a particular brand, but often also refers to share of media spending.

Share is the percentage of HUT tuned to a particular program. It can also be the percentage of PUT, PVT, PUR or Cume rating. It is commonly referred to as *share of audience*.

The same term is used by marketers when assessing their "share of market"—the percentage of total sales volume of a particular product category (e.g., instant coffee) accounted for by product X. This percentage is used as a benchmark to express what portion of total industry sales dollars a company has garnered for itself—what its relative position in the marketplace is. Similarly, in television or radio *share* is used to indicate the percentage of the total viewing/listening audience a program, or station, has. Both the marketer and the media supplier strive for dominant shares, for similar reasons. A high or growing share indicates not only relative strength vis-a-vis competitors, but also consumer acceptance and, to a large degree, business stability.

The mechanics of calculating a program share of audience are shown in Table 6.1. Program A, viewed by two of the five available TV homes in market X, produces a 40 rating; programs B and C each produce a 20 rating. In total, four of the five homes are viewing TV, thereby generating an 80 percent HUT. Because share is a percentage of HUT, HUT becomes the base against which share is calculated. This calculation requires that the program rating be divided by the HUT. Thus, program A's 40 rating divided by an 80 percent HUT gives a 50 percent share of the total *viewing* audience.

TABLE 6.1: Share of Audience—Market X

	# Homes Viewing	Rating	Share
Program A	2	40	50%
Program B	1	20	25
Program C	1	20	25
HUT	4	80	100
Not Viewing	1	—	—
Population Base	5	100%	

TABLE 6.2: Relative Shares

Program	Time	Rating	Share	Women 18+ Rating	Share
A	8–9 p.m.	30.0	50%	—	—
B	8–9 p.m.	15.0	25	—	—
C	8–9 p.m.	15.0	25	—	—
D	1–2 p.m.	—	—	7.5	25%
E	1–2 p.m.	—	—	7.5	25
F	1–2 p.m.	—	—	15.0	50
Total		60.0	100	30.0	100

The share of the program broadcast during the daytime might be the same as that of a program at nighttime, but because HUT levels vary by time of day, the nighttime program will produce a higher rating. (See Table 6.2.) Comparison of program shares, therefore, should be restricted to programs in the same general time periods. It is appropriate, for example, to compare program A to program B if they are on the air at the same time; but it is not appropriate, and possibly misleading, to compare them if they are on the air at distinctly different times. The only valid way to address share of audience for programs that air at different times is to refer to their *relative* strength. For example, one could state that program A, with a 50 percent share, holds a stronger position in nighttime than program D, with a 25 percent share, holds in daytime. Program A is therefore a *relatively* more popular show.

PROFESSIONAL WORKSHOP

1. Program A gets a 40 rating among men 18 and older during its 9:00–10:00 p.m. broadcast. At this time 80 percent of all men 18 and older are viewing television. What is program A's share of audience?

2. Program B garners a 25 household share during its 8:00–8:30 p.m. broadcast. The HUT at this time is 60. What is program B's rating?

3. Program X and program Y each obtained a 50 share among teens. Which program was viewed by a greater number of teens?

Chapter 7

Rating/HUT/Share

This chapter shows the inter-relationship of *rating, HUT*, and *share*. We demonstrate how the numbers for each of these terms are reported by media research suppliers and how a media planner goes about estimating a rating for a future TV program.

Clearly, the terms *rating, HUT*, and *share* are totally interrelated and are often used in conjunction with each other during the media selection process. Because of this interrelationship, by having data for any of the two we can calculate the third. The formulas are these:

- Solving for Rating: HUT × Share = Rating

- Solving for Share: $\dfrac{\text{Rating}}{\text{HUT}} = \text{Share}$

- Solving for HUT: $\dfrac{\text{Rating}}{\text{Share}} = \text{HUT}$

The interrelationship is shown graphically in Exhibit 7.1. We see:

- Four of the five homes owning a TV set are viewing:

  $\dfrac{4}{5} = 80\%$ HUT.

- Program A is viewed by two of the five homes:

  $\dfrac{2}{5} = 40\%$ Rating.

- Of the four TV homes viewing, two are viewing program A:

  $\dfrac{2}{4} = 50\%$ Share.

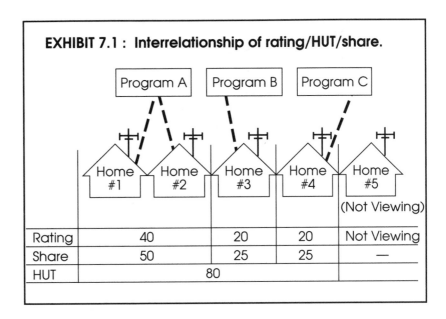

EXHIBIT 7.1 : Interrelationship of rating/HUT/share.

	Program A	Program B	Program C	
Rating	40	20	20	Not Viewing
Share	50	25	25	—
HUT	80			

Exhibit 7.2 gives the reader a sense of how rating, HUT, and share are typically presented in syndicated research sources. Studying this information will reinforce your understanding of how the three terms interrelate, indicate why each term is independently important in a media analysis, and demonstrate the complexity of the information with which a media planner or buyer needs to deal. The following facts, among others, can be gathered from the table:

- From January 30 to February 27, KAAA broadcast three different programs on Wednesdays between 9:30 and 10:00 p.m.

- Program A received a 14 *household* rating on February 6 and a 15 the following week.

- For its two telecasts, program A averaged a 15 household rating and obtained a 21 share based on the average 73 HUT for the time period across the four weeks studied.

- Programs B and C each aired one week, receiving a 9 and a 23 household rating respectively.

- During the four weeks, KAAA averaged a 15 rating with a 21 share.

EXHIBIT 7.2:   Example of Data Found in Syndicated Research Reports

DAY/TIME/STATION/PROGRAM	TV HH RATINGS						PERSONS RATINGS—TV MARKET										
	BY WEEK				AVERAGE				12–24	12–34	18–34	18–49	21–49	25–54	35+	35–64	50+
	JAN 30	FEB 06	FEB 13	FEB 20	RTG	SHR	2+	18+									
WEDNESDAY 9:30–10:00P																	
KAAA Program A		14	15		15	21	9	11	4	4	5	7	7	9	15	12	19
Program B	9				9	13	6	7	8	6	5	5	5	5	8	7	11
Program C				23	23	30	15	16	27	22	22	19	18	16	12	13	10
–4 Wk Avg–					15	21	10	11	11	9	9	10	9	10	12	11	15
KBBB Program D	18	15	14		16	22	10	12	11	10	11	12	12	12	12	12	11
Program E				23	23	29	14	16	10	11	12	13	14	15	18	18	21
–4 Wk Avg–					17	24	11	13	10	11	11	12	13	13	14	14	13
(Remaining programs deleted from chart)																	
HUT/PVT/TOTAL	72	73	69	78	73		48	55	43	45	46	50	51	53	60	59	65

- The ratings of program A varied by demographic group—from a low of 4 among people age 12–24 and people age 12–34, to a high of 19 among people age 50 and older.

- PUT levels for this time period varied by demographic group: 43 percent for people 12–34 and 60 percent for people 35 and older.

- Program C tended to have proportionately greater appeal to younger audience segments, as witnessed by the ratings.

Estimating a Rating

All ratings information from syndicated research sources is for *past* performance. Media buyers need to estimate program ratings for the future. The past might be an indicator of future performance, but does not guarantee it. As shown in Exhibit 7.2, Program D produced ratings ranging from 14 to 18, for an average rating of 16. The challenge is predicting whether the program will hold at an average 16 rating in the future, increase, or decrease.

The first step in estimating a rating is to estimate the level of potential viewing audience (PUT) for the time period in question. History has shown that PUT levels are fairly consistent from one year to the next*—that is, if the 9:00–10:00 p.m. time period produced a 60 PUT during February in market X for the last few years, the probability is it will produce the same level next February.

The next step is to estimate the share you think this program might receive. This is far more difficult to calculate because the estimate is based more on opinion than on hard fact, and is complicated by ever-changing competitive programming environments. Some of the variables that can be considered when estimating a share are these:

- History: What is the track record of similar types of programs?

- The type of program: Will it be a documentary or a situation comedy? The latter generally gets a higher share.

---

* There were HUT aberrations at the beginning of the decade. Although inexplicable, this occurrence does not negate the general reliability of HUT predictions.

- The competition: Will the program be opposite a longstanding top-rated show, or will it compete with average shows?

- Lead-in: Is the show that will precede it on the same channel top-rated or average? Some evidence indicates that a strong *lead-in* carries viewers over to the next program—that is, if a goodly portion of the lead-in program's viewers do not switch channels, they will represent a substantial portion of the next program's audience and therefore help produce a higher rating.

- Producers, directors, cast, and scriptwriters: Have these people produced past successes?

A corollary to Murphy's Law might be "If anything can vary, it will." As we have seen, HUT varies by time of day and share varies for all the reasons stated. These variations occur not only during the duration of a program, but also minute-by-minute while the program is airing. It is not uncommon to find significant rating variation for two consecutive airings of the same program (whether or not each airing is an original or a repeat), or for each quarter-hour segment within each airing. As shown in Table 7.1, "A Team's" average rating over a two-week period was 22.2—with a high of 24.3 and a low of 18.4 depending on the week and the quarter-hour within that telecast.

TABLE 7.1: "A Team" Household Ratings.

Time	Week 1	Week 2	Average
8:00–8:15	20.2	18.4	19.3
8:15–8:30	22.8	19.8	21.3
8:30–8:45	24.3	23.6	24.0
8:45–9:00	24.3	23.6	24.0
Average	22.9	21.4	22.2

Source: A.C. Nielsen

PROFESSIONAL WORKSHOP

1. Market X has 100,000 TV homes. 50,000 homes are viewing TV at 9:00–9:30 p.m., at which time program A is on the air. 25,000 homes are tuned in to Program A.

   a. What is the HUT level at this time?
   b. What is program A's household rating?
   c. What is program A's share?

2. Program B has a 25 share with a 10 rating. What is the HUT at the time program B is broadcast?

3. Programs W, X, Y, and Z each have a 25 share. What is the HUT at this time?

Chapter 8

Gross Rating Points

I n this chapter we show how ratings are combined to produce a combined total known as *gross rating points* (GRPs), and how GRPs are used by the media planner to analyze the relationships of alternative media schedules. We also discuss how GRPs vary by demographic group, by media type, and by time frame.

Gross Rating Points (GRPs)   The sum of all ratings delivered by a given list of media vehicles. Although synonymous with *TRPs*, GRPs generally refer to a "household" base. In out-of-home media, GRPs are synonymous with a *Showing*.

Gross Rating Points are the sum of all ratings. Like ratings, GRPs are expressed as a percentage and can be used for various media forms.

If, for example, you plan to purchase two announcements, one in each of two programs, and each program has a 10 rating, you will be purchasing 20 GRPs (10 × 2). The operative word is *gross*. GRPs describe the total audience of a media schedule without regard to duplication of audiences; that is, the number or percent of people who are exposed to more than one media vehicle. In this example of two 10-rated programs yielding 20 GRPs, there is no consideration for how much of the audience of the first program, if any, is part of the audience of the second program.

Let's say your media budget allows for the purchase of 6 announcements scattered across three TV programs as shown in Table 8.1. By multiplication (average rating times number of announcements) you determine that this schedule will generate 100 GRPs. The "100" is 100 percent. It does not necessarily state that 100 percent of the population will watch these shows or be exposed to your commercials in the shows. The 100 GRPs does indicate, however, that the *equivalent* of 100 percent of the population will watch one or more of these programs. Hypothetically, the 100 GRPs could be composed of 100 percent of the population, who will watch an average of one program (or telecast); one-sixth of the population, who will watch all 6 telecasts; or anything in between.

TABLE 8.1:   Calculating GRPs in Television

Program	# Telecasts in 4 weeks	Average Rating		# Telecasts in which an announcement is purchased		GRPs
A	4	25	×	2	=	50
B	4	20	×	1	=	20
C	4	10	×	3	=	30
TOTAL				6		100

Demography and Target Rating Points (TRPs)

Target Rating Points (TRPs)   Essentially synonymous with GRPs.

TRPs (Target Rating Points) have the same definition as GRPs. It does not matter which term is used in media planning. All that matters is that you state *which demographic* is encompassed in GRPs or TRPs. In the previous explanation of GRPs, there was no reference to a demographic group, but this was only for simplicity in describing the GRP dynamic. In an actual media plan it is imperative that the demographic group to which you are referring be stated—in one fashion or another. Popular notations are these ("GRPs" can be substituted for "TRPs" without changing the meaning):

- HH TRPs (Household)
- A18+ TRPs (Adults 18 & older)
- W18–34 TRPs (Women)
- M25–49 TRPs (Men)
- T12–17 TRPs (Teens)
- K6–11 TRPs (Kids/children)

Just as we saw different demographic ratings for the same program in the chapter on ratings, so GRPs/TRPs will encompass different levels depending on the demographic used. This demographic descriptor becomes critically important when two different media are compared and/or combined in a media plan.

GRPs/TRPs by Media Type

The concept of GRPs/TRPs is the same for all media, although the calculations and terminology used might vary. Tables 8.2 through 8.5 demonstrate the basic math used for establishing TRPs by media type. Note that different demographic descriptors are used in each table, but only for demonstration purposes.

TABLE 8.2: Radio TRPs

Station	Time Period	T12–17 Rating		# Announcements		T12–17 TRPs
A	6–10 a.m.	1.0	×	18	=	18
	10 a.m.–3 p.m.	.5	×	4	=	2
	3–7 p.m.	2.0	×	24	=	48
B	6–10 a.m.	.1	×	10	=	1
	3–7 p.m.	.7	×	10	=	7
	7 p.m.–midnight	1.0	×	24	=	24
Total				90		100

TABLE 8.3: Magazine TRPs

Magazine	% Coverage of W18–34		# Advertisements		W18–34 TRPs
A	25%	×	1	=	25
B	15	×	4	=	60
C	5	×	3	=	15
Total			8		100

TABLE 8.4: Newspaper TRPs

Newspaper	% Household Penetration		# Insertions		Household TRPs
A	40%	×	1	=	40
B	30	×	1	=	30
C	20	×	1	=	20
D	10	×	1	=	10
Total			4		100

TABLE 8.5: Outdoor TRPs

# Poster Units	People 2 & Older Daily Circulation for Average Poster		Gross Daily Circulation	Market Population	People TRPs
50	×	1,000	= 50,000	50,000	100

If, for example, all four of the media forms shown in Tables 8.2–8.5 were used in a media plan, the TRP calculations would have to be made against the same demographic group (the target group of the advertising effort). It would be incongruous to report that the media effort is composed of a total of 400 TRPs (100 in each of the four media types). If you keep in mind that TRPs are an expression, in percentage terms, of coverage of specific population groups, this becomes quite clear.

For the same reason that you cannot add together TRPs for different demographic segments, you cannot add TRPs for combinations of geographic markets. As shown in Table 8.6, for example, scheduling 100, 50 and 25 TRPs respectively in markets A, B and C yields an average TRP level of 50 for the three markets combined —not 175 TRPs (which is the sum of the three levels). The 50 TRPs is obtained by multiplying the TRPs in each market by the population base, adding the products, and dividing by the combined population base. (Note: Remember that TRPs are percentages. For a TRP of 50, multiply by 50 percent or .50, for a TRP of 100, multiply by 100 percent or 1.0.)

TABLE 8.6:   TRPs by Geographic Market (men 18 & older)

Market	Population (000)	TRPs	Equivalent Number of Men (000)
A	10,000	100	10,000
B	20,000	50	10,000
C	40,000	25	10,000
Total	60,000	—	30,000
Average	—	50	—

Time Frame

The time frame for the accumulation of GRPs/TRPs varies by medium and must therefore be considered when evaluating media types:

- Magazines accumulate their readership, and therefore their coverage, over time, depending on how many different people read the magazine and when they physically obtain an issue for reading. Thus, coverage over time can vary from a week or two for some weekly magazines to several months for monthly magazines.

- Newspapers, for the most part, are read the day of issuance. TRP accumulation is therefore in a single day.

- Outdoor TRPs are a reflection of one day's audience accumulation, although nearly all outdoor purchases are made for a duration of at least one month.

- Sunday newspaper supplements have a longer lifespan than daily newspapers. Their TRPs are accumulated primarily on the day of issuance, but also in the ensuing days.

- Television and radio produce a rating when a program airs: the time span of that rating is *at that moment*. If you purchase programs during a one-week period, the accumulated TRPs have a lifespan of one week; programs purchased during a four-week period accumulate TRPs within those four weeks.*

The time frame of TRPs for various media is listed in Table 8.7.

TABLE 8.7: Time Frame of TRPs by Medium

Magazines	As long as an issue physically exists and is read by someone
Newspapers	Generally one day
Outdoor	One day
Radio	During the time the programs air
Sunday Supplements	Mostly in the first day
Television	During the time the programs air, except for VCR viewing

---

Why GRPs/TRPs Are Used

The reason GRPs are used instead of actual population counts is the same reason ratings/penetration/coverage is used: it's easier to calculate and report on percentages than it is on total head counts, and it's easier to demonstrate the relationship of alternatives (e.g., one schedule has 100 TRPs, the other 150). Further (as we will see in later sections) GRPs/TRPs form the foundation for other media dynamics, such as reach/frequency.

---

* With the proliferation of VCRs we see some programs recorded for later viewing. The ratings and, therefore, TRPs produced by these viewings may fall within the period originally purchased, or at some later time.

PROFESSIONAL WORKSHOP

1. If you purchase one commercial announcement in each of four TV programs, each of which has a 25 rating, how many GRPs will you have purchased?

2. If Programs A, B and C have women 18+ ratings of 5, 10, and 15 respectively, and you purchase three announcements in each program, how many TRPs will you have purchased?

3. If you purchase ten announcements on each of five radio stations in market X and produce a total of 100 TRPs, what is the average rating of the average station?

4. Magazine A has a coverage of men 18–34 of 20 percent. Magazine B has a coverage of men 35–49 of 10 percent. If you schedule one advertisement in each publication, how many TRPs will you have produced?

5. If you purchase 100 GRPs in market X and 50 GRPs in market Y, how many total GRPs have you purchased for the two markets combined?

Chapter 9

Impressions

I n this chapter we show how *impressions* are calculated based on ratings or absolute audience measures and demonstrate how impressions are used to compare alternative media schedules.

Impressions The gross sum of all media exposures (numbers of people or homes) without regard to duplication.

Impressions are the sum of all advertising exposures. They are identical to GRPs/TRPs, except they are expressed in terms of *numbers* of individuals (or homes) rather than as a percentage. It is equally correct to refer to them as *gross impressions*.

As shown in the following tables, impressions can be calculated in two ways. For demonstration, let us assume we are analyzing a television schedule geared to reaching adults 18 and older in market X (which has an adult 18+ population of 1 million). The same arithmetic applies regardless of the target audience, the market, or the medium being analyzed.

Method # 1 (see Table 9.1): Multiply the audience of each TV program by the number of announcements scheduled in each. Add the products of the multiplication.

TABLE 9.1: Calculating Impressions

Program	A18+ Viewers		# Announcements		A18+ Impressions
A	250,000	×	2	=	500,000
B	200,000	×	3	=	600,000
C	150,000	×	4	=	600,000
D	100,000	×	3	=	300,000
Total					
					2,000,000

Method # 2 (see Table 9.2): Determine the GRPs (ratings times number of announcements) and multiply by the market population. Keep in mind GRPs are a percentage (200 GRPs = 200 percent = 2.0).

TABLE 9.2: Calculating Impressions

Program	A18+ Rating		# Announcements		A18+ GRPs
A	25	×	2	=	50
B	20	×	3	=	60
C	15	×	4	=	60
D	10	×	3	=	30
Total					200

200 × 1,000,000 population = 2,000,000 A18+ impressions

Impressions are used for various purposes. The first purpose is for use in sales brochures and the like when advertisers inform retailers of the breadth and scope of the advertising planned to support a product. The belief is that retailers are accustomed to seeing delivery figures in gross impressions and are impressed by these statistics: "2,000,000 impressions," for example, sounds like a lot more that "200 GRPs." The expression "boxcar number" is often used when referring to impressions because the magnitude of the numbers is akin to the number of cases of a packaged goods product that can be shipped in a railway boxcar.

The second use for impressions involves media plan comparisons. Because impressions can be calculated for any media form, it is a convenient way to compare gross audience deliveries of different media vehicles or different media plans. Table 9.3 shows two media plans at equal dollar budgets. Both deliver 90 million *women* impressions. If all women are the target, both plans (on the surface) are equal. If, however, the target is women 18–34, then plan I is superior, because it delivers more of your target audience. If women 50 and older are the target, plan II has the advantage.

TABLE 9.3:   Comparison of Alternative Plans Having Equal Expenditures

	Impressions	
	Plan I	Plan II
Total Women	90,000	90,000
18–34	30,000	15,000
35–49	30,000	30,000
50+	30,000	45,000

Two additional uses of impressions are for calculating Audience Composition and Cost-per-Thousand, both of which are discussed in later chapters.

PROFESSIONAL WORKSHOP

1. You intend to purchase 300 TRPs against men in market X, which has a total population of 1 million people. Forty percent of these people are men. How many men impressions will you generate?

2. You've scheduled five national magazines to receive one ad each. Each magazine has a women rating of 10. If there are 90 million women in the United States, how many impressions will you generate?

3. If the magazines in question 2 skew to women 18–34, will you have more or fewer impressions for women 18–34?

4. Your market X media plan calls for 20 announcements on each of three radio stations. Each station has an average 1.0 rating for men. You also schedule a newspaper ad in a metropolitan daily that has a 40 percent coverage of men. What will the impressions you generate be equivalent to?

Chapter 10

Index

> I n this chapter we show how to calculate an *index*. We demonstrate how an index is used to quickly review numerical relationships between different numbers or sets of numbers. We also discuss two specific kinds of index numbers—*Brand Development Index* and *Category Development Index*—that are commonly used in marketing analyses.

Index A number indicating change in magnitude relative to the magnitude of some other number (the base) taken as representing 100. A 110 index indicates a 10 percent positive change in magnitude; a 90 index a 10 percent negative change.

You've heard of the Consumer Price Index (CPI). It's usually up or down or holding at the same level relative to a base level. The same concept applies to **index** when used for media evaluation. An index is a *percentage* which relates one number to another number, called the *base*. An index is used to demonstrate quickly whether a number is average, above average, or below average. Unlike percent increase or percent decrease, an index *includes* the base in the reported number.

Calculating an Index

Calculating an index requires simple division. It follows the same arithmetic relationship as percent increase or decrease, but is accomplished with one less step. To calculate percent increase, for example, you subtract the smaller number from the larger number and divide the difference by the smaller number. To calculate an index for the same increase, you avoid the subtraction step and simply divide the larger number by the smaller number. Because the smaller number is the base against which you are comparing the larger number, you include the base in your index calculation.

	Percent Increase	Index
Number in question:	60%	60%
Base:	− 40%	40%
Math:	20% ÷ 40%	60% ÷ 40%
Result:	50%	150
Conclusion for either:	60 percent is 50 percent greater than 40 percent	

If the 60 percent/40 percent in the above example is reversed, the same procedure applies to both the percent *decrease* and an index—except the base is now 60 percent, so you are dividing by the larger number:

	Percent Decrease	Index
Number in Question:	40%	40%
Base:	− 60%	60%
Math:	(20%) ÷ 60%	40% ÷ 60%
Result:	(33%)	67
Conclusion for either:	40 percent is 33 percent less than 60 percent	

Because an index compares a number to the base, and the base is always 100 (percent), an index of 100 means something is average (the same as the base); an index over 100 means it is above average; an index below 100 means it is below average. The amount by which something is below average is demonstrated by its numerical distance from 100. In the above example, the 67 index is 33 less than 100. Here are some more examples to help reinforce the above/below average designation:

Index	To Read
100	Average
125	25% above average
225	125% above average
75	25% below average
50	50% below average
25	75% below average

Let us assume you are writing a media plan to address adults who went bowling. To determine their age skews you tabulate the number and percent who went bowling and relate this to the population. As shown in Table 10.1, of the 140,000 adults 18–24 in the population, 35,700 went bowling—representing 23.8 percent of *all* adults who went bowling (column labeled "% Down") and 25.5 percent of the total population in this age cell (column labeled "% Across"). By displaying the index for each age group, you can see quickly that younger adults have a greater propensity for bowling than older adults, and you can easily assess the relative intensity of that propensity. Some of the statements you can make about your findings, based on the index, are:

- Adults 18–24 have a 70 percent greater propensity for bowling than the average adult.

- It is 70 percent more likely that adults 18–24 would have gone bowling than the average adult.

- The concentration of adults 18–24 who have gone bowling is 70 percent greater than the concentration of bowlers in the general population.

- If you advertise to adults 18–24, you have a 70 percent greater probability of addressing someone who has gone bowling than if you advertise to the total population at large.

TABLE 10.1: Using an Index

Adults:	Population (000)	% Total	Went Bowling (000)	% Down	% Across	Index
18–24	140.0	14.0%	35.7	23.8%	25.5%	170
25–34	240.0	24.0	46.8	31.2	19.5	130
35–44	200.0	20.0	33.0	22.0	16.5	110
45–54	140.0	14.0	18.0	12.0	12.9	86
55–64	120.0	12.0	9.0	6.0	7.5	50
65 or older	160.0	16.0	7.5	5.0	4.7	31
Total:	1000.0	100 %	150.0	100 %	15.0%	100

Because all the numbers in the table are interrelated, the index can be calculated in either of two ways:

1. Divide the "Percent Across" for the 18–24 age group by the "Percent Across" for the total population (25.5%/15.0% = 170).

2. Divide the "% Down" for the 18–24 age group by the "% Total" that the 18–24's represent of the total population (23.8%/14.0% = 170).

An index can be divided by an index to yield a new index. You might encounter data that show a series of indices, such as the fluctuation in the cost of a 30-second (:30) commercial year to year, with all data relating to a base year. If you wish to change the base year against which you are comparing the cost, you can recalculate the data either by using the actual costs, or by using the index for the new base year. As shown in Table 10.2, if you use year 6 as the new base, you can obtain the 110 index either by using $77/$70 or by using the indices of 154/140.

TABLE 10.2: Indexing an Index

Year	Cost/:30 Commercial	Index Year 1 = Base	Year 6 = Base
1	$ 50	100	
2	55	110	
3	62	124	
4	67	134	
5	68	136	
6	70	140	100
7	77	154	110
8	85	170	121
9	95	190	136
10	100	200	143

Brand Development Index

Brand Development Index (BDI) A numerical display showing the geographic or demographic areas of a brand's relative strength or weakness. See *Index*.

Indices are used to express any relationship of numbers within any category. Commonly, a **Brand Development Index (BDI)** is displayed by geographic area to show how each area is performing relative to the average U.S. performance. As shown in Table 10.3, markets A and D are above average, market B is on average, and markets C and E are below average.

TABLE 10.3:   Brand Development Index

Market	% U.S. Population	% Brand Sales	BDI	Share of Market	BDI
A	10%	11%	110	22%	110
B	15	15	100	20	100
C	20	18	90	18	90
D	25	30	120	24	120
E	30	26	87	17	87
Total	100	100	100	20	100

The indices in Table 10.3 can be calculated in various ways and still yield the same conclusions. Method 1 is to divide the percent of total sales accounted for in each market by the percentage of total population in that market:

$$\frac{\text{Market A}}{\text{\% Brand sales}} \quad \frac{11}{10} = 110 \text{ BDI}$$
$$\frac{\text{\% Brand sales}}{\text{\% Population}}$$

Method 2 is to divide the share of market in each area by the average U.S. share of market. In the above example, this brand commands a 22 percent share of market in market A—that is, of all the product category sold in this market, this particular brand accounts for 22 percent of the total. The average market has a 20 percent share. Therefore, 22 share divided by 20 share equals a 110 index or a 110 BDI.

Category Development Index

Category Development Index (CDI)   A numerical display showing the geographic or demographic areas of a product/service category's relative strength or weakness. See *Index*.

The **Category Development Index (CDI)** is identical to the BDI except in one you are comparing a *brand* and in the other you are comparing a *category* of brands (e.g., "Danny's Lemonade" brand versus the category of all lemonade brands).

Comparisons between BDI and CDI are often made to help a marketer decide relative strengths and weaknesses vis-a-vis the competition.

The following table demonstrates some of the conclusions a marketer could draw from the BDI/CDI analysis shown in Table 10.4:

- "Danny's Lemonade" is selling proportionately more in market A than in the average of all markets, and has a greater relative franchise than the whole category.

- The brand is an average seller in market B, but could have some room for growth given that the category is doing relatively better. There's an apparent 10 percent greater propensity for people in market B to drink lemonade.

- The brand is not doing well in market C (10 percent below average), but the market obviously performs well for total lemonades (50 percent above average). This appears to be a brand problem, not a total lemonade consumption problem.

TABLE 10.4:   BDI versus CDI

Market	BDI	CDI
A	110	100
B	100	110
C	90	150
D	120	80
E	87	80
Average	100	100

Always Show the Components

To fully appreciate the meaning and magnitude of an index, you should always display the two numbers that beget the index. Table 10.5 demonstrates how an index, shown in isolation, can deceive you into thinking that one market is substantially more important than another. Here we see that market B has a 67 BDI, compared to market E with a 200. If only the BDI is considered you might decide that market E should receive more advertising than B. Further inspection, however, reveals that market E accounts for only two percent of all cases sold, compared to market B with 20 percent of the sales volume. Based on case volume, market B would ordinarily be allocated more advertising.

TABLE 10.5:   An Index Can Deceive

| Market | % POP | Brand Sales | | BDI |
		Cases (000)	% Total	
A	40%	200	50%	125
B	30	80	20	67
C	18	72	18	100
D	11	40	10	91
E	1	8	2	200
TOTAL	100%	400	100%	100

PROFESSIONAL WORKSHOP

1. Of all the adults 18 years and older living in market X, 20 percent buy their groceries at the Sigma supermarket chain. Of all the women 18–49 in this market, 30 percent shop at Sigma. Do women 18–49 have a greater or lesser propensity for shopping at Sigma than the average adult? What is the index? What is the magnitude of that propensity?

2. Product X is sold in markets A, B, C and D, which respectively represent 5 percent, 10 percent, 10 percent, and 25 percent of the U.S. population. Product X's percent of total sales in each market is (respectively) 30 percent, 10 percent, 20 percent, and 40 percent. What is the BDI in each market?

3. Television program A had a five-year run, producing an average household rating each year as follows: 10, 15, 20, 20, 10. What is the index of performance each year relative to the average year?

4. In market A, product X has a BDI of 90 compared to a CDI of 110. What does this tell you? If the BDI is 110 and the CDI 90, what does this tell you?

Chapter 11

Audience Composition

I n this chapter we show how *audience composition* of a medium's audience is used to analyze alternative media schedules and how the term is used to describe generally the kind of audiences various media or media schedules attract.

Audience Composition
The demographic profile of media audiences.

Audience composition is the amount or percentage of individuals in each demographic segment being analyzed.

Audience composition (usually referred to as *Audience comp*) indicates the *relative concentration* of different audience segments within a specific media vehicle, for an entire schedule of media vehicles, or for combinations of different media forms. Audience composition answers the question "What part of the total audience is my target audience?"

Table 11.1 demonstrates audience comp for two TV prorams, both of which have a total viewing audience of 500,000 people. Program A delivers 300,000 adults 18 and older, representing 60 percent of its total audience; program B delivers 200,000 adults 18 and older, or 40 percent of its total audience. All other things being equal, if you're trying to target adults 18 and older, program A is the better choice because it has a higher audience composition of your target than program B. It can be said that program A *skews* (is biased) toward an adult audience.

How a TV program (or any media vehicle) skews is an indication of the relative acceptance of that program by a given population group and therefore, by inference, the relative strength and importance of that program to that group. For programs C and D in Table 11.2 we see that both deliver 40,000 adults 18 and older, but

TABLE 11.1:   Audience Composition

	Program A		Program B	
	# Viewers	% Total (Audience Comp)	# Viewers	% Total (Audience Comp)
Adults 18+	300,000	60%	200,000	40%
Teens 12–17	100,000	20	200,000	20
Kids 2–11	100,000	20	100,000	20
Total	500,000	100%	500,000	100%

program C skews much more heavily to an adult audience—that is, a greater percentage of its audience is adults. This skew suggests that the adult is in control of the TV set and has chosen to view this program. If this indeed is the case, a commercial placed in this program, which is directed to an adult, might have a better chance of effectively reaching the adult than if placed in program D.

TABLE 11.2:   Skew

	Program C		Program D	
	# Viewers	% Total	# Viewers	% Total
Adults 18+	40,000	80%	40,000	40%
Teens 12–17	5,000	10	30,000	30
Kids 2–11	5,000	10	30,000	30
Total	50,000	100%	100,000	100%

An audience composition analysis of a medium (or a media category, etc.) is a handy device for describing generally the kind of audiences the medium attracts. When the analysis also includes an audience composition index for each demographic cell, you could "write a story" about the people who consume the medium. For example, Table 11.3 shows such an analysis. The story you could write might read: The people who consume medium A tend to be middle-aged and older, with a household income skewing to the relatively higher level. More often than not they live in a household with two people, which, combined with their age and income level, indicates they fit within the category that is termed "empty

TABLE 11.3: Audience Composition of Medium A

	Total Adults	Medium A	Index
Total U.S.	100%	100%	—
By age:			
18–34	40	30	75
35–54	35	45	129
55+	25	25	100
By Household Income:			
$50M+	25	25	100
$30M–49M	30	40	133
$10M–29M	35	30	86
Under $10M	10	5	50
By Household Size:			
1 person	10	10	100
2 people	35	50	143
3+ people	55	40	73
By Education:			
Graduated College	20	40	200
Graduated High School	40	70	175
By Region:			
Northeast	20	25	125
North Central	25	20	80
South	35	30	86
West	20	25	125

nesters," where the kids are grown and have left the household. Because it is usual for the higher income people to have attained a higher education level, it is not surprising to see that these people are more educated than the average adult. For the most part, these adults are concentrated in the northeastern and western regions of the United States, although half of all these adults can still be found throughout the remainder of the United States.

Despite its usefulness, audience composition cannot stand on its own as the primary reason for selecting a medium or media category, for two reasons. First, other media dynamics, such as reach and frequency, should be part of the selection analysis. Second, the base numbers used in the composition might be very small and therefore not indicative of the main thrust of the medium. This is especially true if you simply review the indices without considering the base numbers. For example, a medium might have an index of 300 for people in its audience who buy a certain product, based on a population base of one percent of people who buy this product. This medium, therefore, has three percent of its audience who buy this product—hardly an indication that this medium skews to people who buy this product.

PROFESSIONAL WORKSHOP

1. Program A delivers 10 million viewers, half of which are women. Half of the women viewers are 18–34, 30 percent are 35–49, and the remainder are older. This compares to a population distribution of these groups of 40 percent, 45 percent, and 15 percent respectively. What is the most pronounced audience skew for program A?

2. Using the same example, does program A deliver more of its audience to women over 34 years of age, or to women under 35 years of age?

3. What is the index of delivery of program B in each age grouping:

	Population	Viewers
18–34	50,000	20,000
35+	50,000	30,000

Chapter 12

Cost-Per-Thousand (CPM)

I n this chapter we introduce a mathematical function known as *CPM* which addresses the advertising cost of media relative to the audiences delivered by these media. We demonstrate how CPM analyses are used by the media planner to decide which media schedule is more cost-efficient.

Cost-per-Thousand (CPM) The cost per 1,000 people (or homes) delivered by a medium or media schedule.

CPM is an abbreviation of **cost-per-thousand**, with the "thousand" from the Latin *mille*. It is the cost per one thousand individuals (or homes) delivered by a medium or media schedule.

Calculating CPM requires simple division and multiplication:

- Divide the cost by the delivery and multiply the quotient by 1,000.

$$\frac{\$10,000.00}{2,000,000} = .005 \times 1,000 = \$5.00 \text{ CPM}$$

- A shorter method is to eliminate three zeros from the delivery and perform the same division:

$$\frac{\$10,000.00}{2,000} = \$5.00$$

The reason CPM is used instead of cost-per-audience-member is convenience in reciting the data. It's easier to say a media vehicle has a CPM of $5.43 than to say it has a cost-per-audience-member of .00543 or 5.43 thousandths of a dollar.

CPM can be calculated for any medium, for any demographic group, and for any total cost. It allows you to compare the relative cost of one medium to another, or of one media schedule to another. It is not unlike the cost-per-ounce information we now find included in supermarket pricing.

Cost Efficiency
Generally refers to the relative costs of delivering media audiences. See *Cost-per-rating-point* and *Cost-per-thousand*.

Calculating CPM allows you to display the **cost efficiency** of various media alternatives. The lower the CPM, the more cost efficient the medium. The more cost efficient a medium, the more audience can be delivered per dollar invested.

As shown in Table 12.1, four media choices cost approximately the same amount of money for the creative units you are considering: a **black and white page** in magazines; a thirty-second commercial in TV. If you are targeting women 18 and older, two choices (at a $2 CPM) are the most cost efficient—magazine B and program B. Program A is the least cost efficient. If you're targeting women 18–49, then magazine B (which has the lowest CPM) is the most cost efficient. (You'll note that the audience headings show [000] which indicate three zeros should be added to the audience shown: 5,000 readers for magazine A is read as 5 million readers.)

Black and White Page
An advertising page that is printed with black on white paper, or in reverse type (white on black paper). Abbreviated as P B/W. In a four-color advertisement, black is considered one of the colors.

TABLE 12.1: CPM Comparisons

	Cost 1P B/W	Women 18+ Readers (000)	CPM	Women 18–49 Readers (000)	CPM
Magazine A	$10,000	4,000	$2.50	2,000	$5.00
Magazine B	$15,000	7,500	$2.00	5,000	$3.00

	Cost :30 Commercial	Women 18+ Viewers (000)	CPM	Women 18–49 Viewers (000)	CPM
Program A	$12,000	4,000	$3.00	3,000	$4.00
Program B	$15,000	7,500	$2.00	3,000	$5.00

Although you can use different cost structures across different media forms (such as a page black/white and a : 30) to determine relative CPMs, you should be careful not to assume that the creative units are necessarily equal to each other. Much research has been conducted, and continues to be done, to determine the "value" of different creative units between different media forms and within media forms. There are *no* general conclusions that can be drawn from this research. There is no evidence, for example, that proves a one-page advertisement for a specific product, executed in a specific creative style, is better than or not as good as a specific 30-second commercial in television. Nor is there evidence that an advertisement in one magazine will perform better or worse than the same advertisement in another magazine. CPM must therefore be used only as a guide in helping decide which media vehicle or media plan is better than another on the basis of cost relative to audience delivery.

It should also be clear that CPM figures must be for the same demographic groups when comparing two vehicles or two plans. It would be pointless, for example, to compare program A's CPM for women 18–34 with program B's CPM for men 18–34.

Because CPM is a function of cost and audience delivery, with one or both of these ingredients changing when vehicle or media plan comparisons are made, it is also incorrect to average CPMs across demographic groups or across media forms. To calculate the average CPM of combinations, you must return to the basic cost and audience ingredients, add these components, and then strike an average. As shown in Table 12.2, the average CPM against women 18+ for magazines A and B combined is $2.17 ($25,000 divided by 11,500,000), not a straight average of $2.50 and $2.00. Likewise, the CPM for adults is not an average of the CPMs for women and men.

TABLE 12.2:   CPM Averaging

	Magazine A	Magazine B	Magazines A + B
Cost 1P B/W	$10,000	$15,000	$25,000
Women 18+ (000)	4,000	7,500	11,500
CPM	$ 2.50	$ 2.00	$ 2.17
Men 18+ (000)	2,000	5,000	7,000
CPM	$ 5.00	$ 3.00	$ 3.57
Adults 18+ (000)	6,000	12,500	18,500
CPM	$ 1.67	$ 1.20	$ 1.35

PROFESSIONAL WORKSHOP

1. A 60-second announcement on a TV program costs $100 and delivers a 5 rating for men and a 2.5 rating for women in a market that has one million of each sex in its population. What is the cost-per-thousand for each group?

2. Using the same example, what is the CPM for men and women combined?

3. Magazine A has a women CPM of $5.00 for a one-page advertisement that costs $10,000. How many women are in the average audience of magazine A?

Chapter 13

Cost-Per-Rating-Point (CPP)

I n this chapter we define another term based on the relationship of a medium's advertising cost and its audience delivery. We show how *cost-per-point* (CPP) varies from one specific media vehicle to another and how it varies by demographic group. We demonstrate how CPP is used by the media planner to project the total advertising cost of a specific media schedule and how it can be used to determine how much media delivery is affordable within a defined media budget.

Cost-per-Rating-Point (CPP) The cost of an advertising unit (e.g., a 30-second commercial) divided by the average rating of a specific demographic group (e.g., women 18–49).

Cost-per-rating-point is the cost of purchasing one rating point. It is commonly referred to as **CPP** (cost-per-point). As we will see, it relates to cost-per-thousand, but is used for entirely different reasons. CPP is most often used for broadcast media.

The calculation for CPP is the same as for CPM, but the components are different. To get a CPP, divide the cost of a unit of advertising (e.g., a 30-second TV commercial) by the program rating. As shown, the CPP for the TV :30 is $50; for the Radio :60, $20:

$$\frac{\$1,000 \text{ per }:30}{20 \text{ rating}} = \$50 \text{ CPP} \qquad \frac{\$100 \text{ per }:60}{5 \text{ rating}} = \$20 \text{ CPP}$$

Because the term is cost-per-*rating-point* you need to define which rating you want before calculating CPPs or before using CPP data to devise a media plan. In the above TV example, if the 20 rating is for homes, the CPP is for homes; if for women, the CPP is for women, etc.

CPP information can be obtained from independent media research sources (e.g., Spot Quotations and Data, *Adweek's Marketer's Guide to Media*), from media buyers (those within your ad agency or independent media buying firms, etc.), or from the TV/radio station's advertising sales representatives.

CPP estimates are based on historical purchases and a prediction of future marketplace conditions. For example, if the CPP for a 30-second TV commercial in daytime in market X was $10 for a schedule that aired in January, and it has become a seller's market (that is, there's more demand than supply), the buyer might estimate that same schedule to have a CPP of $12 in March.

CPPs vary widely—from one market to another, from one calendar quarter to another, from station to station or network to network, and from program to program. Although there may be reason for this variation, there is no yardstick for measuring past or future CPPs—no tried and true formula that can be used. Although Table 13.1 presents hypothetical data, it does reflect typical realities. By studying the data, you'll note that different programs or stations command different CPPs by market and by calendar quarter, but there is no linear relationship of one element to the other. Some examples:

- Station A has the same rating for "News" in each quarter, but the CPP is higher in the second quarter.

TABLE 13.1: Cost-Per-Point Variation

	Market X				Market Y			
Population (000)	500				1,000			
	Jan–Mar		Apr–Jun		Jan–Mar		Apr–Jun	
	Rating	CPP	Rating	CPP	Rating	CPP	Rating	CPP
Station A								
News 6–7 p.m.	5	$10	5	$12	—	—	—	—
Movie 7–9 p.m.	8	$ 8	9	$10	—	—	—	—
Station B								
Sitcom 6–7 p.m.	—	—	—	—	5	$25	5	$20
Games 7–8 p.m.	—	—	—	—	6	$20	7	$30
Special 7–8 p.m.	—	—	—	—	—	—	8	$40

- The CPP for "News" in the first quarter is the same as for the "Movie" in the second quarter, but the ratings for each program are substantially different.

- Station B is in a market twice the size of station A's market, but the CPP for the same rating size is sometimes more than twice the amount, sometimes less.

Using CPP to Estimate Affordability

Most often, cost-per-point data are used to estimate how many GRPs/TRPs can be purchased within a defined media budget. For example, if you have a budget of $1,000 and a predicted CPP of $10, you can purchase 100 TRPs ($1,000 divided by $10 is 100).

Table 13.2 shows an example of how many TRPs can be purchased in various combinations of daytime and nighttime television —beginning with 100 percent of the budget expended in either primetime or daytime, then half the budget in each, and finally one-third in day and two-thirds in night. Calculating TRP affordability requires the budget to be allocated to each TV time in the desired ratios with the appropriate CPP divided into the respective budgets.

A similar mathematical principle applies if you want to allocate *TRPs* in predetermined ratios. As shown in Table 13.3, you must

---

TABLE 13.2: Calculating Affordable TRPs within a $1,000 Budget—Dollar Allocation

Allocation of Budget	Budget	CPP	Affordable TRPs
100% daytime	$1,000	$10.00	100
100% primetime	$1,000	$25.00	40
50% daytime	$ 500	$10.00	50
+50% primetime	$ 500	$25.00	20
Total	$1,000	$14.29	70
33.33% daytime	$ 333	$10.00	33
+66.66% primetime	$ 667	$25.00	27
Total	$1,000	$16.67	60

TABLE 13.3:   Calculating Affordable TRPs within a $1,000 Budget—TRP Allocation

Allocation of TRP delivery	CPP	Affordable TRPs	Cost
100% daytime	$10.00	100	$1,000
100% primetime	$25.00	40	$1,000
50% daytime	$10.00	28.6	$ 286
+50% primetime	$25.00	28.6	$ 714
Total	$17.50	57.2	$1,000
33.33% daytime	$10.00	16.7	$ 167
+66.66% primetime	$25.00	33.3	$ 833
Total	$20.00	50.0	$1,000

first calculate the average CPP for the combination of TV entities. The average CPP for the 50 percent/50 percent combination is $17.50 ($10 plus $25 divided by 2). Next, divide the total available budget by the average CPP to determine total TRPs. Allocate the total TRPs to each TV entity according to the desired ratio. Multiplying the TRPs by TV entity times the respective CPP will yield the budget for each entity. By comparing the two tables (Dollar Allocation and TRP Allocation) you'll note striking differences in the amount of dollars and number of TRPs that each system yields. Neither system is necessarily the better. It all depends on what you're trying to accomplish with the media, which is a rather involved subject and requires a complete understanding of the many dynamics discussed in other sections of the book.

This mathematical principle also applies when calculating the CPP for a group of markets. For example, let us assume you intend to purchase radio in three markets within a $2,000 budget and want to estimate the average TRPs you can buy in the three markets combined. You have estimated the CPP for each of the three markets, as shown in Table 13.4. It would be erroneous to add the three and determine the CPP to be $13, as it would be erroneous to add the three and divide by three to strike a $4.33 average. The correct math requires you to include the *size* of each market rela-

TABLE 13.4:   Calculating an Average Cost-Per-Point for Market Groupings

Market	Population #	Population %	CPP		Product
A	200	50	× $7	=	$3.50
B	100	25	× $4	=	$1.00
C	100	25	× $2	=	$ .50
Total/Average	400	100			$5.00

tive to the other—remembering that CPP is cost-per-*rating-point* and that one rating point produces different audience amounts in different population-size markets. As the table indicates, the average CPP for the three markets combined is $5.00 (obtained by multiplying the CPP in each market by the percent of population it represents of your total three-market universe, and adding the products).

The Relationship of CPP and CPM

Cost-per-point and cost-per-thousand have two things in common: cost and audience delivery. How cost and delivery are expressed for each is different, but both are based on a *rating*. As shown in this example, the CPP of $20 for a 5-rated program results in a cost per unit (e.g., :30) of $100. The 5 rating is equivalent to an audience of 50,000. With a $100 unit cost and a 50,000 audience you can quickly calculate the CPM, which is $2.

			Market Population		Audience Delivery
CPP	$ 20				
× Rating	5	×	1,000,000	=	50,000
Cost/Unit	$100				
CPM					$2.00

If you have an estimated CPP (for a program, a station, a market, etc.) and want to determine the CPM without regard to how many TRPs you might include in your media plan, you can use the following formula. The basis of the formula is the understanding that 100 TRPs is equivalent to 100 percent of the market's population.

Formula		Example	
$\dfrac{\text{CPP} \times 100}{\text{Market Population*}}$	$= \text{CPM}$	$\dfrac{\$20 \times 100 = \$2,000}{1,000}$	$= \$2.00$

Conversely, if you have a CPM and wish to estimate the CPP, the following formula can be used:

Formula		Example	
$\dfrac{\text{Market Population*} \times \text{CPM}}{100}$	$= \text{CPP}$	$\dfrac{1,000 \times \$2.00 = \$2,000}{100}$	$= \$20.00$

*Shown in thousands.

The usefulness of converting CPP to CPM is to provide additional information for the media evaluation process. For example, if you need to choose between two media entities (two markets, two programs, two media vehicles, etc.) you would be hard-pressed to select one on the basis of CPP. As shown in Table 13.5, a $10,000 budget could afford 800 TRPs in market A and 775 in market B, based on their respective CPPs of $12.50 and $12.90. Which choice is more efficient—which will deliver the greatest audience per dollar invested? By calculating CPM we determine that B is more efficient.

TABLE 13.5: CPP & CPM Comparisons

	$10,000 Budget	
	Market A	**Market B**
CPP	$ 12.50	$ 12.90
Affordable TRPs	800	775
Population (= 100 TRPs)	275,000	325,000
Cost/100 TRPs	$1,250	$1,290
CPM	$ 4.55	$ 3.97

PROFESSIONAL WORKSHOP

1. You plan to buy a 10-rated program for a cost/:30 of $100. What is your CPP?

2. You determined that the cost-per-point for primetime is $40, and for daytime $10. You have a $10,000 budget. How many rating points can you buy if:
   a. You want to distribute your budget evenly by daypart?
   b. You want to evenly distribute rating points by daypart?

3. You purchased a program which has a women rating of 20 in a market with a population base of 500,000 women. You paid $10 CPP. What is your CPM?

Chapter 14

Reach

I n this chapter we build on what we learned about ratings and an advertising medium's capability to deliver audiences by introducing the concept of *reach*. We explain how different media vehicles attract different groups of people and how, by combining these media vehicles in a media plan, you can increase the number of people who will be exposed to your advertising message. We examine how reach accumulates by medium, with successive uses of a medium, and by combining media forms.

Reach The number or percentage of a population group exposed to a media schedule within a given period of time.

At this point you should have a good grasp of what a rating point is and how it leads to GRPs/TRPs and eventually to impressions. You've noted that GRPs and impressions are indicators of *gross* delivery, without regard for duplication. Neither indicates how many *different* people will be exposed to a medium; **reach** does. Reach is the number of *different* individuals (or homes) exposed to a media schedule within a given period of time. Reach is generally expressed as a percentage. It applies to *all* media forms.

When media suppliers "send out" their medium every person has the opportunity to receive that medium. For example, when a TV program is broadcast, everyone (with a TV set) has the opportunity to tune their set to the channel on which the program is broadcast; when a newspaper distributes copies of its daily edition, everyone has the opportunity to buy a copy. Obviously, not everyone views a particular TV program or reads a given issue of a newspaper. Those who do view the program or read the newspaper are those who are *reached*.

Audience reach should not be confused with how many people will actually be exposed to and consume the *advertising* in a medium. Reach merely estimates the percentage (or number) of people who can be expected to be exposed to the *medium*, and who, therefore, have the *opportunity* to see/hear the advertising. Media Planners in the United Kingdom use the term **opportunity-to-see (OTS)** instead of *reach* because it clearly states what media reach is all about.

Let's suppose there are 100 TV homes within a market, and each box shown in Exhibit 14.1 represents one home. You decide to schedule commercials in four of the available TV programs. Each of the programs airs at a different time in the week. Each of the four programs has a 20 rating—that is, each is viewed by 20 of the 100 homes in the market. Because some homes view less TV than others, they might see only one of the four programs (as shown by the boxes with only one program listed). Some homes view more TV and see more shows. As demonstrated, a total of 40 homes viewed at least one of the programs. You have therefore reached 40 percent of the TV homes one or more times (40 homes reached divided by 100 TV home population).

OTS (Opportunity to See) A term commonly used in Europe indicating the amount of "frequency" a media audience receives in a media schedule.

EXHIBIT 14.1:   Calculating TV Reach
100 TV HOMES

A	A	A	A	A	B	B	B	C	C
C	C	D	D	D	D	D	AB	AB	AC
AC	AD	AD	BC	BC	BD	BD	BD	ABC	ABC
BCD	BCD	BCD	ACD	ACD	ABDC	ABDC	ABDC	ABDC	ABDC

To calculate reach, viewers are counted only once, no matter how many programs they view or how many commercials they might be exposed to. The same applies to all media. For example, to calculate reach in magazines, readers are counted only once, no matter how many magazines they read. The only variation among media is the time frame for which reach is expressed (as discussed in the chapter on GRPs and reprised in Table 14.1 for convenience).

TABLE 14.1: Time Frame of TRPs by Medium

Magazines	As long as an issue physically exists and is read by someone
Newspapers	Generally one day
Outdoor	One day
Radio	During the time the programs air
Sunday Supplements	Mostly in the first day
Television	During the time the programs air, except for VCR viewing

---

Exhibit 14.2 displays the percentage of women who will be reached with an advertising schedule encompassing three magazines. Again, the dynamics of reach are the same as in television but are displayed differently in this exhibit for greater clarification. Magazine A is read by 20 percent of all women. Some of these women also read magazine B or magazine C, and some read both B and C. The 20 percent that read magazine A is the gross audience of magazine A. Those that read *only* magazine A are its exclusive audience, and those that read A and another magazine are part of a **duplicated** audience.

Duplication The number or percentage of a medium's audience, or of those reached with a media schedule, who are exposed to more than one media vehicle or to more than one advertising message.

14% read only A (exclusive audience)
 2% read A and B
 2% read A and C
 2% read A, B and C
20% read A

To determine the reach of all three magazines combined, we add the exclusive audiences for each to the duplicated audiences, counting the duplicated audience only once:

	Reach
A (Exclusive)	14%
B (Exclusive)	14
C (Exclusive)	14
A + B (Duplicated)	2
A + C (Duplicated)	2
B + C (Duplicated)	2
A + B + C (Duplicated)	2
Total	50%

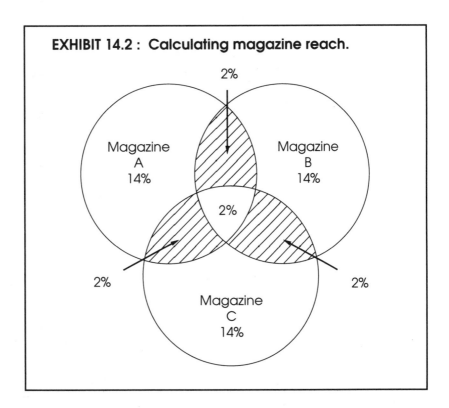

EXHIBIT 14.2 : Calculating magazine reach.

Reach Accumulation

As additional media are added to a media schedule, reach generally increases—unduplicated audiences are *accumulating*, which is why reach is also sometimes referred to as *accumulated reach* or *cume reach*. Continuing with our three-magazine example, we can demonstrate how magazine B increases reach over that of A alone, and how magazine C adds even more reach. Table 14.2 shows audience accumulation. It is constructed to show the number of readers (rather than percent) so you can appreciate that *percent* reach is equivalent to real numbers of people. We see that each magazine is read by 20,000 people. If you buy only magazine A you will have reached 20,000. If you add magazine B, your reach increases to 36,000. Because 4,000 of the readers of magazine B also read magazine A, they are duplicated and thus not counted in the reach calculation. The remaining 16,000 readers of B who do not read A are counted. Likewise, only 14,000 of magazine C readers are *new* and only these are included in the reach calculation.

TABLE 14.2:   Audience Accumulation

Magazine	Total Readers (000)	Also Read Above Magazine(s) (000)	Do Not Read Above Magazine(s) (000)
A	20	0	20
+B	20	4	16
Subtotal	40		36
+C	20	6	14
Total	60		50

It should be clear that within a media form, reach does not generally accumulate along a straight line. As a second vehicle is added to a first, some of the audience is duplicated and therefore counted only once in the reach equation. As more and more vehicles are added, the relative amount of duplication usually increases. This can be seen in Table 14.2: 4,000 readers read both magazines A and C, resulting in a 10 percent duplication (4,000 divided by the combined gross audience of 40,000), and 10,000 readers read all three magazines, resulting in a 17 percent duplication (10,000 divided by the combined gross audience of 60,000). In fact, Exhibit 14.3 demonstrates that it would take 24 different media vehicles, on average, each with a 20 rating, to accumulate nearly a 100 percent reach. The graphical display of the reach accumulation is sometimes called a *reach curve*. It curves because there is an increasing rate of duplication as more media vehicles are added. If there was no duplication between vehicles, reach would accumulate along a straight line.

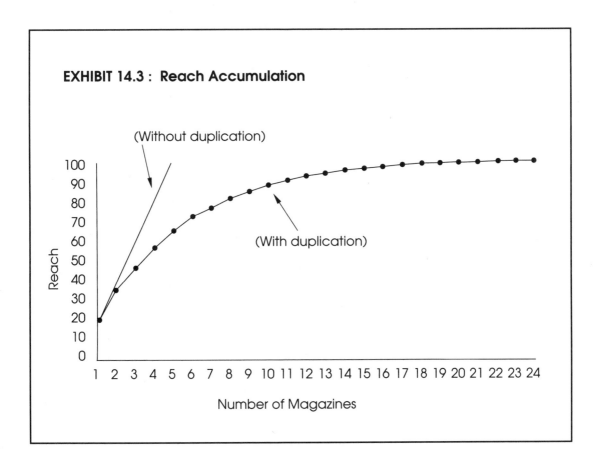

EXHIBIT 14.3 : Reach Accumulation

(Without duplication)

(With duplication)

Reach

Number of Magazines

The percentage of duplication between media vehicles has an inverse relationship with reach accumulation: the lower the duplication, the higher the reach, and vice-versa. As shown in Table 14.3, media vehicles A and B have a combined duplication rate of 16.7 percent (100,000 people are exposed to both vehicles, which represents 16.7 percent of the gross combined audience of 600,000 people). The combination of vehicles A and C has a duplication of

TABLE 14.3:   Relationship of Duplication and Reach

Media Vehicle	Total Audience (000)	Duplicated Audience (000)	% Total	Unduplicated Audience (000)	Reach (000)
A	400	100	25.0%	300	
B	200	100	50.0	100	
Total	600	100	16.7	400	500
A	400	50	12.5%	350	
C	200	50	25.0	150	
Total	600	50	8.3	500	550

8.3 percent. Because A and C have a lower duplication rate than A and B, the total reach of the A/C pair is greater than that of the A/B pair. Also displayed in this table is the duplication rate represented by each vehicle. As shown, the 100,000 people exposed to both A and B represent 25 percent of vehicle A's audience and 50 percent of vehicle B's. Vehicle B, therefore, is adding 100,000 exclusive readers to vehicle A, representing 50 percent of its total audience. This compares to vehicle C, which adds 150,000 exclusive readers, or 75 percent of its total audience. The higher the ratio of exclusive (non-duplicated) audience to a medium's total audience, the greater the reach accumulation.

Generally speaking, and with all other variables held constant, reach accumulates fastest when media are scheduled sequentially from the largest to the smallest vehicle. Shown in Table 14.4 are two listings of the same magazines—on the left in rank-order from largest to smallest; on the right in the opposite order. By scheduling the four largest magazines you can obtain a 36 reach, compared to having to purchase nine magazines if you start at the bottom and work up toward the largest.

Reach Accumulation over Time

As was explored in the chapter on GRPs, different media types accumulate their total audience within various time frames. For the most part, electronic media (radio and television) are instantaneous

**TABLE 14.4:   Audience Accumulation by Rank Order of
Magazine Audience Size**

Magazine	Reach		Magazine	Reach	
	Each	Cume		Each	Cume
A	19	19	J	3	3
B	13	27	I	3	5
C	12	32	H	3	6
D	11	36	G	5	10
E	8	38	F	6	13
F	6	40	E	8	17
G	5	41	D	11	24
H	3	41	C	12	29
I	3	41	B	13	36
J	3	42	A	19	42

—programs are viewed or listened to at the time they are broadcast. With the exception of VCR recording for later viewing (which accounts for a small amount of total viewing) media consumption happens at the time of broadcast because the broadcast intrudes on the consumer with the offer of "watch this *now* or don't watch it." Print media are different. Direct mail, magazines, newspapers, and out-of-home media have permanency. They invite the consumer to "look at this when you decide to." Because of this inherent permanency and sustained offer, print media accumulate their total audiences over time, not instantly.

There are several dynamics that affect how fast print media might accumulate their total audience reach, and how long a specific media vehicle might exist in the consumers' eyes. With magazines, for example, this existence is known as **issue life**. Here are some of the dynamics:

Issue Life   The length of time it takes a magazine to be read by the maximum measurable audience.

- The more material contained in a direct mail piece, and/or the more complicated the offer, and/or the more recipient involvement needed to consume the message, the longer the life of the piece.

- The shorter the time for a consumer to respond to a direct mail offer, the shorter the life.

- The shorter the publication interval, the faster the accumulation. For example, daily newspapers accumulate their

TABLE 14.5:   Percent Total Audience Accumulation over Time

	Weekly Magazines		Monthly Magazines	
Week	A	B	C	D
1	55%	65%	40%	35%
2	80	85	65	55
3	90	95	75	70
4	98	99	85	80
5	100	100	89	85
6			93	90
7			96	93
8			98	96
9			99	99
10			100	100

audiences faster than weekly magazines; weeklies faster than monthlies. Table 14.5 shows the pattern of audience accumulation for two weeklies and two monthlies, all of which have approximately the same total audience level. By the fifth week the weeklies have accumulated their total readership, whereas the monthlies take about ten weeks.

Readers-per-Copy (RPC)   The number of individuals who read a given copy of a publication.

- The higher the number of different people who read a given copy of a publication (known as **readers-per-copy**, or **RPC**), the slower the accumulation—although this can vary substantially according to the editorial focus of the magazine and the amount of time it takes the average reader to read an entire issue. A magazine that continues to be passed along to more and more people accumulates more and more readers per copy, but the passing-along process obviously takes time.

- The greater the proportion of newsstand sales versus subscriptions, the slower the audience accumulation (but this is a broad generality with many exceptions).

- Timely or news-oriented publications are generally consumed faster and therefore accumulate reach faster.

- The greater the need for reference by the consumer, (e.g., a special issue or supplement on first aid care or places to vacation) the longer the issue life of a magazine or newspaper supplement—which could affect reach accumulation as well as repeat readership of the same material.

- The higher the traffic count of an outdoor poster or billboard, the faster the reach accumulation.

Roadblock

Roadblock A scheduling device used with broadcast media to increase reach at a given point in time (e.g., scheduling a commercial on all local market stations at 9:00 p.m.).

In the first example of how reach works we assumed a schedule of four TV programs, each airing at a different time in the week. In this situation, a given viewer has the opportunity to see all four programs. If the programs aired simultaneously, for example, all on Monday from 8:00–8:30 p.m., the average viewer could view only one of the programs at any specific moment. Therefore, if each of the four programs has a 20 rating, then each is attracting *different* viewers. If there is no duplication of audience between the four programs, then the ratings for each are additive, which results in an 80 reach. This tactic of scheduling advertising *at precisely the same time of day* is known as a **roadblock**—a device that intercepts as many viewers as possible in order to maximize reach at a specific time. If commercials are scheduled on *all* TV programs (or radio stations) broadcast at a given time, then reach is equivalent to the PUT (People Using TV) level at that time. Keep in mind, however, that this scheduling tactic is not necessarily as cost efficient as scheduling programs at different times. Two of the disadvantages follow:

Audience Turnover The average ratio of cumulative audience listening/viewing to the average audience listening/viewing.

- Precise timing—Reach will equal the sum of individual ratings *only* if the advertising message airs at precisely the same time on all programs. Because there is **audience turnover** during a typical TV (or radio) program—some program viewers tune out during the program and new viewers tune in—there can be audience duplication among viewers who might have seen your commercial on Program A (at 8:10 p.m.) and on Program B (at 8:20 p.m.).

- Cost efficiency—During any specific time of day, competing TV (or radio) programs have different commercial cost structures. Some programs command a higher commercial cost than others, resulting in different CPMs by program. Buying multiple programs during a given time period, therefore, will force the purchase of relatively inefficient (high CPM) programs. This results in a higher combined CPM than if only the most efficient programs are purchased in the time period or at different times (see Table 14.6).

TABLE 14.6:   Cost Efficiency of a Roadblock

Programs Airing 8:00–8:30 p.m.	Adults 18+ Audience (000)	Cost/:30	CPM
A	10,000	$15,000	$1.50
B	6,000	12,000	2.00
C	5,000	10,000	2.00
D	3,000	9,000	3.00
E	1,000	4,000	4.00
Total Average	25,000	$50,000	$2.00

Media Mix

Media Mix The use of two or more media forms, e.g., TV and magazines or radio, outdoor, and newspapers.

When two or more different media forms are used in a media plan, it is referred to as a **media mix**—mixing media such as TV and magazines, or TV, radio and magazines, etc., as opposed to simply using more than one vehicle within a medium (such as two or more magazines).

When you add a second media form, you generally accelerate reach accumulation beyond what could be obtained by using more of the same media form. For example, if you first buy a 20-rated TV program (and therefore reach 20 percent of your target audience), you can usually generate more additional reach if you add a 20-rated magazine than if you add another 20-rated TV program. Accelerating reach is but one reason to mix media. Here are some more:

- To reach people who do not consume your first medium, or are only lightly exposed to the first medium.

- To provide additional repeat exposure of your advertising in what might be a less expensive secondary medium after you've attained optimum reach in the first medium.

- To utilize some of the intrinsic values of a medium, which may not have been of paramount importance in your original selection of media forms, but which can enhance the creative effectiveness of the advertising campaign (such as music on radio or long copy in print media).

- To deliver coupons in print media when the primary medium selected is broadcast.

- To deliver visible full-color package registration when the primary medium selected is radio (e.g., to register how the packaging of your brand looks).

- To address a different target audience than those targeted with the primary medium (such as using radio to reach teens and newspapers to reach adults).

- To enhance reach during a specific time (that is, to "bump" up delivery during a critical period (such as using one or two weeks of TV in addition to a base schedule of monthly magazines, or adding radio in the summer on top of a year-long TV effort).

- To bring about *synergism*, a term borrowed from chemistry, which describes an effect produced when the sum of the parts is greater than that expected by adding together the individual components (e.g., 2 + 2 = 5).

Random Combination of a Media Mix

Random Combination
A mathematical formula for estimating the reach of two or more media.

There are many computerized mathematical formulas for estimating reach within a media form as more and more advertising is planned, and for estimating the reach of two media forms combined. Some of these formulas are devised by media research suppliers, and some are proprietary to an advertiser or to an advertising agency. Most of the formulas used for estimating reach of a media mix are based, more or less, on an accepted statistical method known as **random combination**. This method assumes that those not reached by the first medium have an opportunity to be exposed to the second medium in direct proportion to the quantity of those not exposed to the second medium. This opportunity increases as the proportion of those not reached by the second medium increases.

Here is how the random technique works, as illustrated in Exhibit 14.4.

- You've established that your television schedule will reach 60 percent of your target audience; magazines will reach 50 percent.

- This means that 40 percent of your target will *not* be reached by TV and 50 percent will *not* be reached by magazines.

- By multiplying the percents not reached by each medium together, you establish the percent that will not be reached by either:

$$
\begin{array}{r}
40\% \text{ not reached by television} \\
\times \quad 50\% \text{ not reached by magazines} \\
\hline
\textit{20\% not reached by either medium}
\end{array}
$$

- Subtracting the 20 percent not reached from the total possible reach of 100 percent leaves 80 percent, which is the percentage the combination in this schedule supposedly *does* reach.

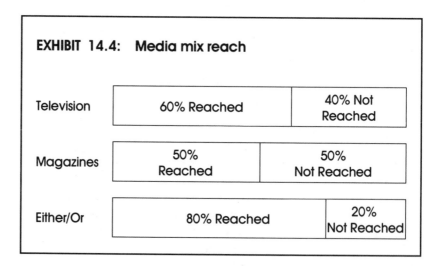

EXHIBIT 14.4: Media mix reach

Television	60% Reached	40% Not Reached
Magazines	50% Reached	50% Not Reached
Either/Or	80% Reached	20% Not Reached

When combining two or more media forms, you must establish reach for each medium on the same population base. For example, you cannot combine the reach of women in one medium with the reach of homes in another. Nor can you combine the homes reached with cable TV (which is not in every home with a TV set) with the homes reached with broadcast TV (which assumes a population base of every home with a TV, whether or not it receives programming via cable or over the airwaves).

Table 14.7 shows the combined reach of two media forms using the random combination technique. To use the table:

- Find the reach of the first medium on the horizontal axis—e.g., 60.

- Find the reach of the second medium on the vertical axis—e.g., 50.

- Read down from the 60 reach and across from the 50 reach. The point of intersection shows the combined reach: 80.

If three or more media forms are combined, the same procedure is used: find the combined reach of the first two media, then find the point of intersection of these two combined plus the third

TABLE 14.7: Random Combination Table.

Reach of First Medium

	25	30	35	40	45	50	55	60	65	70	75	80	85	90	95
25	46	47	51	55	59	62	66	70	74	77	81	85	89	92	95
30	—	51	54	58	61	65	68	72	75	79	82	86	90	93	95
35	—	—	58	61	64	67	71	74	77	80	84	87	90	93	95
40	—	—	—	64	67	70	73	76	79	82	85	88	91	94	95
45	—	—	—	—	70	72	75	78	81	83	86	89	92	94	95
50	—	—	—	—	—	75	77	80	82	85	87	90	92	95	95
55	—	—	—	—	—	—	80	82	84	86	89	91	93	95	95
60	—	—	—	—	—	—	—	84	86	88	90	92	94	95	95
65	—	—	—	—	—	—	—	—	88	89	91	93	95	95	95
70	—	—	—	—	—	—	—	—	—	91	92	94	95	95	95
75	—	—	—	—	—	—	—	—	—	—	94	95	95	95	95
80	—	—	—	—	—	—	—	—	—	—	—	95	95	95	95
85	—	—	—	—	—	—	—	—	—	—	—	—	95	95	95
90	—	—	—	—	—	—	—	—	—	—	—	—	—	95	95
95	—	—	—	—	—	—	—	—	—	—	—	—	—	—	95

Reach of Second Medium

medium. For example, if you have three media forms producing a reach of 50, 40 and 30 respectively, follow this procedure:

	Reach
Medium A	50
Medium B	40
Media A + B	70 (from table)
Medium C	30
Media A + B + C	79 (from table)

To physically appreciate how the random combination technique works, you might try this demonstration. Mark 20 ping pong balls, 10 with the word "TV" and 10 with the word "magazines." Gather 20 people in a room. Randomly toss out the 10 TV balls and ask that no one catch more than one ball. Then toss out the 10 magazine balls, requesting that no one catch more than one of these balls, whether or not they already caught a TV ball. Count the number of people who caught a TV ball (it has to be 10). These 10 represent a 50 reach (10/20 = 50%). Repeat the process for magazines. This will also equal a 50 reach. Then count the number of people who have either a TV ball or a magazine ball or both. It will probably come out to be about 15 people—representing a 75 reach of the group of 20 people.

Only-Only-Both

It is often mistakenly assumed that when two media forms are combined, *all* people reached will be exposed to your advertising in *both* media. Because the usual effect of adding a second medium is to extend reach to those not exposed to the first medium, not all people will be exposed to both media forms. The only way all people reached can be exposed to both media is when each medium produces 100 percent reach of the target, or when media delivery is tightly controlled, such as sending a direct mail piece to every person who receives a subscription-only magazine.

Whenever a media mix reach is calculated you should also indicate the "only-only-both" components—that is, the reach of those who will be exposed *only* to the first medium, the reach of those who will be exposed *only* to the first medium, the reach of those exposed *only* to the second medium, and the reach of those exposed to *both* media forms. If *synergy* is perceived as an important factor in your media evaluation process, then (hypothetically) the "both" reach must be considered more valuable than either of the "only's."

To calculate the "only-only-both" reach, use the following procedure:

1. Combine the two media randomly (or use a computer model): 60 + 50 = 80 (reach of either/or)

2. Subtract the reach of medium A from the combined reach. This yields the reach of those exposed only to medium B: 80 – 60 = 20 (reach of only B)

3. Subtract the reach of medium B from the combined reach. This yields the reach of those exposed only to medium A: 80 – 50 = 30 (reach of only A)

4. Subtract the combined reach of only A and only B from the total combined reach. This yields the reach of those exposed to *both* media: 80 – (20 + 30) = 30 (reach of both)

If the media forms in the media plan are those shown in Exhibit 14.5, the planner can conclude the following:

• Television will reach 60 percent of the population group against which these calculations have been made.

• Magazines will reach 50 percent.

• 80 percent will be reached by TV, or magazines, or both.

• 30 percent will be reached by TV only.

• 20 percent will be reached by magazines only.

• 30 percent will be reached by both TV and magazines.

• 20 percent of the population will not be reached with this advertising schedule.

EXHIBIT 14.5:   Media mix reach

Television	60% Reached	40% Not Reached

Magazines*	30% Not Reached	50% Reached	20% Not Reached

Either/Or	80% Reached	20% Not Reached

	TV Only 30%	TV & Mags 30%	Mags Only 20%	20% Not Reached

*50% not reached shown as 30% and 20% for demonstration only.

While you still have those 20 people in a room counting ping pong balls, you might want to physically examine the only-only-both concept. If you obtained a 50 reach of each medium (TV and magazines) you should have the following array:

	# People with Ping Pong Balls	Reach
TV only	5	25
Magazines only	5	25
Both TV & Magazines	5	25
Total	15	75
Not reached	5	25
Population Base	20	100

The random combination technique should *not* be used for calculating reach *within* a media form, primarily because the rates of duplication between two media vehicles within the same media category are generally higher than between two different media forms. As previously shown in Table 14.4, the combination of magazines A, B, C, and D produced a 36 reach based on *actual* tabulations of the duplication rates between these magazines. A random technique would have produced a much higher total reach:

		Reach	
Magazine	Each	Cume Actual	Cume (Using Random Technique)
A	19	19	19
B	13	27	30
C	12	32	38
D	11	36	45

Two questions remain: At what point should you stop accumulating reach in one medium and start adding a second medium? How do you evaluate reach for those people who are exposed to your advertising more than once?

There are no rules for determining how much reach is enough. Answering this question is the same as trying to answer "How high is up?" We might answer: as high as it needs to be. We have seen that as more and more vehicles are added to a schedule, reach accumulates, but the accumulation produces diminishing returns with each successive addition. You could graph the reach accumulation obtainable within a specific media form, such as that displayed in Exhibit 14.3, and visually pick that point at which you believe the reach curve is "flattening," that is, the point beyond which additional reach is adding proportionately very little to a schedule. Using the same graph you can select what you believe to be a "threshold" level of activity—a point below which you perceive the advertising delivery will not produce a desired consumer response. Using either the flattening or threshold barometer you can determine how much money that level of activity will cost, subtract this cost from your total budget, and use the remaining monies for a second medium.

You could also do a cost analysis to determine the cost per additional reach point to give quantitative substance to your decision. Shown in Table 14.8 is a hypothetical approach to this type of analysis. We see that magazine B adds 8 reach points to magazine A at a cost of $5,000 per reach point, magazine C adds 5 reach points at a cost of $6,000 per reach point, etc. All in all, however, the media planner's judgment must come into play in deciding "how high is up?"

TABLE 14.8:   Increasing Cost per Reach Point

MAGAZINE	Cost 1-Page	Rating	Cume Reach	Additional Reach	Cost per Additional Reach Point
A	$50,000	19	19	—	—
B	40,000	13	27	8	$ 5,000
C	30,000	12	32	5	6,000
D	28,000	11	36	4	7,000
E	20,000	8	38	2	10,000

Exposure   A person's physical contact (visual and/or audio) with an advertising medium or message.

The second question is related to the first. As reach accumulates there are diminishing returns for *reach*, but not for the total **exposure** of your advertising message(s). Total exposure is a combination of reach and *frequency*. The latter is discussed in the next section.

PROFESSIONAL WORKSHOP

1. You purchase two magazines, each with a 10 rating for men. What is the minimum and maximum reach you might obtain?

2. You schedule ten TV programs, each with a 5.0 rating, and five magzines, each with a 10.0 rating. How much reach will you generate?

3. You're considering the purchase of radio stations A and B. Station A has 20,000 listeners and station B has 10,000. The two combined have a 20 percent duplication rate. What is the combined reach of the stations?

4. Using the same example as in question 3, what percent of station A's audience is duplicated with B? What percent of station B's audience is duplicated with A?

5. Your TV schedule has a 50 reach of adults, and your outdoor plan yields a 30 reach. Using the random technique, what is your combined reach?

6. Using the example in question 5, what is the reach of people who will be exposed to *only* TV, *only* outdoor, and *both* media?

Chapter 15

Frequency

I n this chapter we investigate *frequency*, a media dynamic that is used hand-in-glove with the previously discussed dynamic of *reach*. We also discuss the differences between the terms *mean, median,* and *mode* —all of which refer to the overall term of *average*.

Frequency The number of times people (or homes) are exposed to an advertising message, an advertising campaign, or to a specific media vehicle. Also, the period of issuance of a publication, e.g., daily or monthly.

We've seen that a media vehicle produces an audience that can be described in total numbers and as a rating. We've also seen that when different vehicles are used in combination, audience delivery increases—both in gross terms (gross rating points and impressions), and in net terms (reach). We know that all of the people reached will be exposed to at least one advertising message, and some to more than one. Up to this point we have not accounted for those who will receive more than one advertising message. This is where the term **frequency** comes into play. Frequency is the *average* number of times individuals (or homes) are exposed to the advertising messages delivered in a media schedule.

A simple example of frequency: if 10 people took one business trip per year, and 10 others took two trips, you can conclude that the average number of trips this group of 20 took was 1.5 (10 × 1 + 10 × 2 = 30/20 = 1.5).

Let's reprise the schedule originally presented in the previous chapter—shown as Exhibit 15.1, and displayed in an alternate format in Table 15.1. We have a total of 40 people who we estimate will view one or more of the four TV programs: 17 people will view only one program (A or B or C or D); 11 people, two programs; 7 people, three programs; and 5 people, four programs. If we add all of this together then the 40 people will view the *equivalent* of 80

EXHIBIT 15.1: Frequency of advertising exposure

A	A	A	A	A	B	B	B	C	C
C	C	D	D	D	D	D	AB	AB	AC
AC	AD	AD	BC	BC	BD	BD	BD	ABC	ABC
BCD	BCD	BCD	ACD	ACD	ABDC	ABDC	ABDC	ABDC	ABDC

TABLE 15.1: Calculating frequency

	# Homes		# Programs		Equivalent # Programs
	17	×	1	=	17
	11	×	2	=	22
	7	×	3	=	21
	5	×	4	=	20
TOTAL	40				80

$$\frac{80}{40} = 2.0$$

programs and will therefore be exposed to the *equivalent* of 80 commercials. By division, we can establish that the *average* person will be exposed to an *average* of two commercials.

The concept of frequency, like reach, is identical in all media forms. Exhibit 15.2 and Table 15.2 show, for example, how frequency computations are made for a combination of magazines. Here again we see three magazines, each read by 20 percent of the population. In the last chapter we calculated a net audience of 50 (that is, a 50 reach) who read one or more of these magazines. It's obvious that there is duplication of readership between the magazines, with some people reading two of the three magazines and some reading all three. If there was no duplication, the three magazines combined would yield a 60 reach, with each person having an average exposure (average frequency) of one (1.0). But because of duplication, the actual reach is less and the average frequency is, therefore, more than 1.0. This duplication results in

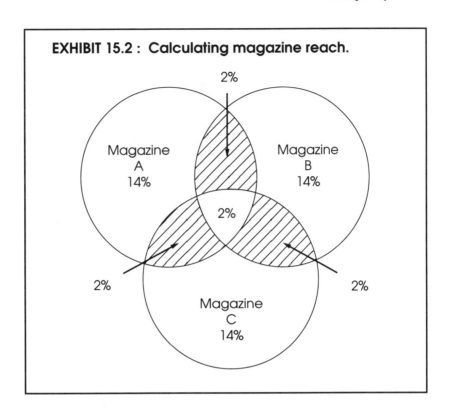

EXHIBIT 15.2 : Calculating magazine reach.

TABLE 15.2: Calculating Average Frequency

Magazine	1 Time	2 Times	3 Times	Total
A	14% × 1	—	—	
B	14% × 1	—	—	
C	14% × 1	—	—	
A + B	—	2% × 2	—	
A + C	—	2% × 2	—	
B + C	—	2% × 2	—	
A + B + C	—	—	2% × 3	
Gross Sum (TRPs)	42	12	6	60
Net Sum (Reach)				50
Average Frequency				1.2

additional exposure—beyond the one-time exposure produced by any one of the magazines.

The arithmetic shown in Table 15.2 is the same as that in our simple example of the business traveler. Each person (or group of people) is counted either once, twice, or three times depending on their exposure to one, two, or three magazines. Those 14 percent of readers who read only magazine A are counted once, as are those who read only magazine B or C. By multiplying the reach of each of these magazines by one and summing the products, and continuing this multiplication for the 2-times and 3-times reach, we find a gross sum of 60 percent—equivalent to 60 TRPs. With a gross sum of 60 and a net sum (reach) of 50, we can calculate an average 1.2 frequency (60/50 = 1.2).

Frequency in a Media Mix

Regardless of the combination of media forms used in a media plan, the concept of frequency remains constant, as does the arithmetic. Table 15.3 shows the reach and frequency we separately

TABLE 15.3:   Frequency in a Media Mix

Schedule 1 Medium	Equivalent # Programs/Insertions	Reach	Frequency
TV	80	40	2.0
Magazines	60	50	1.2
Combined	140	70	2.0

Schedule 2 Medium	Equivalent # Programs/Insertions	Reach	Frequency
TV	60	40	1.5
Magazines	80	50	1.6
Combined	140	70	2.0

established in our previous two examples for TV and magazines. Schedule 1 shows that TV produced the equivalent of 80 programs across 40 people, yielding an average frequency of 2.0. Magazines reached 50 percent of people with an average frequency of 1.2, with the equivalent of 60 insertions. Using the random combination technique, we determine that this schedule will produce the equivalent of 140 advertising messages among 70 percent of the people, with the average person receiving a 2.0 frequency.

You'll note that the frequency for the combination (2.0) is the same as that for TV. This is coincidental. The average frequency for combined media forms cannot be less than either medium alone, but it can be greater than either. This is shown in Table 15.3 in schedule 2, where we have reversed the number of equivalent programs/insertions for demonstration purposes.

Frequency in Only-Only-Both

Frequency for Only-Only-Both cannot be tabulated unless you have precise media consumption data for *each person* you are reaching with your media schedule. Without this precision, you cannot know the average frequency within any of these three groupings. Using schedule 1 in Table 15.3, for example, we can conclude that 20 percent of people will be exposed *only* to TV, 30 percent *only* to magazines, and 20 percent to *both* TV and magazines. We know that the average person reached via TV (either only TV or with TV and magazines) is exposed to an average of 2.0 advertising messages. What we do not know is the frequency composition of the 40 percent of people who are exposed to TV either in the "only" TV segment or in the "both" TV and magazines segment. Hypothetically, of the 40 percent of people exposed to TV, the half exposed *only* to TV could have a frequency lower or higher than the average 2.0. It can be assumed that the group exposed only to TV would have a higher frequency than the group exposed to both media, based on the belief that those who are viewing proportionately more TV than average have a lesser opportunity to be exposed to magazines. But this is only assumption and could lead to misinformation. (See Table 15.4.)

TABLE 15.4:   Frequency Unknowns

	Reach	Equivalent # Programs/Insertions		Average Frequency
TV Only	20	lower:	20?	1.0?
		average:	40?	2.0?
		higher:	60?	3.0?
Magazines Only	30	lower:	30?	1.0?
		average:	36?	1.2?
		higher:	42?	1.4?
Both	20	higher:	38?	1.9?
		average:	64?	3.2?
		lower:	90?	4.5?
Total/Average	70	140		2.0

Mean, Median, Mode

Mean   The sum of all items divided by the number of items. Commonly called "average."

Median   The middle number in a sequence of numbers.

Mode   The number occurring most frequently in a sequence of numbers.

When we speak of average frequency, we are referring to the **mean** average—not the **median** or the **mode**:

- Mean—   the sum of items divided by the number of items

- Median— the middle number in a series of numbers

- Mode—   the number occurring most frequently in a series of numbers

If we take the following series of numbers, for example, we can see that the three definitions have distinctly different meanings:

	Series
	50
	25
	15
	5
	5
Total	100

- Mean (100/5)   =   20
- Median (middle number)   =   15
- Mode (most frequent)   =   5

Whenever the word *average* appears in media data it means the mean average. If the media planner wants to refer to the *median* in discussing media research, this term is usually specified.

PROFESSIONAL WORKSHOP

1. Based on the following information, how many programs did the average person view?

# People	# Programs viewed
5	5
3	3
2	2

2. Magazine A is read by 30 percent of women; magazine B by 20 percent. Half of the women who read magazine B also read magazine A. If you schedule an ad in both magazines, how many ads will the average reader be exposed to?

3. You are analyzing five TV programs which have respective ratings of 1, 1, 3, 5, and 10. What is the mean average rating of these five? The median? The mode?

Chapter 16

Reach/Frequency/GRPs

This chapter examines the interrelationship and interdependence of *reach*, *frequency* and *gross rating points*. We demonstrate how these three media dynamics are used to analyze the audience delivery productivity of various media schedules with specific focus on how each media form, each sub-segment of these forms, or each combination of the media forms produces markedly different audience delivery patterns. We discuss how a media planner can exercise control over how much reach or frequency can be generated within a given number of GRPs. Lastly, we caution about possibly misusing the number of announcements or advertisements in a media schedule to determine the audience reach of that schedule by demonstrating the non-relationship between announcements and reach.

When you devise a media schedule, you should know

- How many of the people you are targeting will be exposed to your advertising—*Reach*;

- How many times the average person you reach will have an opportunity for that exposure—*Frequency*;

- The total gross delivery of the target audience—*GRPs*.

These three terms are totally interrelated, as shown in this simple mathematical formula:

GRPs = Reach × Frequency

If you are scheduling 200 GRPs and have determined that you will produced a 50 reach, you will also produce a 4 frequency (50 × 4 = 200). The 50 reach is of course a percentage (shown without the percent sign). The 4 frequency is an actual number, not a percentage, and is usually shown with one decimal place; thus the "4" would be written as "4.0." GRPs are also a percentage because you are multiplying the percent reach by the number of times (50 percent × 4.0 = 200 percent). Media shorthand is generally used when reporting reach/frequency. It is commonly shown as "R/F" with the slash used as a separator, not as a division symbol. Also, it is not necessary to show "times" or "X" next to frequency because it is assumed. The following iterates the components of R/F/GRPs —both in percentage terms and in actual numbers. You can see that the shorthand does allow for convenient reference.

		Percent	Numbers of People*
	·Reach	50	100,000
×	Frequency	4.0	4
=	GRPs	200	
=	Impressions	—	
	R/F	50/4.0	400,000

* Population base = 200,000

R/F can be estimated for all major media forms, with the basic formula being the same for all forms. We'll first use TV examples to demonstrate R/F dynamics, then show the application in other media.

Reach Curves and Frequency Lines

If you were able to conduct a proprietary survey of consumers each time you devised a specific media schedule—that is, if you could actually interview specific people to determine which TV programs they watch—you could estimate with near precision the reach/ frequency you could deliver with a specific media schedule. This is obviously an unreasonable proposition given the time and expense involved in such a survey. The alternative is to use estimates of the probable R/F for your media schedule as established by researchers.

Using raw data (unaveraged, unprojected) from consumer surveys conducted by syndicated media research companies, researchers and statisticians are able to determine the duplication of audiences between various pairs of media vehicles, and between media schedules composed of more than two vehicles. With this duplication data researchers can estimate how many people could be reached with a given combination of media exposure. By tabulating the survey findings for a wide variety of media combinations, researchers can "plot" how reach levels increase as more media (GRPs) are scheduled. By averaging the findings of these tabulations (using what is known as a *least squares regression analysis*) a reach "curve" can be produced.

Shown in Exhibit 16.1 are 15 hypothetical combinations of media vehicles (let's assume these are TV programs) and the actual reach

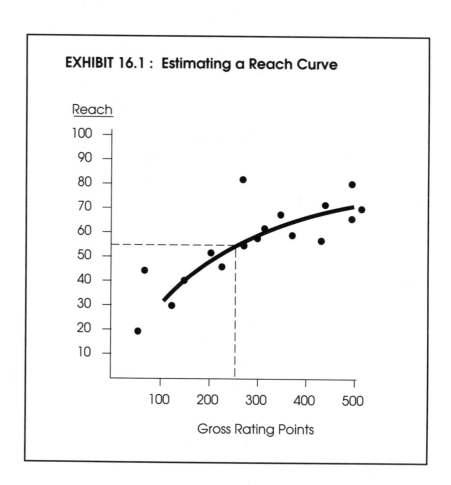

EXHIBIT 16.1 : Estimating a Reach Curve

Reach

Gross Rating Points

these combinations produced according to the raw survey data. The least squares analysis forces an average line (the reach curve). Using this curve, you can estimate the reach of any level of GRPs, whether or not that particular level was part of the researcher's original tabulations. For example, if the schedule for which you want to estimate reach contains 250 GRPs, you can read the graph and determine it will produce a 55 reach.

You must keep in mind that the reach curve is an *estimate*. It does not pretend to identify the exact reach within a given level of GRPs; it does tell you that, on average, a given schedule should produce approximately the reach shown.

Because reach and frequency are both functions of GRPs, you can determine the average frequency level by knowing the GRPs and the reach: GRPs divided by reach equals frequency. The pattern of reach accumulation is one of diminishing returns—as

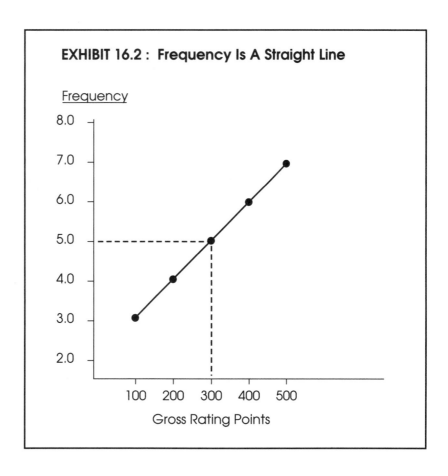

EXHIBIT 16.2 : Frequency Is A Straight Line

more and more GRPs are added to a media schedule, proportionately less and less reach is accumulated, thereby flattening the curve at the higher GRP levels. Frequency, however, remains a straight line, regardless of the number of GRPs within a media schedule. This phenomenon is displayed in Exhibit 16.2, which was constructed based on the reach curve shown in Exhibit 16.1. The specific R/F from these two exhibits is:

GRPs	R/F
100	32/3.1
200	48/4.2
300	60/5.0
400	66/6.1
500	70/7.2

Because frequency remains a straight line, you can graph the line based on two different GRP levels and use the line to estimate reach and frequency for any level of GRPs. For example, if you estimated R/F for the levels of 100 and 500 GRPs, and plotted the frequency line on a graph, you would effect what is shown in Exhibit 16.2. If you then wanted to estimate the reach for 300 GRPs, you would read up from the 300-GRP point until it intersects the frequency line (at 5.0), and then divide 300 GRPs by a 5.0 frequency to yield a 60 reach.

The reach curve and frequency line are affected by these truths:

- The more duplication of audience between media vehicles, the lower the rate of reach accumulation; conversely, the less the duplication, the greater the rate.

- The lower the rate of reach accumulation, the faster the rate of frequency accumulation; conversely, the greater the rate of reach, the slower the frequency accumulation.

An additional dynamic at play in a reach curve is the point at which reach—for all intents and purposes—ceases to accumulate. Obviously, reach cannot exceed 100 percent of a population group. In fact, based on typical media consumption patterns, reach might be substantially less than 100 percent. For example, if your media plan schedules only daytime television, the probability is that your reach will never exceed 60 percent of adult women because, on average, 40 percent of women typically do not view daytime TV.

The graphs shown in Exhibit 16.3 demonstrate reach and frequency accumulation for six different television time periods (dayparts). In scanning these graphs, you'll note different rates of reach accumulation, different GRP points where the reach curve begins to "flatten" (i.e., where little additional reach is accumulated with the scheduling of additional GRPs), and different slopes for the frequency lines.

All of the graphs shown in Exhibit 16.3 were constructed to display R/F of *households* based on household GRPs. Household reach simply means *someone* in a household will be reached (exposed to the media forms in your schedule). Household R/F does not indicate *who* will be reached. Because different population groups have varying media consumption patterns, you cannot assume that (for example) a household reach of 50 will mean that you will reach 50 percent of women, or men, or women 18–34, or any given group. Table 16.1 shows the R/F that is produced by a schedule of 200 household GRPs. If the 200 household GRPs are scheduled in early morning TV, for example, they will produce a 35 reach among households, but far less reach against women 18 and older and substantially less against men 18 and older.

TABLE 16.1:   R/F by Demographic Group within a Schedule of 200 Household GRPs

	Household	W18+	M18+
Early Morning	35/5.7	25/5.6	19/4.5
Day	52/3.9	43/3.7	N.T.
Early Fringe/News	35/5.7	27/5.4	31/4.3
Prime Access	66/3.0	55/2.8	54/2.2
Prime	69/2.9	59/2.6	53/2.3
Late Fringe/News	49/4.1	40/3.5	42/3.0

N.T. = Not Tabulated

You'll also note in Table 16.1 that if you multiply reach by frequency for the people demographic, your product will always be less than 200—you will produce fewer than 200 GRPs against women 18 and older or men 18 and older if you schedule 200 GRPs against households. The reason for this ties back to viewing patterns and the different rates of media consumption by different demographic groups. Table 16.2 on page 140 shows the average number of GRPs that are produced among women 18 and older and men 18 and older by 100 household GRPs scheduled in each of six

EXHIBIT 16.3 :   Reach Curves / Frequency Lines by Daypart — Households

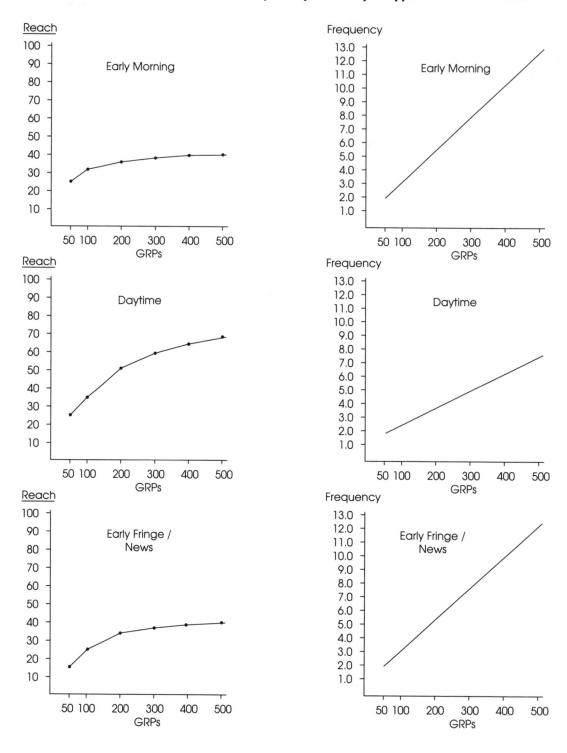

EXHIBIT 16.3   Continued

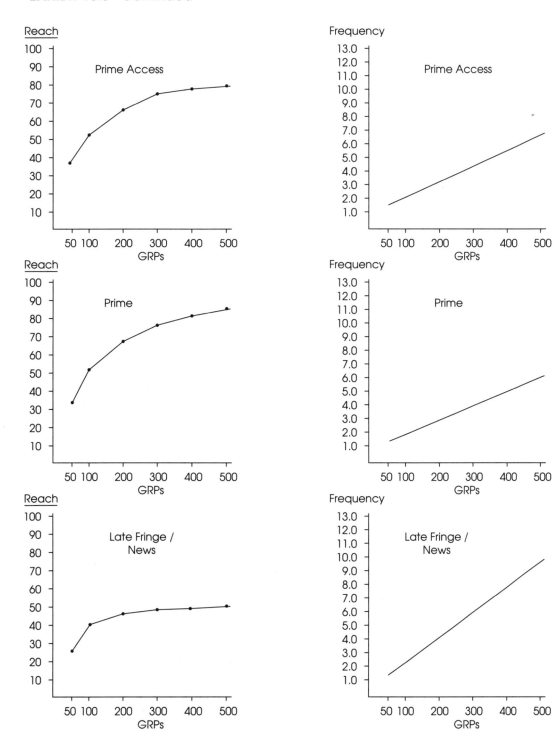

Conversion Factor   A percentage applied to a number (e.g., a household rating) to obtain a different number (e.g., a women 18–34 rating).

television dayparts. The people GRPs can be read as a **conversion factor** and applied to any level of household GRPs. For example, if you want to determine how many women 18+ GRPs will be generated by 200 household GRPs scheduled in early morning, multiply 200 by 69 percent to yield 138 W18+ GRPs.

TABLE 16.2:   GRP CONVERSIONS

	Household GRPs	W18+ GRPs	M18+ GRPs
Early Morning	100	69	43
Day	100	78	N.T.
Early Fringe/News	100	73	66
Prime Access	100	77	60
Prime	100	76	61
Late Fringe/News	100	71	63

N.T. = Not Tabulated

Using GRP conversion factors which might be available to you, you can set out to calculate R/F. This calculation can be done from reach curves designed for that population segment, or by using various formulas which are generally computerized, or by using published tables. Computer models and published tables are generally available from syndicated media research companies, media suppliers, or a company's proprietary systems. The larger advertising agencies, for example, generally develop their own proprietary R/F models.

As shown in Table 16.3, the same level of GRPs scheduled against different demographic groups produces different R/F levels. For example, 200 women 18+ GRPs in early morning will generate a 26/7.8, compared to 200 men 18+ GRPs in the same daypart yielding a 21/9.6. You'll note the substantial differences between this R/F pattern and the one in Table 16.1, where R/F among these groups was a result of scheduling household rating points. Whenever you schedule *people* GRPs, you will produce more reach and/or frequency against these people than if you schedule the same amount of *household* GRPs. This happens because household GRPs are people-indiscriminate. For example, two TV programs, each with a 10 rating, could produce widely varying ratings for women, men, etc.

TABLE 16.3:   R/F by Demographic Group with a Schedule of 200 Targeted Rating Points

	200 Household GRPs	200 W18+ GRPs	200 M18+ GRPs
Early Morning	35/5.7	26/7.8	21/9.6
Day	52/3.9	47/4.2	N.T.
Early Fringe/News	35/5.7	29/6.9	34/5.8
Prime Access	66/3.0	60/3.3	66/3.0
Prime	69/2.9	65/3.1	62/3.2
Late Fringe/News	49/4.1	40/5.0	42/4.7

N.T. = Not Tabulated

In our examples so far, we have been discussing R/F patterns with all GRPs scheduled in only one TV daypart. When a combination of dayparts is used in a media schedule, different patterns emerge. Generally, as additional dayparts are added to a media schedule, reach accumulates faster than might ordinarily be achieved by concentrating activity within one daypart. This phenomenon is akin to our earlier discussion on media mix in Chapter 14, "Reach." The scheduling of additional dayparts affords the opportunity to reach people who are ordinarily not viewing the first daypart.

Shown in Table 16.4 is the R/F of various combinations of two dayparts—such as a schedule composed of 100 women 18+ GRPs in daytime and another 100 in primetime. If you compare the R/F results shown in this table to the results shown in Table 16.3, you'll

TABLE 16.4:   Reach/Frequency for Daypart Combinations

	W18+ GRPs				
	1	2	3	4	5
Day	100	—	—	—	—
Early Fringe/News	—	100	—	100	—
Prime Access	—	—	100	—	—
Prime	100	100	100	—	100
Late Fringe/News	—	—	—	100	100
Total TRPS	67/3.0	62/3.2	72/2.8	52/3.9	67/3.0

R/F

see major differences. For example, 200 W18+ GRPs scheduled *only* in daytime produce a 47/4.2 and, if scheduled only in prime, a 65/3.1. By scheduling 200 W18+ GRPs in daytime *and* prime, you produce a 67/3.0—a higher reach than either daypart alone, and a lower average frequency. Generally speaking, when you want to produce more reach, it's best to have a mixture of dayparts rather than concentrating in one daypart. Concentration in one daypart will generally have the effect of increasing frequency at a proportionately greater rate than reach.

If indeed you are setting out to produce as much reach as possible, and you've tabulated (for example) the five schedules shown in the above table, clearly you will select schedule 3. But, you could be deceived by the R/F information as presented. None of the R/F data reflects what it will *cost* to deliver that level of R/F. Because the cost of commercial time varies from one daypart to another (see Chapter 13 on cost-per-rating-point) schedule 3 might cost more than the other schedules, or it might not be affordable within your media budget. To compare R/F of various schedules, you must first determine how many GRPs you can purchase within your budget. As shown in Table 16.5, a given budget in market X affords the purchase of 200 GRPs in prime, and up to 600 GRPs in early morning. The respective affordable GRPs within each daypart yield different levels of R/F.

TABLE 16.5:   Reach/Frequency Possibilities for Equal Expenditures

	W18+ GRPs Affordable	R/F
Early Morning	600	27/22.2
Day	500	56/9.0
Early Fringe/News	300	32/9.5
Prime Access	250	62/4.0
Prime	200	65/3.1
Late Fringe/News	325	40/8.1

Reworking our hypothetical schedules from Table 16.5, we might find that schedule 5 is superior because it allows the purchase of more GRPs and produces a slightly higher reach *and* frequency. Table 16.6 demonstrates this possibility. Keep in mind, however, that the one percentage point difference in reach between these schedules should not be definitive in making a decision. Given that all R/F schedules are estimates, small differences between one schedule and another are not necessarily definitive. Still, if reach is your *only* concern in selecting one schedule over another, and all other variables are constant, then schedule 5 is probably the better choice.

TABLE 16.6:   Affordable W18+ GRPs—R/F

	Schedule 3	Schedule 5
Prime Access	100	—
Prime	100	140
Late Fringe/News	—	70
Total	200	210
R/F	72/2.8	73/2.9

Reach/Frequency in Radio

The same general dynamics hold true for radio as for TV. In fact, both of these electronic media forms are planned on the basis of GRPs (as opposed to, say, magazines). The only difference between radio and TV media planning is that radio usually also refers to the number of announcements that are placed on each station because the activity *by station* has a direct effect on reach/frequency accumulation, as do these additional factors:

1. The GRP level

2. The number of stations purchased

3. The average rating of the purchased stations

4. The dispersion of announcements across different times of the day on each station

Assume you intend to purchase 100 GRPs targeted to adults 18 and older. You've decided to analyze three alternative schedules, as shown in Table 16.7. If you place a schedule on five average stations in market X, you'll purchase 111 announcements to generate 100 GRPs and will produce a reach/frequency of 28/3.6. If you place a schedule on the top five stations, which by definition have a higher average rating, you'll need to purchase only 83 announcements to yield 100 GRPs, for a reach/frequency of 32/3.1—more reach, less frequency. If you scatter your announcements across the top ten stations, your R/F will be 42/2.4—the highest reach of the three, and the lowest average frequency. The dynamics at work in these schedules deal with the audience accumulation patterns for each of the stations, as well as the duplication of audiences between stations. Generally,

- The more stations purchased, the greater the reach potential;

- The higher the average rating of the stations, the greater the rate of reach accumulation;

TABLE 16.7: Dynamics of Radio R/F—Adults 18+

Description/# Stations	Average 5	Top 5	Top 10
Average Rating	.9	1.2	1.0
# Announcements	22	17	10
Total # Announcements	111	83	100
GRPs	100	100	100
R/F	28/3.6	32/3.1	42/2.4

Reach/Frequency in Print Media

Because of the nature of the audience data collected by syndicated research companies, GRPs need not be used to estimate reach and frequency for magazines and newspapers, but the basic R/F formula is still used and the display of R/F estimates can be the same as that shown for TV or radio.

Several media research companies collect readership information for many magazines and newspapers. Through their survey techniques, they can determine duplicated readership of pairs of vehicles—how many people read *both* magazine A and magazine B, *both* C and D, etc. Using accepted statistical formulas, research suppliers (or independent media research services, etc.) can estimate the total reach of any combination of magazines or newspapers.

Table 16.8 shows an example of three magazines (you could just as easily substitute newspapers) in market X. Magazine A reaches (is read by) 300,000 people, 125,000 of whom also read magazine B and 75,000 of whom do not. Magazines A and B produce a gross audience of 500,000 readers and a net unduplicated audience of 375,000. Magazine C added to this schedule increases gross delivery to 600,000 and net delivery to 400,000. Using the R/F calculation, we can determine that the average person reached with this schedule will have the opportunity to be exposed to your advertising message an average of 1.5 times each. The data in the right portion of the table are identical to those in the left, except they are shown as percentages rather than actual numbers.

TABLE 16.8:   R/F in Print Media

Magazine	Total Readers (000)	Cumulative Net Unduplicated Readers (000)	Coverage	Cume Reach
A	300	300	30%	30.0
B	200	75	20	7.5
Total	500	375	50	37.5
C	100	25	10	2.5
Total	600	400	60%	40.0

$$\frac{600}{400} = 1.5 \qquad \frac{60}{40} = 1.5$$

(Market Population Base = 1 Million)

If duplication rates were reported for all TV and radio programs, the same kind of formulas could be developed to calculate broadcast reach and frequency. The media planner would not have to rely on the generalities of GRPs and general audience accumulation data. However, because of the dynamic and ever-changing program environment in broadcast media, such duplication information would be relatively unreliable for predicting future media consumption patterns.

Reach/Frequency in Out-Of-Home Media

Reach and frequency in out-of-home media are generally used more for information devices than as evaluation tools. With the exception of periodic national studies conducted by syndicated research companies and a few basic formulas created by media suppliers, there are little data available to determine the reach and frequency of specific out-of-home vehicles.

The preponderance of R/F data is based on the placement of outdoor 30-sheets (see Chapter 3) used at a level of a #100 showing. A #100 showing is equivalent to the purchase of 100 GRPs *daily* against people age two and older in the market. There are no data to help discriminate between one poster unit and another, nor between different poster combinations. R/F data used to decide if outdoor should be used in a media plan, or how much should be used, or which specific schedules should be used, are therefore wanting.

For general information purposes, Table 16.9 displays the R/F predicted for a #100 showing of 30-sheets in an average market among various demographic groups.

TABLE 16.9:   R/F in Outdoor—#100 Showing

Demographic	Reach	Frequency
Adults 18+	88	28.4
Men	88	29.4
Women	88	27.5
18–34	90	32.9
35–49	89	27.5
50+	84	23.6

Media Mix Reach/Frequency

We use the same math for calculating R/F for a media mix as we do for one medium. To establish R/F for a mix, follow these steps:

1. Determine the GRPs and reach for each medium.

2. Add the total GRPs.

3. Calculate the combined reach of the first two media using computer formulas available to you, or using the random combination technique.

4. Divide the total GRPs by the combined reach to yield average frequency. Do not average the individual frequencies.

5. Continue this process for each successive medium added to the schedule.

Table 16.10 demonstrates the above steps for a hypothetical situation in three media forms.

TABLE 16.10:   R/F in a Media Mix

	GRPs	Reach	Frequency
TV	80	40	2.0
Magazines	60	50	1.2
Combined	140	70	2.0
Radio	100	35	2.9
Combined	240	80	3.0

Controlling Reach/Frequency within GRPs

We have seen that reach accumulates as more GRPs (or coverage) are added. We've also seen that frequency levels are calculated by dividing GRPs by reach. By controlling the rate of reach accumulation, we can control, to some extent, the amount of frequency.

To demonstrate this control let's use marbles. Lay 100 marbles on a flat surface, forming a ten-by-ten square. Assume that each marble represents one percent of the population (a one rating); 100 marbles, therefore, equals 100 GRPs. Further, assume the height of your square represents reach and the width represents frequency. In this 10 × 10 array, therefore, you have displayed a reach of 10 and a frequency of 10.0. If you change the shape of your display to 5 high and 20 across, you've displayed the equivalent of a 5 reach and a 20.0 frequency (5/20.0). With just these 100 GRPs, you can effect 100 different combinations—ranging from a 1/100.0 to a 100/1.0. So if all you can afford is 100 marbles (that is, your media budget allows the purchase of just 100 GRPs) you can keep changing the matrix to display a variety of different shapes—to offer many different reach/frequency patterns. You probably will not deal with 100 different combinations because you'll have some notion of the minimum or maximum reach you want to attain. Besides, if you did deal with 100 different combinations, you'd wind up losing some of your marbles.

To reinforce this concept of *control*, let's use yet another device —this time two pieces of 8 1/2" × 11" paper. Lay one sheet on your desk, vertically. Assume that the height (11") is 11 percent and the width (8 1/2") is 8.5 frequency. Now lay the second sheet over this, horizontally, as shown in Exhibit 16.4. The top sheet is equivalent to an 85 reach with an 11 frequency. Both sheets encompass the same number of square inches—both the same quantity of GRPs: 93.5 (8.5 × 11). As H × W = Area, R × F = GRPs.

To use an example from advertising, if you scatter TV commercials across five different TV programs which have relatively little duplication from one to another, you will accumulate

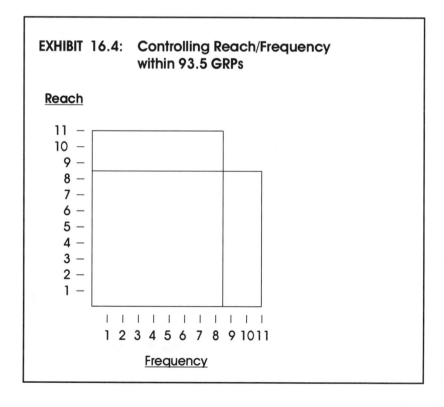

EXHIBIT 16.4:   Controlling Reach/Frequency within 93.5 GRPs

Reach

Frequency

proportionately more reach than frequency—reaching more new viewers with the addition of each new TV program. Conversely, if you concentrate all commercials in one TV program (and let's assume successive airings of this program do not attract additional new viewers), you've limited reach for the sake of accumulating frequency. Table 16.11 demonstrates the kinds of R/F effects possible with these two hypothetical schedules.

TABLE 16.11: Different Patterns of R/F

Program	Rating	Schedule 1 Announcements	GRPs	Schedule 2 Announcements	GRPs
A	10	1	10	5	50
B	10	1	10	—	—
C	10	1	10	—	—
D	10	1	10	—	—
E	10	1	10	—	—
Total		5	50	5	50
R/F		40/1.3			10/5.0

The real application of this R/F control requires that you have some understanding of the duplication rates between media vehicles within a media form, and between different combinations of media forms. It is logical to assume, for example, that programs within a given TV time period probably have more duplication than programs in different time periods. Also, magazines within an editorial category (such as women's magazines) will have more duplication than magazines in divergent categories. But even with this understanding, you should test your notions by conducting a reach/frequency analysis of alternative combinations.

Number of Spots

It has become common to refer to the number of commercial announcements in television or radio as the *number of spots*. Although grammatically questionable, referring to commercial announcements as "spots" is semantically proper—everyone knows what you are referring to. It is also sometimes common to confuse the number of spots with the intensity of advertising delivery. The number of spots you schedule in television or radio, in and of itself, has little to do with how many people you will reach with that schedule, or how often they will be exposed to your advertising message.

As we've seen, average program ratings vary by daypart and are a function of the homes-using-TV (or people-using-radio) at any particular time of day. We've also seen, for example, that HUT levels increase as we move from morning to evening, and then decrease as the evening wears on. It's logical, therefore, that *average* ratings would be higher at night than in the day. For example, if there are ten programs being telecast in daytime, and ten at night, and the HUT level during the day is 30 and at night 60, then the average program, by definition, will get a lower rating in

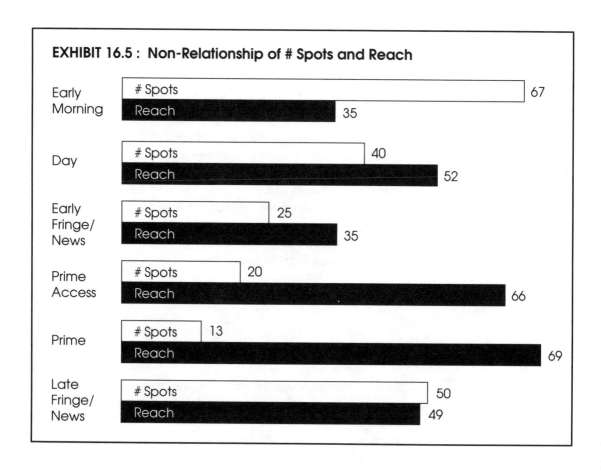

EXHIBIT 16.5 : Non-Relationship of # Spots and Reach

	# Spots	Reach
Early Morning	67	35
Day	40	52
Early Fringe/ News	25	35
Prime Access	20	66
Prime	13	69
Late Fringe/ News	50	49

daytime than at night—in this case, a 3 rating in the day and a 6 at night. To produce 60 GRPs you would have to schedule, on average, 20 programs in the day or 10 at night. We've also seen that equivalent levels of GRPs scheduled in different dayparts produce varying levels of reach—for the most part, lower in daytime and higher at night (primetime). In this example, therefore, 20 spots in daytime will produce a lower reach than half as many spots in primetime. The number of spots you schedule does not, per se, have anything to do with reach/frequency. There's almost a non-relationship between number of spots and R/F. Exhibit 16.5 demonstrates this non-relationship across various television dayparts.

PROFESSIONAL WORKSHOP

1. Your media plan contains a schedule encompassing 1,000 TRPs and you've determined that you will produce an 80 reach. What is the average frequency?

2. Your plan generates a 60/4.0 against women at a CPP of $10. How much have you spent for this schedule?

3. You've reached 10,000 men an average of five times each in a market with a population of 50,000 men. What are your reach and frequency?

4. There are 100 million women in the United States. Your media schedule generates 500 million impressions, and you've calculated that each woman reached will be exposed to an average of 10 advertising messages. What is your R/F?

5. You purchased a combination of radio stations which yield a 50/3.0 against men and a 25/2.0 against women in a market which has a population of two million adults (half within each sex). How many adult TRPs have you purchased?

Chapter 17

Frequency Distribution

I n this chapter we extend our understanding of frequency by discussing *frequency distribution*. We demonstrate how different media audience members receive different levels of advertising exposure and how, by combining these levels, we arrive at *average frequency*. We also examine how different components of a media form produce varying frequency patterns.

Frequency Distribution The array of reach according to the level of frequency delivered to each group.

In all our examples on reach and frequency we demonstrated *average* frequency among those people reached with a media schedule. As you digested those tables and charts you noted that some people received more than average frequency, and some less than average. For example, when we spoke of magazine reach and frequency we saw that some people read only one magazine, some read two, and some read all three. Each of these groups of people (each of these *reach* segments) received different *rates of exposure*, that is, different levels of frequency.

Let's use the combination of three magazines that was originally displayed in Exhibit 15.2. We saw that 42 percent of people read only one of the three magazines, six percent read any two, and two percent read all three. If you array this reach and exposure level (as shown in Table 17.1), you will have calculated a **frequency distribution**. The usual way of showing this distribution is displayed in the lower part of the table.

You'll also note that the three magazines produced a total of 60 GRPs. With a combined 50 reach, the *average* frequency is therefore 1.2—even though none of these people is exposed to the medium exactly 1.2 times. A frequency distribution overrides the necessity

TABLE 17.1:   Magazine Frequency Distribution
3 Magazines—60 GRPs

Magazine(s) Read	Frequency Level	Reach at Each Level
Only A	1	14
Only B	1	14
Only C	1	14
A + B	2	2
A + C	2	2
B + C	2	2
A + B +C	3	2
Total		50
Average Frequency	1.2	
	1	42
	2	6
	3	2
	Total	50

of displaying the average frequency because it addresses the amount of reach obtained at *each* level of frequency. Semantically, it would be better to call a frequency distribution "a distribution of reach by each level of frequency," but media shorthand prevails.

The frequency distribution of ten 20-rated announcements scheduled in ten primetime TV programs is displayed in Table 17.2. The 200 women 18+ GRPs generated by this schedule produce a reach of 64.9 and an average frequency of 3.1. Some of the women reached will view only one program, some more than one—up to the possible total of all ten programs. The specific distribution for this schedule indicates that 20.6 percent will view only one program, a different group of women representing 13.9 percent of the population will view only two programs, etc. Because there is no duplication between these *only* groups, the reach against each frequency level can be added together to get total reach. Going back to our previous discussion on mean average, you'll see that the average frequency is 3.1. The median average frequency is 4.0, but median averages are not used in frequency distributions.

TABLE 17.2: Frequency Distribution Pattern Schedule: 200 W18+ GRPs in Primetime

Frequency	Reach at Each Level
1	20.6
2	13.9
3	9.7
4	6.8
5	4.7
6	3.3
7	2.3
8	1.5
9	1.3
10	1.2
Total Reach	64.9
Average Frequency	3.1

Exhibit 17.1 displays the frequency distribution in Table 17.2 graphically. Typical frequency distributions follow this same pattern —less and less reach as the level of frequency increases. The reasons for this pattern are twofold:

1. Some people view only a little bit of TV and therefore will automatically not have the opportunity to be exposed to many commercials. Some people view a lot of TV and will therefore receive proportionately higher levels of advertising exposure.

2. The chances of hitting everyone with the same level of frequency diminish as more and more TV programs are added to a media schedule, because different programs attract different people. In our schedule of ten primetime programs, for example, it's unreasonable to believe that most of the people reached will be part of the viewing audience of most of the programs.

Although the general pattern of a frequency distribution is as shown, specific patterns vary according to the rates of duplication

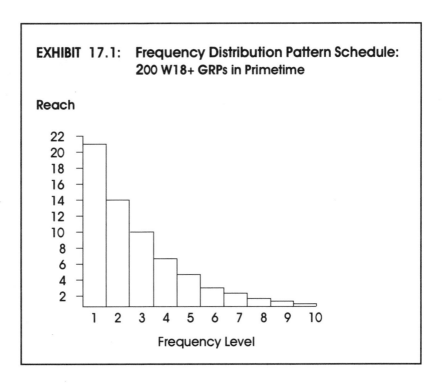

**EXHIBIT 17.1:   Frequency Distribution Pattern Schedule:
200 W18+ GRPs in Primetime**

Reach

Frequency Level

between media forms and between vehicles within a form. If you schedule one announcement in each of two TV programs that have no duplication (no one views both programs), your average frequency will be one. If these two programs have total duplication (everyone reached views both programs), your average frequency will be two. Because of varying duplication rates between vehicles, coupled with the available audience size at any given time (HUT levels), frequency distributions vary by television daypart. Those dayparts, such as daytime, that have proportionately more duplication between programs tend to have proportionately more reach at the higher frequency levels; those with proportionately less duplication (e.g., primetime) tend to have proportionately less reach at the higher frequency levels.

Shown in Table 17.3 are frequency distributions for a schedule of 200 women 18+ GRPs in each of five TV dayparts. Total R/F varies between dayparts (for reasons explained in the previous section), as does the amount of reach at each frequency level between and within dayparts. For ease in reviewing these data, arithmetic changes are included: first, all reach numbers are rounded to the nearest full number; second, frequency is displayed only up to a level of "8 or more." Although technically a frequency distribution can be displayed for every level of frequency (up to the total number of announcements contained in your media schedule) it is customary to group the higher frequency levels into an "or more" statement because the absolute reach at the very high levels of frequency is usually very small (often less than one percent).

TABLE 17.3: Frequency Distribution by Daypart Schedule: 200 W18+ GRPs in Each Daypart

		Reach at Each Level			
Frequency	Day	Early Fringe	Prime Access	Prime	Late Fringe
1	14	7	19	21	12
2	8	4	12	14	7
3	6	3	8	10	5
4	4	2	6	7	3
5	3	2	4	5	3
6	2	1	3	3	2
7	2	1	2	2	2
8 or more	8	9	6	4	7
Total	47	29	60	65	41
Avg. Frequency	4.2	6.8	3.3	3.1	4.9

Another way to evaluate a frequency distribution is to calculate the gross delivery at each frequency level to determine how much relative pressure (or weight) is directed to each frequency group. Using the information from Table 17.3 for 200 W18+ GRPs in primetime, for example, we can calculate how many GRPs are generated by each frequency level. As shown in Table 17.4, the 20.6 reach at one frequency level equals 21 GRPs; the 13.9 reach at the two-level equals 28 GRPs, and so forth. Adding GRPs for each frequency level produces the total GRPs of 200. Of the total

200 GRPs, 10.5 percent are represented by women who will, on average, be exposed to only one TV program; 14 percent are accounted for by women who will be exposed to two programs, etc.

TABLE 17.4:   R x F = GRPs at Each Level
Primetime— Women 18+

Frequency	×	Reach	=	GRPs	Percent Total
1		20.6		21	10.5%
2		13.9		28	14.0
3		9.7		29	14.5
4		6.8		27	13.5
5		4.7		23	11.5
6		3.3		20	10.0
7		2.3		16	8.0
8+		3.6		36	18.0
Total		64.9		200	100.0%

If you tie this GRP information into cost considerations, you can determine the *relative* investment you are making for the schedule you are analyzing. In the above primetime frequency distribution, for example, you can correctly state that 10.5 percent of the media budget you want to expend in primetime for 200 GRPs is accounted for by women who will be exposed to only one commercial announcement.

By displaying the GRPs generated at each frequency level for different media schedules, such as for 200 women 18+ GRPs in daytime versus primetime, you can both evaluate the concentration of GRP "weight" and make some judgments on whether or not your media budget is providing the kinds of frequency concentrations you are seeking. Exhibit 17.2 demonstrates the vast differences between daytime and primetime. The 200 GRPs in daytime show a definite skew to the higher frequency levels, whereas primetime exhibits a generally flat concentration pattern.

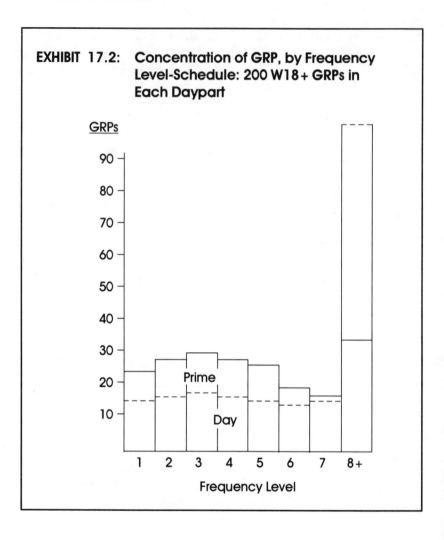

EXHIBIT 17.2: Concentration of GRP, by Frequency Level-Schedule: 200 W18+ GRPs in Each Daypart

PROFESSIONAL WORKSHOP

1. You've scheduled one announcement in each of five TV programs which, combined, produced 117 GRPs. You've instructed your PC to compute R/F and a frequency distribution, but the printer ran out of paper and only the following information was shown:

   Frequency: 1   2   3   4   5
   Reach: 20 10 8   7   5

   You can't access the PC to rerun the data because there's a power outage. You're not having a good day, but you still must know the R/F. Can you figure it out?

2. The multimedia schedule you are running produces an 80/4.0 against men 18–34. How many of these men will be exposed to one or more commercial messages?

3. You decided to run in two magazines, each of which reaches 20 percent of women in an average issue. If there is no duplication of audience between these magazines, what will your frequency distribution look like? If there's 50 percent duplication, what will it look like?

Chapter 18

Quintile Distribution

I n this chapter we focus on *quintile distributions*. We show how these distributions are related to the previously discussed frequency distributions, and how quintiles are calculated. We demonstrate how different uses of media, or different combinations of media, produce different quintile patterns. We also show how media research suppliers' definitions of quintiles are not necessarily in concert with how media planners use quintile analyses to assess media schedules.

Different people consume different media with varying intensity. This consumption pattern is generally fairly habitual. Although consumption patterns may change as a person changes (for instance, as they get older, or become more educated, or attain a different income level), at any given point in time a person tends to fall within a defined level of media exposure. Some people, for example, spend a great deal of time reading magazines. Others spend less. Some view a great deal of TV. Some watch very little. If you were to randomly select any five people and query them on how much TV they view in an average day, we would find five different levels of viewing—from the light viewer who might view only an hour or less each day, to the heavy viewer who might view five hours or more per day. By arraying these people into five different groups (each containing one person), we have effected a **quintile distribution**. A quintile distribution is like a frequency distribution, but rather than displaying reach at each frequency level, it groups the audience reached into five equal parts and averages the frequency for each group. Although quintiles (fifths) will be discussed

Quintile Distribution
A display of frequency (or related data) among audiences grouped into equal fifths of reach.

Tertile Distribution
A display of frequency
(or related data) among
audiences grouped into
equal thirds of reach.

in this chapter, the same concept applies to any equal division of people or homes, such as **tertile** (one third) or decile (one tenth) distributions.

Continuing with our example on viewing hours, Table 18.1 shows a quintile distribution of time spent viewing TV during the average day among all the one million households in market X. The hypothetical survey that was conducted in this market revealed that the average home viewed TV for seven hours (that is, one or more people in the household were viewing TV and collectively produced a viewing level of seven hours). Of these homes, 200,000 averaged only one hour of viewing, another 200,000 averaged four hours, etc. Each of these household segments represent one-fifth (20 percent) of the total market population. The 200,000 households that viewed the least are designated as the "lightest" viewing quintile; those that viewed the most are referred to as the "heaviest" viewing quintile. The "next" groups, each accounting for one-fifth of the total, have viewing levels somewhere between light and heavy.

TABLE 18.1:   Quintile Distribution of Hours Spent Viewing TV

Quintile	# Households (000)	% Total Household	# Viewing Hours/Day	% Total Viewing Hours
Lightest	200	20%	1	3%
Next	200	20	4	11
Next	200	20	6	17
Next	200	20	9	26
Heaviest	200	20	15	43
Total/Average	1,000	100%	7	100%

Total viewing hours in the market are seven million (7 hours × 1 million households). The light viewing quintile accounts for 200,000 hours (1 hour × 200,000). The lightest viewing quintile, therefore, accounts for three percent of all viewing hours (200,000/7,000,000). Conversely, the heaviest viewing quintile accounts for 43 percent of total market viewing hours. In nearly all quintile distributions, you will find that the heaviest group always accounts for significantly more consumption than the lightest group.

Calculating Quintile Distribution

Rest assured that if you will be dealing with quintile distributions you will not, in all probability, have to calculate them manually. Nevertheless, you should understand how one is calculated to gain a greater appreciation for what the distribution indicates.

To calculate a quintile distribution, you must first have a complete frequency distribution—generally available via various computer programs. Using these data, you can re-array the reach for each frequency level in order to put reach into equal fifths and recalculate average frequency. At first glance, it's a complicated procedure, but after calculating one quintile distribution you'll fully understand the mechanics and can let the computer do all the calculations for you in the future. The steps, as shown in Exhibit 18.1, are:

1. Refer to the frequency distribution as shown on the left side of the exhibit.

2. Divide the total reach into five equal parts. One-fifth (20 percent) of 75 is 15.

3. Move down the frequency distribution (starting at the 1.0 level) to find audience segments that represent a 15 reach. Here we find that the most lightly exposed 15 percent is contained within the 20 reach of those exposed at the 1.0 level. You have therefore accounted for the lightest viewing quintile, who will receive, on average, a frequency of 1.0.

4. Tally any portion of reach you have not accounted for, such as the 5 percent within the 20 at the 1.0 frequency level. This remaining audience (the 5 percent) becomes part of the next viewing quintile.

5. If you have not obtained a 15 reach with the carryover of reach from the previous quintile, accumulate more audience until you reach the level of 15. Here we see that we need an additional 10 reach points (in addition to the 5 we already have) to equal a 15 reach. We can find this additional 10 reach at the 2.0 frequency level. Therefore, for this "next" viewing quintile, we have a 5 reach plus a 10 reach equaling a 15 reach. We also have 5 percent of the people receiving a 1.0 frequency and 10 percent receiving a 2.0 frequency.

6. You need to average the frequency for this "next" group by performing the R × F = GRPs equation and striking an average. The mathematics look like this:

$$5 \text{ reach} \times 1.0 \text{ frequency} = 5 \text{ GRPs}$$
$$+ \underline{10} \text{ reach} \times 2.0 \text{ frequency} = \underline{20 \text{ GRPs}}$$
$$\text{Total} \quad 15 \text{ reach} \qquad\qquad 25 \text{ GRPs}$$

$$\frac{25 \text{ GRPs}}{15 \text{ Reach}} = 1.7 \text{ frequency}$$

7. Continue the same procedures as above to account for all reach at all frequency levels.

8. Check your findings by first adding the GRPs at each quintile level. This should equal the total GRPs of the schedule.

EXHIBIT 18.1 : Television quintile analysis

		Equal Fifths			Quintiles		
Frequency	Reach	Reach	Frequency	GRPs	Reach	Frequency	
		15	1.0	15	15	1.0	Lightest
1.0	20						
		5	1.0	25	15	1.7	Next
		10	2.0				
2.0	15						
		5	2.0	40	15	2.7	Next
3.0	10	10	3.0				
4.0	10	10	4.0	65	15	4.3	Next
5.0	5	5	5.0				
6.0	5	5	6.0				
7.0	4	4	7.0				
8.0	3	3	8.0	110	15	7.3	Heaviest
9.0	2	2	9.0				
10.0	1	1	10.0				
Total Average:							
3.4	75	75		255	75	3.4	

9. Also check your findings by multiplying the reach at each quintile level by the average frequency and adding the products.
The sum of the products should equal the total GRPs of the
schedule.

You can now make the following observations about this quintile
distribution:

- You'd probably rather have a computer do the calculations.

- The lightest viewing quintile has an average frequency of one.

- The heaviest viewing 20 percent has an average frequency of
7.3.

- The "top two" viewing quintiles have an average frequency of
5.8. The "top" quintiles are those with the heaviest level
of exposure—not necessarily those which are displayed at
the top of a chart. The top two quintiles in our example are
therefore composed of the 15 reach with 4.3 frequency and the
15 reach with 7.3 frequency. The 5.8 average frequency is
calculated by adding the GRPs for these two groups and
dividing by the combined reach:

$$\frac{(15 \times 4.3) + (15 \times 7.3)}{30} = 5.8$$

Quintile Distributions of a Media Mix

Whenever a second medium is added to the first, the frequency
distribution (and therefore the quintile distribution) flattens. Disproportionately more frequency is added to the more lightly
exposed groups than to the most heavily exposed group.

There is a mistaken belief that heavy users of one medium are
light users of another. This appears logical if one concludes that
people, in general, spend about the same amount of time each day
with their preferred media forms. Therefore, if people view television for most of that time, they will have less time to spend with
other media. While logical, this is not a real-world phenomenon. The
fact is that people spend varying amounts of time with media. Some
are heavy consumers of media overall; some are light consumers.
As a result of this pattern, consumers of one medium (e.g., magazine

readers) have an equal propensity to be heavy, moderate, or light consumers of another medium.

The logical and real-world assumptions are displayed in the following two tables. Table 18.2 shows what might happen if people, in general, spend about the same amount of time with their preferred media forms. For example, most of the heavy radio listeners would be light TV viewers. To read the chart: 20 percent of adults are considered *heavy* radio listeners. These 20 percent view television for varying amounts of time. Ten percent of these 20 percent are *heavy* viewers, compared with 30 percent who are *light* TV viewers. At the other end of the spectrum are light radio listeners. A large portion of these are concentrated within the heaviest viewing quintile, that is, they tend to view TV more than they listen to radio.

TABLE 18.2:   Hypothetical inter-media quintile distributions.

	Radio Quintiles				
% Adults	Heaviest 20%	Next 20%	Next 20%	Next 20%	Lightest 20%
Prime TV Quintiles					
Heaviest	10	15	20	25	30
Next	15	20	25	30	10
Next	20	25	30	10	15
Next	25	30	10	15	20
Lightest	30	10	15	20	25

Source: Simmons

Table 18.3 displays the real-world situation. It shows that heavy radio listeners are almost equally distributed among each of the TV quintiles. To read the chart: 20 percent of adults are considered *heavy* radio listeners. Of this 20 percent, 19 percent are heavy viewers of primetime TV, and 23 percent are light viewers. The same holds true for light radio listeners; that is, 21 percent of all listeners are heavy TV viewers, and 20 percent are light TV viewers.

Because of what happens in the real world, the frequency distribution tends to flatten whenever a second medium is added to

TABLE 18.3:   Real-world inter-media quintile distributions.

% Adults	Radio Quintiles				
	Heaviest 20%	Next 20%	Next 20%	Next 20%	Lightest 20%
Prime TVQuintiles					
Heaviest	19	20	20	21	21
Next	19	21	20	20	19
Next	19	21	22	19	19
Next	19	20	21	20	20
Lightest	23	19	18	20	20

Source: Simmons

the first. Adding magazines to a base of television, for example, delivers equal frequency to each TV quintile but *disproportionately* more frequency to the lighter viewing quintiles than to the heavier viewing quintiles. As shown in Exhibit 18.2, the addition of magazines increases frequency among the lightest viewing fifth by 200

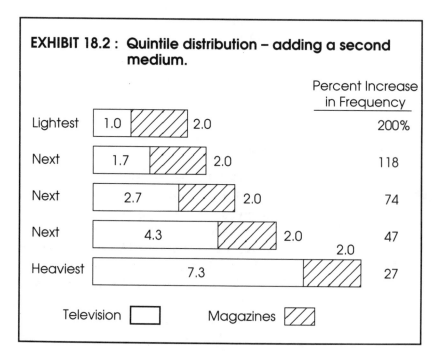

EXHIBIT 18.2 : Quintile distribution – adding a second medium.

Percent Increase in Frequency

Lightest	1.0 / 2.0	200%
Next	1.7 / 2.0	118
Next	2.7 / 2.0	74
Next	4.3 / 2.0	47
Heaviest	7.3 / 2.0	27

Television ☐   Magazines ▨

percent, compared with a 27 percent increase in frequency of the heaviest viewing fifth.

In this example, television provides a frequency of one to the lightest quintile, 1.7 to the next quintile, up to a 7.3 average frequency to the heaviest viewing quintile of reach. Magazines, with an average frequency of 2.0, deliver the same level of frequency to each of the TV viewing quintiles.

This "flattening" phenomenon occurs only when different media forms are combined, not when more of the same medium is used. Using more of the same medium results in delivering messages in approximately the same proportions as a lesser use of the medium. People who are light consumers of that medium will continue to be relatively lightly exposed; those who are heavy users will continue to be relatively heavily exposed. Table 18.4 demonstrates quintile distributions for two levels of radio usage. The "5 station" level is composed of a schedule of 18 spots (announcements) placed on each station; the "10 station" schedule also has 18 spots on each station. Comparing these two schedules, we see that the 10 station schedule produces:

- twice as many spots (index of 200)

- 68 percent more GRPs

- a 54 percent greater reach

- a 9 percent increase in average frequency

TABLE 18.4:   Quintile Distribution of Two Levels of Radio Usage

	5 Stations		10 Stations		
Quintile	Reach	Frequency	Reach	Frequency	Index
Lightest	6.4	1.0	9.9	1.0	100
Next	6.4	1.6	9.9	1.8	113
Next	6.4	2.6	9.9	2.8	108
Next	6.4	4.1	9.9	4.5	110
Heaviest	6.4	7.3	9.9	7.8	107
Total	32.0		49.5		154
Average		3.3		3.6	109
GRPs	106		178		168
# Spots	90		180		200

- a relatively *flat* increase in frequency across each of the listening quintiles—certainly flatter than that exhibited for the previous media mix of magazines added to television.

Predefined Quintiles

All of the quintile distributions displayed so far have been based on specific media schedules in each of the various media forms. All have also been devised using the frequency distribution of those schedules. Many syndicated media research companies report media audiences by quintile (or equivalent), but these designations do not necessarily jibe with the quintile distribution that will be obtained for a specific media schedule. Syndicated research companies classify audiences into one or another quintile based on their findings of media consumption intensities—either by arraying segments, each of which encompasses 20 percent of the population base, and determining their overall level of media consumption, or by defining an array of media intensity and determining the portion of the population within that array. Shown in Table 18.5 is an example of two major syndicated research reports listing their definitions of each quintile for magazine readership along with the corresponding percent of total U.S. population within each segment. If you use this information in planning a media schedule, you need to understand that different sources reveal different information, and that overall general information may or may not indicate the quintile distribution of a specific media schedule.

TABLE 18.5: Quintile Definitions Used by Syndicated Researchers—Women 18 and Older

	Number of Issues in a Month				
	I (Heavy)	II	III	IV	V (Light)
MRI	18+	11–17	7–10	3–6	2 or less
Simmons	10+	6–9	4–5	2–3	1 or less

	Percent of Total Reading Audience				
	I (Heavy)	II	III	IV	V (Light)
MRI	20.0	20.0	20.0	20.0	20.0
Simmons	20.4	23.8	18.6	19.8	17.5

Why Quintile Distributions Are Used

Quintile distributions are a better descriptor of frequency among different groups of people than average frequency, but less discriminating than a complete frequency distribution. Nevertheless, quintile distributions are used to assess the dynamics of a media schedule—to determine the impact of a second medium, and sometimes to decide when an additional commercial or advertisement should be put into the pool of creative executions. This last notion is discussed in the next section under the general description of commercial "wearout."

PROFESSIONAL WORKSHOP

1. What is the reach of the heaviest viewing quintile in a TV schedule that produces a 50 reach overall?

2. What is the reach of the lightest viewing tertile in a magazine plan that produces a 75 reach overall?

3. Having the following quintile distribution data, what is the reach for the missing segment (shown with an asterisk) for this 180 GRP schedule?

Quintile	F	R
I	1.0	20
II	2.0	15
III	5.0	10
IV	8.0	5
V	10.0	*

4. If you have a base plan using only one medium, what will happen to the lightest quintile if you add more of the same medium? If you add a second medium?

5. If the lightest quintile of medium A represents a 10/2.0 and the lightest quintile of medium B represents a 10/2.0, what will the lightest quintile of the combined schedule be?

Chapter 19

Effective Reach

I n this chapter we go beyond the basic concepts of reach and frequency by combining these separate terms into one media dynamic known as *effective reach*. We show how effective reach is calculated by using a frequency distribution. We examine the various patterns of effective reach which emerge through the use of alternative media schedules. We discuss possible answers to a question that has plagued advertisers: How much frequency is enough? We conclude with a discussion on advertising *wearout* by reviewing pertinent research conducted on the issue and by demonstrating some techniques for deciding the proper level of effective reach.

Effective Reach The number or percentage of a population group reached by a media schedule at a given level of frequency.

Effective Frequency The level of exposure frequency at which reach is deemed "effectively" delivered. See *Effective Reach.*

We have spoken of total reach, average frequency, frequency distribution, and quintile distribution. All of these are obviously interrelated and basically address the same thing: the quantity and intensity of potential advertising exposures. From a numerical standpoint the aim of the media planner is to maximize this total exposure—to provide the most delivery per dollar invested. Maximization of exposure opportunities goes beyond delivering reach and frequency. It involves reaching people with frequency. Enter the media dynamic known as **effective reach**—often also called **effective frequency**. It is the percent (or number) of people reached by a media schedule at a frequency level deemed *effective*.

This effective frequency level is not the overall average frequency nor the average frequency within any quintile. It is the frequency level that you have defined as being the right level to get your creative message across to the consumer. You might decide, for example, that you must reach people with your advertising message at least three times within a four-week period for them to absorb the message and take action as a result of this absorption— action such as buying the product you are advertising. If a 3.0 frequency is your chosen level of effectiveness, you will analyze alternative media combinations to select that combination that delivers the most reach among people who will be exposed *at least three times*. Those reached one or two times (frequency level of 1.0 and 2.0) will be considered ineffectively reached and are therefore excluded from your analysis.

Calculating effective reach is an offshoot of a frequency distribution. Table 19.1 shows the frequency distribution we derived for 200 women 18+ GRPs scheduled in primetime TV (on the left side of the table), with the effective levels on the right. The effective levels are listed as "reach at each level." For example, the total reach of this schedule is 64.9 percent—that is, 64.9 percent of women will be exposed to *one or more* commercial announcements. Moving down this distribution we see that 44.3 percent will be exposed two or more times, 30.4 percent three or more times, etc. These "or more" reach levels are tabulated by adding the reach at each frequency level starting at the bottom and working up: 3.6

TABLE 19.1 : Frequency Distribution Schedule: 200 W18+ GRPs in Primetime

Frequency	Reach at Each Level	Frequency	Reach at Each Level
1	20.6	1+	64.9
2	13.9	2+	44.3
3	9.7	3+	30.4
4	6.8	4+	20.7
5	4.7	5+	13.9
6	3.3	6+	9.2
7	2.3	7+	5.9
8+	3.6	8+	3.6
Total	64.9		
Average frequency	3.1		

percent will be exposed eight or more times, added to 2.3 percent exposed only seven times equals 5.9 percent who will be exposed seven or more times. If you have decided that a "three or more" frequency level is effective, you can determine that this schedule delivers a 30.4 percent reach to women who will be exposed at the 3+ level.

Using the frequency distributions tabulated in the previous section, Table 19.2 shows that "reach at 3+" varies from one daypart to another—just as total reach and average frequency vary. The primetime schedule has a 30 reach at 3+, daytime has a 25 reach, early fringe has 19, etc. If you needed to decide which of these dayparts should be selected for your media plan (all other variables held constant) you would select primetime—it has the highest 3+ reach. Likewise, if you analyzed combinations of dayparts (as shown in the lower half of Table 19.2), with each combination delivering 200 GRPs, you would select either daytime plus primetime or prime access plus primetime, each delivering a 3+ reach of 31.

TABLE 19.2:   Effective Reach at Constant GRPs

	GRPs	+Additional Prime	R/F	Reach @ 3+	Reach @ 6+
Day	200	—	47/4.2	25	12
Early Fringe	200	—	29/6.8	19	12
Prime Access	200	—	60/3.3	29	11
Prime	200	—	65/3.1	30	9
Late Fringe	200	—	41/4.9	22	12
Day	100	100	67/3.0	31	9
Early Fringe	100	100	62/3.2	30	10
Prime Access	100	100	73/2.8	31	7
Late Fringe	100	100	67/3.0	30	9

Hypothetically, if you decided that a 6.0 frequency is the effective level you need to seek, you would choose 200 GRPs in daytime, early fringe, or late fringe, each of which delivers the highest level of 6+ reach—12.

We've noted, however, that you should not compare equal GRPs from one media schedule to another inasmuch as the costs might differ. You need to determine affordability first and then calculate an effective reach. As demonstrated in Table 19.3, plans A, B, C, and D each cost $60,000 and produce GRP levels ranging from 200 to 600. Although the all-daytime plan has the most GRPs, and plans C and D both have the highest reach (at 1+), plan D is the clear winner on reach at 3+.

TABLE 19.3:   Effective Reach—Plan Comparisons—Equal Expenditures—Market X

	Cost			
	Plan A	**Plan B**	**Plan C**	**Plan D**
Daytime	$ —	$60,000	$15,000	$30,000
Primetime	60,000	—	45,000	30,000
Total	$60,000	$60,000	$60,000	$60,000
	Women 18+ Delivery			
	Plan A	**Plan B**	**Plan C**	**Plan D**
Daytime	—	600	150	300
Primetime	200	—	150	100
Total	200	600	300	400
R/F	65/3.1	55/11.0	75/4.0	75/5.3
Reach at 3+	30	38	43	48

Bear in mind that the effective reach concept applies to all media. Just as all media can be analyzed on the basis of total reach/frequency, they can be analyzed on effective reach levels. Also keep in mind that when combining media, some people who are exposed at the 1.0 level for medium A and the 1.0 level for medium B move into the 2.0 level for a combination of both media (i.e., receive two exposures from either medium A or B or both). Table 19.4 shows frequency distributions for two schedules—one encompassing 200 GRPs in TV and the other one a schedule for one insertion in each of seven women's magazines. You'll note that in the combination the percent reached at the 1.0 level is less than the reach obtained by either medium alone.

TABLE 19.4:   Media Mix Frequency Distribution

Frequency	Women Reach at Each Level		
	TV	Magazines	Combined
1	21	19	16
2	14	12	15
3	10	8	12
4	7	6	10
5	5	4	8
6+	8	4	23
Total	63	53	84
Average Frequency	3.1	2.6	4.0
GRPs	200	137	337

How Much Frequency Is Enough?

The often asked question is: How much frequency constitutes *effective* frequency . . . how much is enough? The simple truth is that no one knows the answer. This underscores the importance of being totally conversant in the science of media planning *and* using judgment to adapt scientific (quantitative and qualitative) data to create what you believe is the best media plan. As to the scientific component, the following discussion reviews popular thoughts and research on how much frequency *might* be needed to constitute effectiveness.

Many in-market and laboratory studies have addressed this question—dating as far back as 1947, when a steering committee representing business publications attempted to determine whether the same ad could be run more than once without losing effectiveness. Interestingly, modern research studies incorporate the same human memory dynamics that Herman Ebbinghaus investigated in 1885—before advertising (as we know it) existed. Ebbinghaus made up lists of nonsense syllables, memorized them, and then tested his memory capability by recording how little or how much he could remember after certain periods of time had lapsed. This learning process required repetitive reviews of the nonsense syllables—either all at once, or over a period of time. Such review is identical to what we now call frequency. Ebbinghaus found that the more frequent the review of the syllables, the greater the buildup of memory retention: as he stated, the forgetting rate of human memory decelerates with repetition. While this is an argument for more frequency, rather than less, in a media plan, it is not a statement on the definitive level of frequency required for *effective* communication.

We can refer to several other studies to help decide the question. Stephen Greyser[1] outlined a six-stage sequence for how consumers respond to commercials. His stages are:

1. Exposure to the message on several occasions prior to serious attention (given some basic interest in the product to begin with)

2. Interest in the advertisement on either substantive (informative) or stimulus (enjoyment) grounds

3. Continued but declining attention to the ad

4. Mentally tuning out the message due to familiarity

5. Increasing re-awareness of the ad, now as a negative stimulus

6. Growing irritation

These presumptions could also be expressed as shown in Exhibit 19.1, which is based on the work conducted by Leon Jacobovits[2]. He identifies three stages:

- *Learning* involves taking from the commercial new knowledge or information which is valuable, interesting or relevant;

- Satiation is the absorption and comprehension of all the elements of the commercial message;

- *Decay* sets in after the satiation period, which can lead to irritation: the consumer knows all he or she needs to know of the message, does not need more stimulation, and probably doesn't want it.

The satiation area is the ideal frequency range—starting at some minimum level after sufficient learning has taken place, and ending at some later point on the frequency scale before decay sets in. Alvin Achenbaum[3] refers to this satiation range as *Effective Rating Points (ERPs)*. Given that this sequence of events "makes sense," the next step for determining effective frequency level

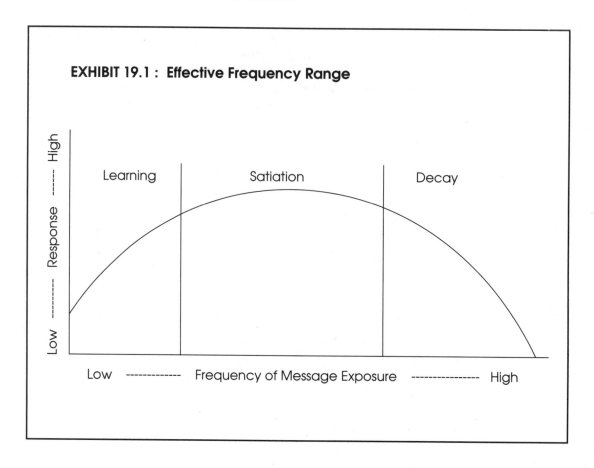

EXHIBIT 19.1 : Effective Frequency Range

is quantifying the frequency level at each of the critical satiation points. We also need to understand that the corollary to remembering is forgetting.

Ebbinghaus found that after one week, 75 percent of "learned" information was forgotten; after four weeks 95 percent was not remembered. Hubert Zielske[4] also investigated learning and forgetting (in 1959 for print media and, joined by Walter Henry, again in 1980 for television advertising). A summary of the 1980 findings appears in Exhibit 19.2. The graph shows the unaided recall level obtained by various scheduling patterns, each totalling 1,300 GRPs. The first schedule, for example, allocated 100 GRPs per week for 13 consecutive weeks. This schedule achieved the highest recall score, but was followed by a rapid decay rate which ended in week 52 with the lowest recall of any of the studied schedules. Other scheduling patterns produced varying recall/decay patterns—all producing accelerated recall during advertised weeks and decelerated recall (decay) during hiatuses. The major point that relates to an effective level of frequency is that without frequent repetition, the learning curve accelerates slowly; with frequent repetition, recall accumulates more rapidly.

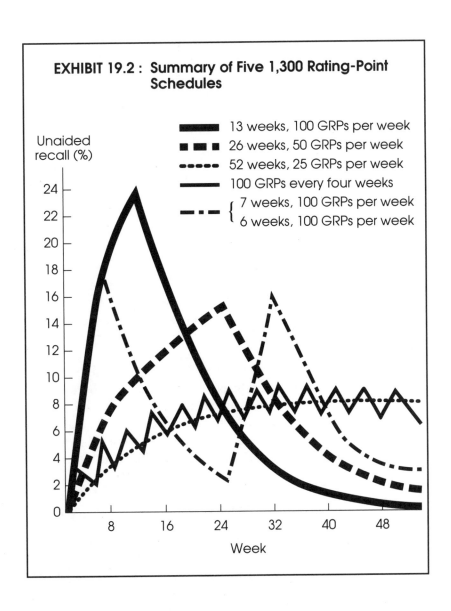

EXHIBIT 19.2 : Summary of Five 1,300 Rating-Point Schedules

Unaided recall (%)

Legend:
- 13 weeks, 100 GRPs per week
- 26 weeks, 50 GRPs per week
- 52 weeks, 25 GRPs per week
- 100 GRPs every four weeks
- { 7 weeks, 100 GRPs per week
- 6 weeks, 100 GRPs per week

Week

Effectiveness = 3+

A very popular notion is that a frequency of three or more is the ideal level. Much of this theory is based on the work of Herbert Krugman[5], who in 1972 postulated that the first two segments of the learning-satiation-decay sequence required just three exposures, which he entitled "What is it," "What of it," and "The true reminder." To use the author's words in describing this concept:

Exposure No. 1 is by definition unique. Like the first exposure of anything, the reaction is dominated by a "what is it?" type cognate response—i.e., the first response is to understand the nature of the stimulus.

The second exposure to a stimulus has several implicit qualities. One is that the cognitive "What is it?" response can be replaced by a more evaluative and personal "What *of* it?" response. Another element ... is the startled recognition response, "Ah ha, I've seen this before!" So the second exposure is the one where personal responses and evaluations —the "sale" so to speak—occurs.

By the third exposure the viewer knows he has been through this "What *is* it?" and the "What *of* it," and the third becomes, then, the true reminder—that is, *if* there is some consequence of the earlier evaluations yet to be fulfilled. But it is *also* the beginning of disengagement, of withdrawal of attention from a completed task.

I suggest that this pattern holds true for all larger number of exposures. That is, most people filter or screen-out TV commercials at any one time by stopping at the "What is it?" response, without further personal involvement. The same person, months later, and suddenly in the market for the product in question, might see and experience the 23rd exposure to the commercial as *if it were the second*. That is, now the viewer is able to go further into the nature of his or her reaction to the commercial—and then the 24th and probably the 25th might finish off that sequence with no further reaction to subsequent exposures.

Krugman's "three-hit" theory gained further popularity in 1979 when Michael Naples[6] authored a review, appraisal, and summary of studies and key case histories concerned with frequency and its effects. Naples' conclusions are these:

1. One exposure of an advertisement to a target group consumer within a purchase cycle has little or no effect in all but a minority of circumstances.

2. Since one exposure is usually ineffective, the central goal of productive media planning should be to place emphasis on enhancing frequency rather than reach.

3. The weight of evidence suggests strongly that an exposure frequency of two within a purchase cycle is an effective level.

4. By and large, optimal exposure frequency appears to be at least three exposures within a purchase cycle.

5. Beyond three exposures within a brand purchase cycle, or over a period of four or even eight weeks . . . increasing frequency continues to build advertising effectiveness at a decreasing rate, but with no evidence of a decline.

6. The frequency-of-exposure data from this review strongly suggests that wearout is not a function of too much frequency per se.

7. . . . very large and well-known brands—and/or those with dominant market shares in their categories and dominant shares of category advertising weight—appear to differ markedly in response to frequency of exposure from smaller or more average brands.

8. Perhaps as a result of the differing exposure environments of television dayparts, frequency of exposure . . . has a differential effect on advertising response by daypart.

9. . . . the amount of money a brand spends on advertising as a percent of total category advertising expenditures has a significant positive effect on brand users' purchase probabilities.

10. Nothing we have seen suggests that frequency response principles or generalizations vary by medium.

11. Although there are general principles with respect to frequency of exposure and its relationship to advertising effectiveness, differential effects by brand are equally important.

12. . . . the leverage of different equal-expenditure media plans in terms of frequency response can be substantial.

At this point you might conclude that a frequency of three *is* the minimum level that is required to effectively communicate with consumers. There are, nevertheless, a number of variables that might have an impact on your decision. Joseph Ostrow[7] put a handle on these variables by outlining how a media planner should think about frequency requirements for a specific product or service. He sees three major considerations (clusters) involved in this decision-making process. Placing your brand on the left or right side of his matrix, shown in Table 19.5, can help you decide which proportionate level of frequency is most appropriate.

A review of Ostrow's list of considerations clearly points to the fact that any preconceived frequency level, be it 1, 3, 3+, or anything in between, cannot apply to every advertising message in every situation. Nevertheless, you might still decide, absent of any counterargument, that 3+ is the place to be—but you will have to consider yet another phenomenon before exercising that decision. We must keep in mind that all media frequencies reflect exposure to the medium, not necessarily to the advertising within that medium. A frequency of three as reported in media analyses is the "opportunity to see" (*OTS*) three commercial messages—not necessarily the conclusive and absolute number that the consumer *will* see.

Here again we embark on a journey of trying to understand consumer behavior as it relates to media consumption and the consumption of *advertising* within the media to which consumers are exposed. And here again no one knows what portion of the people who are part of the media audience actually *watch* the commercial (or actually read an advertisement or listen to a radio commercial, etc.). We can, however, look to syndicated research, customized studies, or proprietary research for guidelines that are based on past performance of specific creative executions within particular marketplace conditions. All of these guidelines, of course, are based on a sampling of the population, not the entire population. Notwithstanding these limitations, judgment suggests that some portion of the people in a medium's audience do not watch the commercial, or do not pay sufficient attention to it to warrant being counted as *exposed*. One such indicator is shown in Table 19.6. The Simmons Market Research Bureau reports on the levels of attentiveness to TV programming claimed by the

---

TABLE 19.5:   Ostrow's Frequency Matrix

Marketing Cluster:

Low Frequency	High Frequency
Established brand	New brand
High brand share	Low brand share
Dominant brand	Small, lesser known brand
Loyal users	Sometime users
Long purchase cycle	Short purchase cycle
Occasional use	Daily, more often use
Low competition level	Highly competitive environment
Adult—old target	Children—teen target

Message Cluster:

Low Frequency	High Frequency
Simple message	Complex message
Unique message	Non-unique message
Continuing campaign	New campaign
Product sell	Image appeal
Small ad unit pool	Large ad unit pool
High wear-out potential	Longer-wearing message
Large ad unit	Small, short ad unit

Media Cluster:

Low Frequency	High Frequency
Uncluttered medium	Heavy clutter
Complementary editorial environment	Neutral editorial environment
High-attention vehicle	Low-attention vehicle
Continuous schedule	Pulsed on flighted schedule
Fewer media	Many media
Repeat exposure per vehicle	Single exposure per vehicle

---

respondents in their self-administered questionnaire. For example, of all the adults 18 and older who claim to be part of the early morning TV audience, 9 percent say they are generally out of the room during the telecasts, 54 percent claim to pay some attention, and only 37 percent claim to pay full attention.

TABLE 19.6: Attentiveness of TV Program Viewing by Daypart—Adults 18+

	Average 1/2 Hour Audience	Full Attention	Some Attention	Out of Room
Early Morning	100%	37	54	9
Daytime	100	57	39	4
Early Fringe	100	58	38	4
Prime	100	69	29	2
Late Fringe	100	69	29	2
Average	100	62	35	3

Source: Simmons, 1990

If you are running an average (though effective) commercial, in an average schedule in TV across many dayparts, in an average competitive marketplace, you might conclude that only 62 percent of the people watching the TV programs in which you have placed your commercial *might* pay full attention. Conceivably, the percentage paying full attention to your commercial could be more or less than 62 percent, but let's stick with this ratio for the purpose of demonstration. Applying this 62 percent to a desired 3+ frequency level would lead you to need a 5+ media exposure frequency:

$$
\begin{array}{ll}
5 \text{ frequency} & \text{(Media audience OTS)} \\
\times\, 62\% & \text{(Possible "full attention" exposure to your} \\
& \quad \text{commercial)} \\
\hline
3 \quad \text{frequency} & \text{(Effective frequency level)}
\end{array}
$$

A decision to choose a particular effective frequency level is not easy to make. It is, nevertheless, important to make a choice. To not decide on a level is to decide that it does not matter—and evidence suggests it very much matters. Regardless of the level that is chosen, it appears that you would be better off to be roughly right than exactly wrong—better to go for something in the range of a 2+ or 3+ or 4+ level than to just settle for a 1+ level. But even after you make this decision, you need to concern yourself with the

"+" portion of the effective frequency level—that is, how much frequency is too much.

Wearout

Wearout A level of frequency, or a point in time, when an advertising message loses its ability to effectively communicate.

There are many definitions for **wearout**, and all address the same phenomenon. For example, wearout can be seen as:

- Where decay sets in. Referring back to our learning-satiation-decay curve, there probably is a point at which the consumer has absorbed as much as he or she needs to (or wants to). Any additional exposure beyond this point is wasteful and possibly harmful to the advertised product.

- Communication inability. There is a level at which a commercial is felt to lose its ability to communicate, persuade, or create positive attitudes. Further exposure beyond this point can be considered to have either a negative or, at best, a neutral effect.

- Non-achievement of goals. "A commercial wears out when it fails to achieve the campaign goal as it has before."[8]

Whether you use one of the definitions above or one of your own, the logical fact remains that there is most probably a maximum frequency level within the effective reach concept. Effective reach may start (for example) at the 3.0 frequency level, but it certainly ends somewhere before infinity.

Specifying this finite maximum is impossible. A host of variables, many of which are also important in defining the minimum level, come into play when thinking about the maximum. We can speculate, with some confidence in our judgment, that wearout occurs for different individuals at different points in time (in the frequency continuum) depending on their demographics and lifestyle characteristics, the creative execution, their propensity to be within the product's consumption group, the number of competitive product advertisements to which they are exposed, etc. Nevertheless, there are some indications of what this maximum level *might* be.

The findings of various major research studies are shown in the following table:

	Wearout Point (The point—frequency— at which "satiation" passes into the "decay" stage.)
Marplan Research	15
Communications Research	13–14
Tele Research	15–20
Market Evaluation Study	20–25
Benton & Bowles	20
TVC	12
Procter & Gamble	20–25

It is not an uncommon practice to use information like the above, tied to a quintile distribution, to decide the point of wearout for a given advertising campaign. Table 19.7, for example, shows a television schedule that produces a 25.0 frequency among the heaviest-viewing 20 percent of the total reach. If a 25 frequency is considered the maximum level of effective communication—that is, a 26 frequency is the point where decay starts—then the commercial(s) being used in this campaign have worn out, suggesting that a new commercial, or pool of commercials (or a print ad, etc.) should be produced. There are several factors to consider, however, in making this decision:

TABLE 19.7: Wearout Based on Quintile Distribution

Quintile	Reach	Frequency
Heaviest	19	25.0
Next	19	12.1
Next	19	7.2
Next	19	4.2
Lightest	19	1.9
Total/Average	95	10.1

---

1. All the research conducted on the subject of wearout was for specific commercial executions under specific conditions and may or may not apply to *your product* in *your media choice* and given *your chosen schedule*.

2. The competitive environment (within the product or service category you are analyzing) is seldom stagnant. For example, new products are constantly being introduced that add to the competition and also to the absolute amount of advertising to which the consumer will be exposed. If you assume that wearout begins with the 26th exposure (for example) in the average situation, might it begin at the 12th exposure in a highly competitive marketplace . . . or at the 50th exposure in an extraordinarily noncompetitive environment?

3. Based on Ebbinghaus (and others), we've seen that the duration of time between exposures can affect learning and recall. To say that 25 exposures constitutes wearout without considering the amount of time between exposures is to deny the scientific data at hand. Put yourself in the consumer's seat and then decide if a *good* commercial will wear out if you've seen it 25 times in a year. Consider that 25 times a year translates to once every 14–15 days, or once every 233.6 of your total wakeful hours (assuming you sleep eight hours a day), or conceivably to one commercial message out of the 300–1,000 you might be exposed to in an average day across all media forms.

4. Assessing the amount of frequency delivered to only the heaviest viewing quintile eliminates, by default, consideration for all other quintiles—i.e., the remaining 80 percent of the people reached by your advertising schedule. The question is: are the people within the heaviest quintile your best prospects, or are there better prospects in other quintiles? If the answer is other quintiles, then your decision on wearout at the 26th exposure level is premature, given that other quintiles will not be exposed nearly this many times.

Methods for Analyzing Effective Reach

There are basically two methods you can use in this evaluation process—the first very straightforward; the second requiring value judgments:

1. Decide the minimum and maximum frequency level you deem "effective" and calculate the reach within these ranges. Using Table 19.8, for example, if you decide that the effective range is from 3.0 to 8.0 exposures, the schedule shown will generate a 28 reach.

TABLE 19.8: Method #1—Effective Reach

Frequency	Women Reach	Effective Reach
1.0	25%	
2.0	20	
3.0	10	
4.0	5	
Effective 5.0	5	
Range 6.0	4	28
7.0	2	
8.0	2	
9.0	1	
10.0	1	
Total Reach	75	

TABLE 19.9: Method #2—Effective Reach

Frequency	Women Reach	×	Value	=	Product
1.0	25%		50		12.5
2.0	20		75		15.0
3.0	10		100		10.0
4.0	5		100		5.0
5.0	5		100		5.0
6.0	4		100		4.0
7.0	2		100		2.0
8.0	2		100		2.0
9.0	1		0		—
10.0	1		0		—
Total Reach	75				
Effective Reach					55.5

2. Assign a value to each frequency level (or range of frequency), using the value as a multiplier against reach to produce what Jules Fine[9] terms *Real Effective Reach*. As shown in Table 19.9, lower frequency levels receive lower values than those in the 3–10 range; frequency levels above 8.0 are given a zero

value. By multiplying the reach at each frequency level by the predetermined value, and adding the products, you can obtain effective reach. The values you use are up to you, based either on known information or informed judgment.

Clearly, analyzing media alternatives on the basis of *average* reach/frequency is wanting. It is also clear that there are no rules as to how much frequency is enough—or for that matter, how much reach is enough. As we have said before, however, to not decide a level is to decide that it does not matter—and evidence suggests it matters very much.

References

1. Greyser, Stephen A., "Irritation in Advertising," *Journal of Advertising Research*, April, 1980.

2. Jackobovits, Leon, "Semantic Satiation and Cognitive Dynamics," American Psychological Association meeting paper, September, 1966.

3. Achenbaum, Alvin, "Effective Exposure: A New Way of Evaluating Media," Association of National Advertisers Workshop, February, 1977.

4. Zielske, Hubert A., and Walter, A. Henry, "Remembering and Forgetting Television Ads," *Journal of Advertising Research*, April, 1980.

5. Krugman, Herbert, "Why Three Exposures May Be Enough," *Journal of Advertising Research*, April, 1980.

6. Naples, Michael, *Effective Frequency: The Relationship Between Frequency and Advertising Effectiveness*, Association of National Advertisers, 1978.

7. Ostrow, Joseph, Advertising Research Foundation Workshop, 1982.

8. Priemer, A. B., "You Can Measure Wearout; However...," Association of National Advertisers Workshop, February, 1981.

9. Fine, Jules, "Using Media Effectively," *Marketing Communications*, January/February, 1978.

Chapter 20

Media Audience Definitions

M ost of our previous discussion has centered on media audiences: how different media vehicles produce different audience numbers (or percentages), how audience accumulates over time or with repeated use of a medium, how reach and frequency are affected by different combinations of media, and so forth. We have referred to readers or viewers or listeners within a given demographic group—women or men of a certain age, total people, etc. Although we have spoken of the rating for program A or the readers of magazine B, we did not discuss how that rating or number of readers came to be, nor did we speak of the computation mechanics that led to the audience count with which we were dealing. This chapter will first concentrate on the definitions of what an audience is in terms of demographics, product usage habits, and psychographics. We will discuss two popular research studies that are used to describe consumers. We will also introduce an increasingly popular analytical device known as *geodemography*. In the latter part of the chapter we will investigate how the major mass media report their audiences to demonstrate the kinds of information with which a media planner deals in analyzing media alternatives.

Demography

The first part of understanding media audiences requires you to understand demography. **Demography** is the study of the characteristics of populations related to age, sex, income, education level, and a host of other descriptors. Demographic analyses permeate marketing and media planning. Nearly all investigations of a brand's strengths and weaknesses, and of a medium's strengths and weaknesses, involve a critical analysis of how *people* consume the product and consume media. To make the right decisions in choosing specific media, you must know *who* should be addressed in the media plan.

A copywriter who creates an ad may have a great deal of latitude in defining the audience for whom the advertising is being created. It's not uncommon, for example, to define a target audience in terms of one person, such as "a 30-year-old man, married with one child 11 years old, who has a white collar job, earns $40,000 a year, and enjoys playing racquetball." This is all well and good, on two counts. First, advertising indeed is talking to one person at a time. The message is usually personal—"you" should know this or do that, not "all people within your general demographic group" should know this or do that. Secondly, the copywriter does not have to be concerned, per se, with how media deliver their audiences or what information is available to find specific audiences within each media type.

The fact is, however, you are inhibited from addressing a specific person when you are trying to choose media to carry the copywriter's advertising. There is no media audience information available for a particular person, only for *groups* of people who share general demographic descriptions. You will not find, for example, how many 30-year-old men read a magazine or view a TV program. You will have to place the specific target audience within a broader group, such as men who are age 18–34 or 25–34, because these age groupings are the only kinds are audience data available to you.

Demographic descriptions are available from many sources, not the least of which is the Bureau of the Census. Many of these sources are discussed in the next chapter. All provide data on the basis of demographic *cells* (specified groupings of particular population groups, such as men 18–34 or men in households with incomes of $30,000–$49,999). The cells reported by the various media are relatively consistent from one medium to another, allowing audience evaluations to be made against the same groups of people by medium. The reason groupings of people are reported has to do mostly with research sampling techniques and reliability of the reported data (which is discussed more fully in a later chapter).

Product Users

Although demographic studies are important in your planning process, they are usually considered of secondary importance to studies that define product *users*, or users of products within a given category. An assessment of product users is a more effective method of analysis because media selection is predicated on the ability to reach very specific groups of people who are most apt to purchase a particular product or service.

A product user study can give you a more precise definition of each medium's ability to reach these users. If you are advertising tennis shoes, for example, you certainly would want to reach men and women 18–34 years old, as this demographic group has an above-average propensity to buy tennis shoes. The inference is that if you advertise to this group you have a better than average chance of talking to people who are likely to buy your tennis shoes. With a product user study showing how many people within the audience of each medium actually buy tennis shoes, however, you have an even better chance of finding the specific people you want to reach.

Although user profiles are more useful, and directionally more precise, than demographic profiles, they are not always reported by syndicated research sources, nor are they necessarily available for all media. You might find that tennis shoe buyers are reported for a long list of magazines, but not for network TV or radio; you might find they are reported for broad television dayparts, but not for specific programs. To the extent you can find user information, you should use it. But you certainly should not select one medium versus another simply because this kind of information is available for one medium but not another.

Psychographics/Lifestyles

Lifestyle Pertains to the nondemographic characteristics of people in describing their behavior (e.g., recreational habits).

Psychographics Pertains to the identification of personality characteristics and attitudes that affect a person's lifestyle and purchasing behavior.

It is becoming increasingly common to view consumers as more than their demographic descriptors or product consumption patterns, and to group or categorize them according to various pyschometrics—their **lifestyles** and attitudes. Descriptions of two **psychographic** research suppliers follow.

Simmons

In addition to reporting on the product and media consumption patterns of more than 20,000 adults in the United States, Simmons Market Research Bureau provides information on *self concept*—how a person views himself or herself. Interviewees are asked to rate themselves on 60 adjectives using a five-point scale: 1—"agree a lot", 2—"agree a little," etc. Grouping like adjectives, Simmons reports up to 20 psychological descriptors for which the interviewee scored "1" and/or "2," as follows:

Affectionate:	passionate, loving, romantic
Amicable:	amiable, affable, benevolent
Awkward:	absentminded, forgetful, careless
Brave:	courageous, daring, adventuresome
Broadminded:	openminded, liberal, tolerant
Creative:	inventive, imaginative, artistic
Dominating:	authoritarian, demanding, aggressive
Efficient:	organized, diligent, thorough
Egocentric:	vain, self-centered, narcissistic
Frank:	straightforward, outspoken, candid
Funny:	humorous, amusing, witty
Intelligent:	smart, bright, well-informed
Kind:	good-hearted, warm-hearted, sincere
Refined:	gracious, sophisticated, dignified
Reserved:	conservative, quiet, conventional
Self-Assured:	confident, self-sufficient, secure
Sociable:	friendly, cheerful, likeable
Stubborn:	hardheaded, headstrong, obstinate
Tense:	nervous, high-strung, excitable
Trustworthy:	competent, reliable, responsible

It is important to note that a person's self view is not necessarily the true psychological makeup of that person. Had Simmons queried respondents on tendencies toward child abuse, for example, it is doubtful that anyone would "agree a lot." Despite the possible polarity of self concept and "real behavior," it is believed that as one projects his or her personality he or she is influenced by stimuli that contain similar personality traits. A person who wants to think of himself as passionate will probably be positively stimulated by a display of passionate behavior in advertising.

By cross-tabulating the self concept data with product and/or media consumption habits, not only could you provide a more enhanced description of your target audience, you could also have the basis for selecting media forms and specific media vehicles beyond what is obtainable through usual and conventional forms of demographic and product usage analysis.

VALS 2

VALS 2   A research study developed by SRI International which describes eight distinct population groups according to their Values and Lifestyles.

Another research supplier is SRI International, which developed **VALS 2** (Values and Lifestyles), a consumer segmentation system. Based on a national probability sample, the system divides the adult consumer population into eight mutually exclusive segments; all consumers can be assigned to one of these eight types. The types are arrayed within a framework that defines fundamental contrasts in consumer attitudes and behavior based on the pattern of relationships between psychological and demographic attributes and consumer behavior. Table 20.1 displays some basic descriptors for each of these eight segments.

Two syndicated media research suppliers (Mediamark Research, Inc. and Simmons Market Research Bureau) include the basic VALS 2 questionnaire as part of self-administered questionnaires they use to obtain marketing and media consumption data for their research reports. Because the Mediamark and Simmons consumer panel responds to the VALS 2 questionnaire, marketing and media data can be cross-tabulated with VALS 2 lifestyle descriptors. For example, you can determine how many Actualizers use product X, or how many readers of magazine A are Achievers, or how many Believers use product Y and view program B.

Following Table 20.1 is a synopsis of each VALS 2 segment.

TABLE 20.1: Demographic Characteristics of VALS 2 Segments

Segment	% Adult Population	Median Age	Median Income (000)	% Some College	% White Collar	% Married
Actualizer	8%	43	$58	95%	68%	72%
Fulfilled	11	48	38	81	50	73
Believer	16	58	21	6	11	70
Achiever	13	36	50	77	43	73
Striver	13	34	25	23	19	60
Experiencer	12	26	19	41	21	34
Maker	13	30	23	24	19	65
Struggler	14	61	9	3	2	47

Source: 1987 Leading Edge survey; SRI International

Actualizers—Successful, sophisticated, active, take-charge people with high self-esteem. They are among the established and emerging leaders in business and government. Their self-image focuses on personal growth and they seek to develop, explore, and express themselves in a variety of ways, enjoying challenges in all areas of their lives. They have a wide range of interests, are concerned with social issues, are open to change, and have a global perspective. Image is important—not as evidence of status or power, but as an expression of taste, independence, and character. Their lives are characterized by richness and diversity. They show a cultivated taste for the "finer things in life." As innovators, they like to try new products and services. Their widespread interests are evidenced by the variety of magazines they read. They are light TV viewers who favor informational and public affairs programs.

Fulfilleds—Mature, satisfied, comfortable people who value order, knowledge, and responsibility. They are well-informed about world and national events and are alert to opportunities to broaden their knowledge. They have a moderate respect for the status quo, institutions of authority, and social decorum, but are open-minded about new ideas and social change. They tend to rely on strongly held principles in their choices and decisions, and many present an appearance of calm self-assurance. Content with their careers, families, and station in life, their leisure activities tend to center around their homes. They are conservative and practical consumers. Prestige and image are less important than functionality, value, and durability in the products they buy. Many of the products they buy center around the home. Exhibiting a varied media consumption pattern, their reading encompasses books and magazines of general interest, home and garden, epicurean and news. Their TV viewing includes public affairs and prime-time programs.

Believers—Conventional people with concrete beliefs and strong attachments to traditional institutions: family, church, community, and nation. Many express moral codes that are deeply learned and literally interpreted. They enjoy settled, comfortable, predictable lifestyles that follow established routines which are organized around their homes, families, and groups to which they belong. They are politically and socially conservative people who are reasonably well informed. As consumers, they are conservative, predictable, and slow to change. They tend to favor American products and established brands. They are cost-conscious consumers who watch for sales and bargain prices. They watch TV and read magazines on home and garden, health, retirement, and topics of general interest.

Achievers—Successful career and work-oriented people who value hard work, responsibility, structure, and predictability in their lives. They seek recognition and acknowledgement for their achievements. Their lives are structured around family and business. They are politically moderate, respect authority, and are content with the status quo. Image is important to them. They like their success to be reflected in the products they buy—premium, prestigious products and services. They read a variety of magazines including those on news, business, and home and family, and are average TV viewers.

Strivers—Seek motivation, self-definition and approval from the world around them. Many are fascinated with status and power. Money defines success for many, who never feel that they have enough of it. They are easily bored and have difficulty controlling their impulses. They are uninformed about current and world events and feel powerless to effect political change. They follow fashions, trends, and fads. They are impressed by what others own and often emulate them, but lack financial resources to keep up. Purchases of clothes and personal care products keep their credit card balances high. They read selected lifestyle magazines and view the top ten TV programs.

Experiencers—Young, vital, enthusiastic, impulsive, and rebellious. They seek experiences, savoring the new, offbeat and the risky. They are still in the process of formulating life values and patterns of behavior. Their energy finds an outlet in exercise, sports, outdoor recreation, and social activities. At this stage in their lives, they are politically uncommitted, uninformed, and highly ambivalent about what they believe. As avid consumers they spend a high proportion of their disposable income on clothing, beer, fast food, music, film, and video. They are impulse buyers. They read sports, lifestyle, and fashion magazines, are ardent rock music fans, and enjoy TV and movies.

Makers—Value self-sufficiency and live their lives within a traditional context of family, practical work, and physical recreation. They epitomize the do-it-yourselfer and fixer of the world and have sufficient skill, income, and energy to carry out their plans. They are politically conservative, suspicious of new ideas, and respectful of government intrusion on individual rights. They are practical consumers, unimpressed by luxury, status, or image. They base their purchases on practical or functional aspects of products such as comfort, durability, and utility. They prefer prime-time action programs on TV and read magazines on topics such as automobiles, home mechanics, and outdoor activities.

Strugglers—Deprived of many economic, social, and emotional resources, their lives are focused on coping with the present moment. Many are burdened by old age and health concerns. They are politically conservative and feel powerless to influence others. They rely on organized religion for moral direction. They are cautious consumers but are strongly brand-loyal in the products they buy. Their purchases are limited to essentials. They are heavy TV viewers and read tabloids and women's service publications.

Geodemographic Areas

Based on the concept that people tend to live near others who share similar demographic and lifestyle characteristics ("birds of a feather flock together"), geodemography focuses on the statistical similarities of people in neighborhoods. Although all individuals are different, members of a small neighborhood unit often share certain characteristics such as income, education, housing type, and presence (or absence) of children. Households within these areas also tend to exhibit similar purchasing patterns. Knowing which geographic segments people reside within—and therefore knowing something about their demographics, lifestyle characteristics, and product and media consumption habits—you have a yardstick for predicting how they will behave as consumers and how they might react to advertising stimuli.

Geodemographic areas are quite different from all the basic geographic areas which will be discussed in Chapter 22, "Geographic Areas." The other areas are based, for example, on "who can receive a TV signal" or "what the social and economic relationship is of people living in and around a central city." Geodemographic definitions go well beyond *basic* descriptors and include hundreds of demographic/lifestyle variables.

Geodemographics
The demographic description of people living in specific geographic areas.

Statisically, **geodemography** is the grouping, or clustering, of descriptive variables (demography, consumer behavior, etc.) whereby each neighborhood in the United States is placed into one of many classifications. There are four geodemographic segmentation systems (also called "cluster," "lifestyle," and "neighborhood" systems) available: "ClusterPLUS," a product of Donnelley Marketing Information Systems, "PRIZM," a product of Claritas: The Target Marketing Company, "ACORN" from CACI, and "Microvision" from National Decision Systems.

All of the companies offer linkage to some of the databases of other specialty research firms—Arbitron, MRCA, MRI, NFO, Nielsen, BPD, Simmons, and others (see Chapter 21, "Media Audience Research"). The cluster system owners are given geocoded listings of the survey respondents which are matched to the appropriate cluster codes based upon ZIP Code or complete street address of the respondent. This marriage of data allows all forms of geographically coded marketing or media data to be profiled and evaluated across geodemographic groups. A very simple example might be: if you input addresses for a listing of retail outlets and defined their trading area as a ten-mile radius around each store, you could determine which magazines or newspapers or TV programs or radio stations the people residing in that area most heavily consume, as well as determining product and service consumption patterns for these people. The amount and kinds of information obtainable using a geodemographic database married to marketing and/or media database is staggering.

Following are brief descriptions of two widely used geo-demographic systems:

ClusterPLUS®

ClusterPLUS A geodemographic clustering system.

Donnelley developed **ClusterPLUS** lifestyles by analyzing 1600 characteristics of Census Block Groups. Subsequent analysis resulted in 64 key demographic variables driving the cluster algorithm, which categorizes every neighborhood into one of 47 clusters. Each cluster can be found, for example, in many TV markets in varying concentrations representing minor to major coverage of the TV market. Although the clusters are numbered 1 to 47 based on socioeconomic standing, this is but one descriptive ingredient. Table 20.2 lists the 47 clusters and displays the index of concentration for only three of the 64 demographic variables. To give you an idea of the kind of information known about these clusters, the following provides an enhanced description of two clusters:

Cluster 1. Characterized as the established wealthy, members enjoy the fruits of residing at the top of the socioeconomic scale. Highly educated, higher-income professionals, these individuals are likely to reside in very-high-value homes in prime real estate areas. Established members of the community, they are likely to be well settled in their neighborhoods. They have a proportionately high preference for having an American Express Gold Card and other travel/entertainment cards, conducting frequent stock transactions, purchasing imported beers and gourmet ice cream, and frequently taking foreign trips and playing tennis.

Cluster 27. Contains slightly-below-average-income families living in single-family homes. Home values are generally lower, reflective of their development in the fifties and sixties—America's suburban boomtown era. With incomes slightly below the national average, these families have financial habits that suggest an effort to stretch their purchasing potential, making use of home equity loans and bank lines of credit. They display an above-average preference for sugarless gum, health and beauty aids, camping, bowling, and attending movies.

TABLE 20.2:　ClusterPLUS Clusters

		Index of Concentration		
	%	Median	Median	
	U.S. Adult	Household	# Years of	Median
Cluster	Population	Income	Education	Age
1	1.5	271	126	116
2	1.2	234	120	101
3	2.2	192	117	95
4	1.7	191	113	103
5	2.7	185	118	117
6	3.1	142	105	87
7	2.9	122	113	99
8	2.0	122	107	118
9	4.2	134	104	103
10	1.4	110	116	89
11	2.9	142	102	103
12	3.8	122	106	82
13	2.1	129	102	122
14	1.2	118	106	134
15	2.6	120	105	117
16	3.1	142	102	105
17	2.2	89	115	70
18	1.4	128	103	94
19	2.1	129	102	93
20	1.3	91	95	84
21	3.9	103	100	101
22	1.6	86	96	119
23	1.8	84	99	110
24	2.6	71	101	82
25	2.6	83	98	93
26	2.1	78	98	132
27	2.0	95	98	95
28	3.7	84	92	89
29	2.2	94	94	116
30	2.0	81	79	109
31	1.8	69	93	126
32	1.3	66	95	136
33	1.9	91	93	115
34	1.3	78	98	115
35	1.8	72	98	91
36	1.7	94	92	97
37	1.6	92	96	98
38	1.2	51	91	135
39	2.3	78	94	114
40	1.1	57	86	120
41	2.2	73	92	105
42	2.9	54	75	107
43	2.7	69	86	105
44	1.6	50	91	92
45	1.3	52	85	113
46	2.0	58	70	96
47	1.3	53	89	97
Total U.S.	100.0%	$24,533	12.2 Yrs.	40.0 Yrs.

Source: Donnelley Marketing Information Systems

PRIZM

PRIZM A
geodemographic
clustering system.

Originally conceived and pioneered by Claritas in 1974, **PRIZM** is a market segmentation system that classifies every American neighborhood into one of 40 basic clusters. In its initial seventies version, the clustering system was based on the geography of the 37,000 five-digit ZIP codes—PRIZM is an acronym for Potential Rating Index of ZIP Markets. Today, PRIZM is available for 5-digit ZIP codes, 9-digit ZIP codes, postal carrier routes, census tracts, and Census Block Groups/Block Numbering Areas. Based on the combination of Census demographics and actual consumer behavior data since 1983, the most recent behaviorally based update of PRIZM utilized over 500 million consumer records summarized to ZIP +4 and Census Block Group levels.

Table 20.3 lists some basic information about each of the 40 clusters. Thumbnail descriptions for two of these groups follow:

Blue Blood Estates These are America's wealthiest socio-economic neighborhoods, populated by super-upper-established managers, professionals, and heirs to "old money." They are accustomed to privilege and living in luxurious surroundings. One in ten millionaires can be found in this cluster. They exhibit an above-average tendency to own United States Treasury notes and Rolls Royces, visit Europe, downhill ski and drink bottled water and low-fat skim milk.

Shotguns and Pickups This is an aggregate of hundreds of small, outlying townships and crossroad villages which serve the nation's breadbasket and other rural areas. It has a more easterly distribution than other clusters and shows peak indices for large families with school-age children, headed by blue-collar craftsmen, equipment operators, and transport workers with high school educations. These areas are home to many dedicated outdoorsmen. They exhibit an above-average likelihood of owning wood-burning stoves and truck-mounted campers, drinking powdered soft drinks, and eating frozen potato products.

TABLE 20.3: PRIZM Clusters

ZQ*	Title	% U.S. Households	Index of Concentration Median Income	% College Graduates
1	Blue Blood Estates	1.1	290	313
2	Money & Brains	.9	189	281
3	Furs & Station Wagons	3.2	206	235
4	Urban Gold Coast	.5	152	312
5	Pools & Patios	3.4	148	174
6	Two More Rungs	.7	129	175
7	Young Influentials	2.9	125	222
8	Young Suburbia	5.3	159	147
9	God's Country	2.7	151	159
10	Blue-Chip Blues	6.0	133	81
11	Bohemian Mix	1.1	90	240
12	Levittown, USA	3.1	118	97
13	Gray Power	2.9	104	113
14	Black Enterprise	.8	137	99
15	New Beginnings	4.3	102	110
16	Blue-Collar Nursery	2.2	124	63
17	New Homesteaders	4.2	107	98
18	New Melting Pot	.9	91	118
19	Towns & Gowns	1.2	74	170
20	Rank & File	1.4	108	57
21	Middle American	3.2	101	66
22	Old Yankee Rows	1.6	102	68
23	Coalburg & Corntown	2.0	99	64
24	Shotguns & Pickups	1.9	100	56
25	Golden Ponds	5.2	83	79
26	Agri-Business	2.1	88	71
27	Emergent Minorities	1.7	91	66
28	Single City Blues	3.3	74	115
29	Mines & Mills	2.8	89	54
30	Back-Country Folks	3.4	82	50
31	Norma Rae-Ville	2.3	76	59
32	Smalltown Downtown	2.5	71	62
33	Grain Belt	1.3	89	52
34	Heavy Industry	2.8	76	40
35	Share Croppers	4.0	69	44
36	Downtown Dixie-Style	3.4	63	66
37	Hispanic Mix	1.9	67	42
38	Tobacco Roads	1.2	55	45
39	Hard Scrabble	1.5	53	40
40	Public Assistance	3.1	45	39
Total U.S.		100.0%	$24,269	16.2%

* ZQ, or ZIP Quality, is a socioeconomic ranking based on income, home value, education and occupation.

Source: Claritas Corporation. PRIZM is a registered trademark of Claritas Corporation, Alexandria, VA.

How Media Report Audiences

We'll deal with only the five major media forms. We can divide these into three groups on the basis of their audiences, which are roughly the same within each of the categories—broadcast media, print media, and out-of-home media.

Broadcast Media Audiences

The absolute foundation of radio and television audience is the rating: the percentage of a population group exposed to a program or station. There are, nonetheless, different types (or designations) of ratings presented by media research suppliers in their periodic reports. These are the ones most commonly used:

AQH The average quarter-hour rating for broadcast programs as reported by several media research suppliers (e.g., A.C. Nielsen).

Average Quarter Hour Rating (AQH) The **AQH** refers to the percentage of a population group that is counted as being exposed to TV or radio during some period within a given quarter-hour time span. The amount of time a viewer or listener must spend with the medium can vary depending on the medium and the definition imposed by the research supplier. In radio, one supplier might require listening for at least five minutes while another requires listening for at least three minutes within the quarter-hour. In TV, one supplier might require at least five minutes of viewing while another records viewing for each minute and averages the 15 separate audience counts to arrive at an AQH rating.

Average Audience (AA) In broadcast, the number of homes (or individuals) tuned to the average minute of a program. In print media, the number of individuals who looked into an average issue of a publication and are considered "readers."

Average Audience Rating (AA) The general reference to an **average audience** rating is to either the full duration of a TV program or the average within a particular time span. For example, a half-hour TV program might have successive AQH ratings of 10.0 and 12.0, which would result in an AA rating of 11.0. Likewise, separate quarter-hour ratings during the 8:00–11:00 p.m. time period would be averaged to yield the average audience rating for this time period.

Here again, however, different media research suppliers have varying definitions. One supplier might fall back on the basic definition of the AQH rating in calculating the AA rating while another might report an average audience composed of anyone within their survey sample who claimed to have viewed the program.

Cumulative Audience (Cume)   As time lapses for a TV or radio broadcast from the first to the last minute of that broadcast, some people tune in and some people tune out. For example, let us say 100 people tune in to program X at 9:00. After a while, half these people tune out, but an additional 50 people tune in. The cume audience in this example is 150 people: the 100 who tuned in early, plus 50 who tuned in later. The 50 people who tuned out are counted in the cume audience inasmuch as they were part of the audience for some duration.

Cume ratings can apply to an individual program broadcast or to multiple airings of the same program, depending on the designation listed by the research supplier. Likewise, cume ratings can apply to a particular radio program or to the daypart (timespan) being reported.

Cume estimates are sometimes called *unduplicated* or *reach* estimates. Cume is also synonymous with *total audience*.

Viewers per 1,000 Households   When the average household had only one TV set, researchers would report people audiences as *Viewers Per Set* which, when multiplied by the number of TV sets tuned to a particular program, would yield the total people audience of that program. For example, if a program was viewed by 10,000 households (i.e., on 10,000 different TV sets) and had a men viewers per set of 1.25, multiplication would reveal that the program was viewed by 12,500 men. Now that we are in an age where the vast majority of homes have more than one TV set, the "per set" definition is antiquated and has been replaced by the current "per household" term. Additionally, for ease in listing and reading audience data in research reports, the number of people per household is multiplied by 1,000 and reported as **Viewers Per 1,000 Households**—thereby eliminating decimal points.

Table 20.4 shows a hypothetical example of a network TV program's audience. All the audience information is reported in a typical audience measurement report. In this example, we see that the program got a 10.0 household rating—equivalent to 10 million households. There are 800 men viewers per 1,000 households which, when multiplied by the 10,000 households, yields 8,000,000 men viewers (8,000 thousands [000] in the table). Dividing the total number of men who viewed the program by the number of men in the U.S. population yields an average audience rating for men of 9.4.

Viewers per 1,000 Households The number of people within a specific population group tuned to a TV program in each 1,000 viewing households.

TABLE 20.4:   Conversion of Viewers Per 1,000 Households

	U.S. Population (000)	Viewers/ 1,000 Households	AA Delivery (000)	Rating
Households	100,000	—	10,000	10.0
Men	85,000	800	8,000	9.4
Women	95,000	500	5,000	5.3
Teens	20,000	100	1,000	5.0
Kids	35,000	100	1,000	2.9
Total	235,000	1,500	15,000	6.4

The above four audience measurement designations—AQH, AA, Cume, and Viewers per 1,000 Households—are in common use. They are, however, by no means the only designations available in syndicated media research reports. Therefore, whenever you seek audience data for a specific designation, you should also review the entire research report to discover what other kinds of measurements are available.

Print Media Audiences

The concepts of rating, average audience, and total audience also apply to magazines and newspapers, although the ingredients that drive these audience measurements are quite different from those used for broadcast media. The primary distinction between print and broadcast media is how their physical form dictates how they are consumed: broadcast media are consumed simultaneously by more than one person, while print media are nearly always consumed by one individual at a time.

Three major factors are used to determine the size of print media audiences:

Circulation In print media, the number of copies sold or distributed by a publication.

Circulation   This is the number of copies of a magazine or newspaper issue in distribution and available for purchase and reading. If, for example, a publisher prints and distributes one million copies of a magazine, only one million people have the opportunity to purchase that magazine. But, because of the physical nature of the magazine, each of these one million copies stays in existence for an extended period of time. The amount of time varies between magazines and newspapers, and between specific publications in each category. You will recall from Chapter 14 that this time duration is called the *issue life* of a publication.

All print media have an issue life—as compared to broadcast media, which are generally fleeting in nature. With the exception of video/audio cassette recording, TV and radio programs can be viewed or heard only at the time they are circulated. **Circulation** in broadcast media refers to the homes or people who can physically receive the transmission being broadcast. For example, if you live in Miami, you are able to receive the signals from Miami radio stations but not from Los Angeles stations.

Circulation In broadcast, the number of homes owning a TV/radio set within a station's coverage area.

A publisher always attempts to print and distribute as many copies of a publication as can be sold. Distributing more than will be purchased results in wasted production and distribution costs; distributing too few copies results in lost revenue from both consumers and advertisers. (Generally, the more copies sold, the higher the advertising rates charged by publishers.) Broadcast media, on the other hand, do not control their circulation in the same way.

Thus, much more than for broadcast media, the foundation of all print media audiences is circulation. Once circulation is set, the next crucial factor is how many people will read a given issue of a publication.

Readers-Per-Copy This is the total number of people who read a given copy of a magazine or newspaper. By multiplying readers-per-copy by the circulation of an average issue, we arrive at *total audience*. If two people read each copy of the June issue of magazine X, which has a circulation of one million, the magazine will have a total audience of two million people.

Generally, magazines have a longer issue life than newspapers due primarily to the inherent qualities of the medium. As you can well guess, there are differences from one magazine to another, from one newspaper to another, and from one magazine to one newspaper. For purposes of comparison let us consider only the generalities of these distinctions. A daily newspaper, for example, provides readers with "today's" information while a magazine is written to incorporate news and information which does not have to be read "today." Readers respond to these editorial focuses by reading a newspaper the day it is published, and reading a magazine sometime before the next issue is published. There are significant exceptions, of course. Some readers read a newspaper the nex day, or read a specific section or item many days later; some readers read a magazine the day it's on the newsstand or arrives at their home. Nevertheless, and generally speaking, magazines have a longer issue life than newspapers and therefore have the opportunity to accumulate more readers-per-copy than newspapers. It is not unusual, for example, for a magazine to have five or more readers per copy, compared to a daily newspaper, which might have about two readers per copy.

Several factors affect the number of readers per copy a publication will garner, such as:

- The distribution pattern used by the publisher in circulating the publication. If the publication is distributed only by subscription, the number of different readers who will pick up and read it is generally limited. Compare this to a distribution plan that places the periodical on an airplane or in a doctor's office, where there is significant opportunity for many people to read it. Such a plan would generate a very high number of readers per copy.

- The amount of editorial in the publication. Generally, the more words contained in a publication, the longer it takes to read. The person who purchased the publication might, therefore, hold the copy longer and not give it to another to read for some time. By the time this second reader has a chance to read it, the third potential reader might have no interest, preferring to read something more current.

- The type of editorial. Some publications have a tendency to be retained by the purchaser because of the reference material in the publication—people might keep it on their coffee table as a decorative item or house it in their library.

Table 20.5 gives figures that illustrate some of the dynamics discussed above, showing how these various factors generate fewer or more readers per copy for a publication. Magazine A, for example, has fewer readers per copy than magazine B—caused primarily by the high percentage of readers who read the magazine in their home and the number of days spent reading the magazine. Magazine D has more readers per copy than C—caused by a greater proportion of readers consuming the magazine outside their home and by the relatively few number of days the average reader spends reading it.

TABLE 20.5: Readership Dynamics

	Daily National Newspaper	Weekly Magazine A	Weekly Magazine B	Monthly Magazine C	Monthly Magazine D
Readers per Copy:	2.0	2.9	10.2	3.4	6.0
Place of Reading:					
In-Home	40	90%	45%	58%	39%
Someone Else's Home	1	7	7	8	11
Place of Work	55	2	19	12	17
Doctor's/Dentist's Office	—	—	13	11	14
Beauty/Barber Shop	—	—	7	3	9
Other	4	1	9	11	10
Total	100	100%	100%	100%	100%
Mean Number of Reading Days Average Per Reader:	1.0	4.5	1.5	2.1	1.5

Regardless of the number of readers per copy a publication generates, the accumulation nevertheless takes time for the first reader to read it, pass it to the second reader, and so forth. For newspapers, this amount of time is generally brief—often the same day. Magazines are another story. For the most part, magazines take much longer to accumulate their total number of readers per copy and therefore their total audience. Table 20.6 displays a typical accumulation profile for weekly and monthly magazines. Although there are some differences by magazine within each category of issuance, the general patterns are similar. The pattern for any particular publication is a result of what that publication is and how readers consume it. For example:

- The shorter the publication interval, the faster the accumulation.

- The higher the readers-per-copy, the slower the accumulation.

- Timely or news-oriented publications are consumed faster and therefore accumulate faster.

- The higher the percentage of newsstand circulation, the more rapidly the primary audience is accumulated.

- The larger the percentage of in-home audience a publication has, the faster its audience accumulation.

The pattern of audience accumulation also varies by type of reader. People who purchase the magazine and read it at home have the first opportunity to read the issue. This category of reader therefore accumulates early, before the type who pick up the

TABLE 20.6:   Percent Total Audience Accumulated

	Weekly Magazines		Monthly Magazines	
Week	A	B	C	D
1	55%	65%	40%	35%
2	80	85	65	55
3	90	95	75	70
4	98	99	85	80
5	100	100	89	85
6			93	90
7			96	93
8			98	96
9			99	99
10			100	100

magazine and read it someplace else. Table 20.7 shows the variation in type of audience accumulation for a typical weekly magazine.

TABLE 20.7:   Variation in Audience Accumulation by Type of Reader—Magazine A

Week	Total Audience	In-Home Audience	Out-of-Home Audience
1	65%	75%	40%
2	85	95	70
3	95	100	85
4	99		95
5	100		100

Primary/Passalong/In-Home/Out-of-Home   As we have noted, readers are categorized according to whether they read the publication in their home or elsewhere, and whether they purchase the magazine or not. These different types of readers are depicted in Exhibit 20.1 and are defined below:

Primary Readers
Readers who purchase a magazine or who are members of a household where the publication is purchased.

- **Primary Readers**—The readers in the household in which the magazine is purchased. This includes the specific purchaser and anyone else living in that household who also reads the magazine.

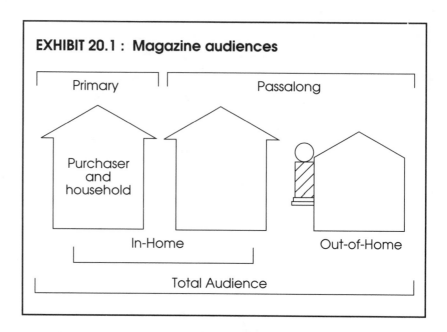

EXHIBIT 20.1 : Magazine audiences

Passalong Readers
Readers of a publication who are not primary readers. Also called *Secondary Readers*.

In-Home Readers
People who read a magazine or newspaper in their own home.

Out-of-Home Readers
People who read a magazine someplace other than in their own home.

- **Passalong Readers**—Any readers who are not primary readers.

- **In-Home Readers**—Anyone (primary or passalong) who reads the magazine in their own home.

- **Out-of-Home Readers**—Anyone who reads the magazine outside their own home, such as at work, on an airplane, in a doctor's office, etc.

There are some research studies that indicate a greater "value" for the primary versus the passalong reader, and for the in-home versus out-of-home reader, in terms of the opportunity for a reader to be exposed to an advertisement. Clearly, not all readers read every page of a magazine. Even those that read the vast majority of a publication do not necessarily *see* a particular advertisement. The more time people spend reading a publication, however, the more likely they are to go through it page by page—thus the greater the opportunity for them to see a particular advertisement. Table 20.8 demonstrates this reading time dynamic for four different magazines. You'll note that regardless of the magazine, primary readers spend more time reading than passalong readers; in-home readers spend more time than out-of-home readers.

TABLE 20.8:   Number of Minutes Spent Reading an Average Issue

	Weekly Magazines		Monthly Magazines	
	A	B	C	D
Total Audience	45	40	40	60
Type of Reader:				
Primary	65	60	50	80
Passalong	35	40	35	40
In-home	65	55	50	80
Out-of-home	30	25	30	30

You should not, however, jump to the conclusion that *only* primary readers should be analyzed, or *only* in-home readers. Passalong and out-of-home readers also have an opportunity to see your advertisement and should therefore be counted as part of the medium's audience. It is your call whether or not you "value" these passalong and out-of-home audiences to the same degree as primary and in-home readers. No research exists that can direct you to give full value to all types of readers, or diminished value to some types.

You should also keep in mind that not all magazines fall within the generalizations shown above. For example, in-flight publications are usually read on an airplane. These are neither purchased by a reader nor generally read in one's home, but this alone should not suggest to the media planner that the audiences should be devalued. Similarly, business magazines and newspapers have a proportionately higher percent of readers who read at their place of work, but this does not mean readers will spend less time reading or read less thoroughly.

Out-of-Home Media Audiences

There are two audience measurements commonly used for out-of-home media—specifically for outdoor (poster panels, etc.) and transit media (bus ads, etc.):

Daily Effective Circulation (DEC) is the number of people exposed to an advertising display in one day. The length of exposure (the day) can vary from 12 to 24 hours depending on the

Daily Effective Circulation The gross number of people (without regard to duplication) exposed to an out-of-home advertising display in one day.

period of illumination of the unit. Circulation of every advertising unit in a market is counted either by using official government machine counts or by hand (described in a later section). The total circulation count for all units combined is divided by the number of units in a market to yield the average DEC for the average unit. DEC currently refers to the number of people in a market age two years and older. Future circulation counts will be based on adults age 18 and older. Once a DEC is established for a market, plant operators or sales representative organizations can convert the DEC to reflect circulation for most standard demographic age groups (e.g., adults 18–24).

Gross Rating Points   GRPs in outdoor media have the same meaning as in other media forms—essentially they are the sum of all rating points in a media schedule. The basis for GRPs in outdoor media is the daily effective circulation. DEC is divided by the market's population to yield the rating for the average out-of-home advertising unit. By multiplying the number of units in a media schedule by the average rating, you obtain GRPs. Keep in mind that the rating for a unit is the daily rating. GRPs are therefore *daily*.

Showing Gross rating points within out-of-home media, or number of posters displayed in transit media.

Showing   Outdoor advertising is ordinarily planned (and sold) in GRP packages called **showings**. For example, a "#100 showing" (verbally referred to as a 100 showing) comprises the number of poster panels needed to deliver a daily effective circulation equal to the market's total population. This is identical to buying 100 GRPs in TV or radio or print—each medium will produce impressions that are equivalent to 100 percent of the market's population. The primary difference with outdoor advertising, however, is that it is usually sold for a one-month period. A #100 showing, therefore, results in an actual purchase of some 3,000 GRPs (100 GRPs × 30 days/month).

Now that you have an understanding of what media audiences are, you need to understand how media research suppliers obtain these numbers—which is the subject of the next chapter.

Chapter 21

Media Audience Research

I n this chapter we will discuss how several media research suppliers collect media audience data for the major mass media by using various interviewing or questionnaire techniques as well as through the use of electronic devices. We precede that discussion with one on *sampling error*, in which we describe how all media audience information is based on a sampling of the population, and why media audience data should be viewed more as an indication of possibility rather than an absolute.

With rare exception, you will have to rely on audience research data to compare one medium to another and to create an overall media plan. It is incumbent on you to understand what kind of data are available so you can seek out the information you need. It is also important that you understand the genesis of the reported information so you can appreciate that the audience data are merely *estimates* based on a sampling of the population.

There is a growing trend to go beyond simple demographic descriptors (such as age and income) in analyzing and selecting media. Increasingly, media vehicles are being chosen based on the lifestyle characteristics of the audience who consume the media vehicle, or on the product/service usage patterns of these audiences. Notwithstanding this trend, the majority of media audience data available to the media planner are based on demographics. Further, the evaluation tools, such as reach and frequency for combinations of media, continue to be based on demographic information and formulas that rely on demographics.

Some research suppliers provide information on media audiences only, some include product or service consumption patterns, and some report only on psychological/lifestyle descriptors (psychographic data). Often, reported data on any of these three categories are cross-tabulated and published by the research supplier or made available to the media planner via various on-line media timesharing computer networks. As you delve into media planning, you should investigate the specific data available to help you decide which media vehicle or media form is most appropriate. This certainly can include lifestyle or product/service consumption characteristics, and will, more often than not, include media audiences based on demographics.

Before reviewing the basic techniques used by research suppliers, it is important to understand that the reported audience data are based on a sampling of the population—not a complete census. This sampling leads to *sampling error.*

Sampling Error

With the possible exception of information provided by the Audit Bureau of Circulation (which is discussed later) *all* audience data are *estimates*—projections based on a sampling of the total population. Inherent in using a sample rather than the entire population is **sampling error**, the possible deviation for the reported finding from what might be the actual finding had the entire population been studied. It is important for you to fully appreciate what sampling error is and why you should keep it in mind whenever comparing one media vehicle to another or one media form to another.

Sampling Error The possible deviation in the reported finding of media audience research based on a sample from what might be the actual finding had a complete census been done. Usually reported as "±" the reported number.

If you took a cup of water from a salt lake and weighed the salt in the water, you could with great accuracy determine the total volume of salt in the entire lake by multiplying your finding by the total amount of water in the lake. There would be little or no question that the sample cup was representative of the whole. On the other hand, if you measured the depth of the lake at any given point, you could not accurately determine the average depth of the entire lake; the one measurement point might be a typical. To increase the accuracy of your estimate, you could take depth measurements at various points (the more the better), combine the measurements to get an average, and state with some degree of accuracy the average depth of the entire lake. The measurement points are the *sample* used to project your estimate of the whole.

The same estimating process is used in media research. Research companies select members of a population group who are ostensibly representative of the total population. The sample group, therefore, supposedly replicates the media consumption and product consumption patterns of the entire population being studied. But because the entire population is not studied, the projections based on the sample have a ± *error factor*: the actual number for the entire population could vary up or down from the projection. The amount of up or down variation depends largely (but not totally) on the size of the sample *relative to the total population being studied*. Basically, the larger the percentage the sample is of the total population, the lesser the ± error—that is, the lesser the up or down variation. Further, the greater the percentage of the people in the sample who report a given activity (e.g., viewing a specific TV program), the less the ± error. If samples of 100 people were chosen in market A (with a population of 100,000) and market B (with a population of 500,000), the estimated projections in market A would be more reliable (have a lower ± error) because the sample represents a greater percentage of the total population in market A than it does in market B. Likewise, if 5 percent of the people in a sample indicate that they viewed program A and 50 percent report viewing program B, the estimated audience projection is more reliable for Program B than that for Program A because the number of respondents represents a greater percentage of the total population.

There is no reasonable way to have total accuracy of reported audience information. The cost of increasing the sample sizes (i.e., having more people respond to questions about media consumption) would be prohibitively expensive. Conceivably, it could cost more to obtain audience estimates than it would to advertise in a media vehicle.

Making media decisions based on small differences among alternatives is therefore a shaky process. You must keep sampling error in mind whenever numerical comparisons among alternative media solutions are made because, in the real world, the exact opposite of what the research says *could* be true. Let's examine this.

First, some definitions and summary explanations:

- The ± error is known by, or related to, other terms: *standard error, sampling error, standard deviation, tolerance,* and *sigma.* All terms relate to similar sampling concepts, although not necessarily to the same specific mathematical function.

- The ± error is usually reported as a number in the same fashion as the number to which it refers. For example, if a 10 rating is reported with a ± 2 error, the "2" refers to plus or minus two rating points.

- The ± error is calculated and presented in various magnitudes, with these magnitudes representing the "chances" that the sample reflects the population within the given ± error range.

- *Sigma* is the term usually used to signify the magnitude of these chances. The three most common sigma references used in audience measurement data are these:
  - 1-sigma (or one standard error)—This means the chances are about 68 out of 100 that the reported audience (e.g., the rating) would not differ from the findings of a complete census of the population by more than the ± number reported. For example, if a 10 rating has a 1-sigma of 2, and you conducted the same audience survey among 100 different samples of people, you would find a rating between 8 and 12 (10 ± 2) in at least 68 of them. In the remaining 32 samples you might find a rating that varies from 10 by more than ± 2. Therefore, you can be confident of the ± range 68 percent of the time—a 68 percent *confidence level.*
  - 2-sigma (or two standard errors)—This means the chances are about 95 out of 100 that the ± number is accurate—a 95 percent confidence level.
  - 3-sigma (or three standard errors)—meaning the chances are about 99 out of 100 that the ± number is accurate—a 99 percent confidence level

As you can see, the greater the magnitude of the sigma, the relatively more reliable is the reported number *including* the sampling error—that is, the higher the confidence level. To demonstrate, let's use a hypothetical ± error for a 10 rating. As shown in Exhibit 21.1:

- At one standard error (1 sigma), the chances are 68 out of 100 (68 percent confidence level) that the actual rating would fall within the range of 9–11.

- At 2 sigma, the chances are 95 out of 100 that the actual rating would fall within the range of 8–12.

- At 3 sigma, the chances are 99 out of 100 that the actual rating would fall within the range of 7–13.

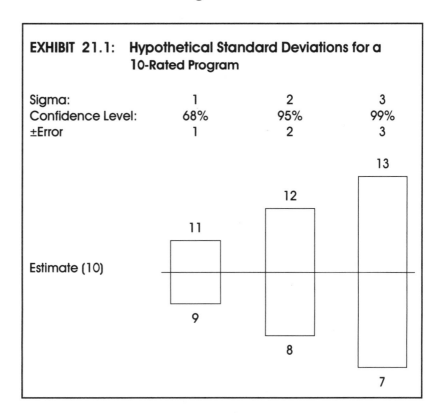

EXHIBIT 21.1:   Hypothetical Standard Deviations for a 10-Rated Program

Sigma:	1	2	3
Confidence Level:	68%	95%	99%
±Error	1	2	3

Shown in Table 21.1 is the ± error for each of a series of household rating estimates for a specific media research report. A program estimated to have a 10 rating has 2-sigma tolerance of ± 1.6 error, meaning the actual (real) rating could be as low as 8.4 or as high as 11.6. A ± 1.6 error for a 10-rated program is equivalent to a 16 percent swing up or down—i.e., 16 percent *relative error* (1.6 divided by 10 = 16 percent). You'll note that the higher the

TABLE 21.1:   Sampling Error

Household Rating	Error +/– (*)	Rating Range	Relative Error
5	1.2	3.8–6.2	24%
10	1.6	8.4–11.6	16
15	1.8	13.2–16.8	12
20	2.2	17.8–22.2	11
30	2.4	27.6–32.4	8
40	2.6	37.4–42.6	7

* At 95% confidence level.

reported rating, the lower the relative error. But even at the high level (40 rating) you are still dealing with ± 7 percent error—the actual rating could be 2.6 rating points less or more.

The next example demonstrates the possible decisions that might be made to purchase time on radio station A or B. On the surface, station B appears to be superior with a higher rating and the same cost as A. However, when the sampling error is applied we find that actual ratings (and therefore actual number of listeners) could be more or less than reported. Station A, therefore, *could* have a larger audience than station B. (See Table 21.2.)

TABLE 21.2:   Application of Sampling Error in Purchase Decisions

	Station A	Station B
Average Rating	3.0	4.0
Cost	$ 100	$ 100
Sampling ± Error*	1.1	1.2
Possible Rating		
low	1.9	2.8
high	4.1	5.2
Possible New Listeners**		
low	1,900	2,800
high	4,100	5,200

  * At 95% confidence level
** Market population = 100,000 men

Most of the major syndicated media research companies publish the sample sizes used to tabulate their total audience projections, as well as the formula that can be used to estimate the sampling error, such as the following:

2 standard deviations = $2 \left(\sqrt{P \, (100 - P)/n} \, \right)$
where P = audience rating and n = the sample size;
2 standard deviations = 95% confidence level.

Using the 4 rating of station B in the table above, the ± error can be calculated as follows:

1. $100 - 4 = 96$

2. $96 \times 4 = 384$

3. $\dfrac{384}{1032^*} = .3721$

4. Square root of $.3721 \times 2 = 1.2$ (rounded)

5. ±error on this 4 rating = 1.2

6. At the 95 percent confidence level, a 4.1 rating can range from $(4.1 - 1.2) = 2.8$ to $(4.1 + 1.2) = 5.2$

Although you don't need to calculate standard errors each time media forms are evaluated, it is nevertheless beneficial to read the technical appendixes of the various media research reports used in the evaluation process to better understand how data are collected, and to serve as a reminder that all audience data are no more than estimates.

Media Research Suppliers

There are basically three categories of media audience research data that might be available to you:

- Proprietary research commissioned by an advertiser for self-use. Generally this is not published for general industry use.

- Proprietary research commissioned by one or more media outlets for use in promoting and selling their medium to

---

* Sample size of this particular study.

advertisers. An example of this is a survey of a magazine's subscribers (*subscriber study*) to determine reading intensity, product consumption, etc. This research is paid for by the media outlet and is generally available to the advertising industry.

- Syndicated media research, which is conducted by independent research suppliers to assess media audiences across one or more media forms. This research is sold to media outlets, advertisers, advertising agencies, independent media buying companies, etc.

The following pages will concentrate on the major syndicated media research resources because these represent the majority of available information. Although there are research suppliers in addition to those discussed, those listed are the most commonly used. The intent of this discussion is to provide a superficial summary of each of these resources, not to elaborate on the highly technical and exhaustive procedures undertaken by each supplier in collecting media audience information.

Arbitron Radio Market Reports

The Arbitron Company utilizes an open-ended, individual radio listening diary to collect audience data among people age 12 and older who are in households with telephones. The self-administered diary allows the respondent to record times of listening, station call letters (or dial setting) and the place of listening (at home, in car, some other place). People are counted as listeners if they listened for five or more minutes during any quarter-hour segment.

As of this writing, Arbitron issues reports for 262 radio markets in the United States, reporting "average week" listening during a 12-week survey period. Audience data are reported primarily for two types of geographic area: Metropolitan Statistical Area (a.k.a. **Metro Area** or MSA), and **Total Survey Area (TSA)**, which may include counties from an adjacent Metro. Another geographic area,

Metro Area   A geographic area defined by the U.S. Government's Office of Management and Budget. Also called a Standard Metropolitan Statistical Area (SMSA).

Total Survey Area (TSA)   The geographic area in which radio signals from an originating market can be received.

ADI (Area of Dominant Influence) Arbitron Company's definition of a TV market.

the **ADI (Area of Dominant Influence)**, is also available in the top 50 radio markets.

Audience estimates for specific age groups for teens and adults by sex are reported for various dayparts and times. The kinds of estimates reported are as follows:

- Average quarter-hour number of persons and cumulative audience by daypart for metro, TSA and ADI

- Average quarter-hour rating, share, and cumulative rating by daypart for metro area

- Location of listening (at-home, car, or other) for metro area

- Exclusive cumulative number of persons listening within the metro area

- Two-station duplication within the metro area

- Hour-by-hour average quarter-hour ratings in the metro area

Criteria for Reporting Stations   Not every radio station in a market is necessarily reported by Arbitron. To be reported, the following minimum reporting standards must have been met for persons 12 and over during the Monday-through-Sunday 6:00 a.m. to midnight daypart during the most recent 12-week survey period:

a. The station must have received five or more minutes of listening in a quarter-hour in at least ten in-tab metro diaries, or must represent at least one percent of the metro (in-tab diaries).

b. The station must have an unrounded metro cume rating of 0.5 or greater.

c. The station must have an average quarter-hour metro rating of at least 0.1.

Arbitron Television Market Report

The Arbitron Company samples the viewing habits of television households and individuals to produce television audience estimates in all markets in the United States. As of this writing, this encompasses 209 Areas of Dominant Influence (ADIs). A TV household is an occupied dwelling unit that has one or more TV sets. Estimates of the number of television households in each surveyed county in the United States are prepared annually based upon total U.S. household data obtained from Market Statistics. The estimated total number of television households in each ADI is used to project TV audience estimates.

Arbitron uses a one-week, self-administered diary to collect viewing data in most markets, and an electronic meter (household meter) in 13 markets. There are three additional meter markets referred to as Local Market Scanamerica (people meters). Meter measurement provides the metro and ADI household and demographic viewing levels for both individual stations and Households Using TV (HUT) estimates. A combination of meter and diary measurements is the basis for ADI demographic audience estimates in the 13 household meter markets. Table 21.3 lists the types of measurement used for deriving audience estimates for some of the classifications of data reported by Arbitron. The Scanamerica markets use a meter to collect both household and demographic viewing. This service also provides product purchase information keyed to individual households.

Audience estimates are reported for households and for various age/sex demographics including all people age 2 and older. A household or a person is counted as a viewer if they view for five minutes or more during an average quarter-hour.

TABLE 21.3: Type of Measurement Used for Deriving Arbitron TV Audience Estimates.

Reported Information	Metro Area	ADI	Total Survey Area
TV HH rating, share, HUTs	M	M	—
ADI demographic ratings, PVTs	—	M/D	—
All TSA estimates	—	—	M/D
TV HH cumes	—	M/D	M/D
TVHH ratings in adjacent ADIs	—	—	D

M = Meter measurement
D = Diary measurement
M/D = both

Audience estimates are shown for each televised program for which a minimum number of the sample respondents report viewing for each half hour, as well as for broad TV dayparts. The kinds of data shown vary according to the geographic area reported by Arbitron. Several examples of the reported data follow:

- ADI TV HH rating and share
- Metro TV HH rating and share
- ADI ratings by age/sex—e.g., women 12–24 or 18–34, teens 12–17; children 2–11 or 6–11
- Number of people viewing within the TSA
- TV HH rating in adjacent ADIs
- Share and HUT trends
- ADI and TSA Cume Households
- Station break averages by ADI and TSA; ratings; thousands of viewers

VCR Viewing   Metered households using a videocassette recorder are also included in the Arbitron audience estimates for the time period when the show is being recorded. Playbacks of recorded programs are not credited in the audience estimates. For non-meter markets Arbitron issues a separate VCR diary to retrieve similar program recording data.

ABC (Audit Bureau of Circulation)

The ABC collects circulation information from an extensive number of magazines and newspapers and issues various reports used by media planners to evaluate and monitor circulation delivery for these periodicals.

Twice a year ABC requires each publication to submit a statement of its circulation—called a Publisher's Statement. The statements, which are subject to audit, cover circulation for a six-month period.

Annual ABC audits either substantiate or correct the information that was reported in the two previous statements. Each audit is based on detailed in-person inspection of the publication's records by an ABC auditor, and the findings are published in an audit report.

ABC releases data via three basic reports:

1. *Publisher's Statements*: Magazine statements are issued for the periods ending June 30 and December 31; newspaper statements for the periods ending March 31 and September 30. At

the publisher's request, newspaper statements can be issued for an interim three-month period. Each statement contains various categories of information to help media planners make informed media buying decisions, such as

- Average total paid circulation and non-paid distribution.

- Circulation by editions (national, regional, etc.) and by issues (January, February, etc. for magazines; daily, Sunday, etc. for newspapers).

- How subscriptions are obtained or renewed (full price, at discount, use of premiums, etc.)

- Circulation by county size and geographic area.

2. *FAS—FAX*: Immediately after the deadline for filing a statement, ABC compiles a summary from all statements received, listing information such as the following (depending on whether the report covers magazines or newspapers):

- Number of issues in the six-month period

- Frequency of issue

- Rate base of circulation guarantee (magazines only)

- Number of subscriptions

- Single-copy price

- Number of single-copy sales

- Average total paid circulation

- Changes in circulation versus the previous year

- Number of occupied households in the newspaper's city zone and retail trading zone or Newspaper Designated Market.

- Circulation in the above market designations

- Total average paid circulation for the current period and for the same period in the previous year

3. *Audit Report*: On an annual basis, an ABC auditor gathers detailed information from each publisher's records to issue the magazine or newspaper's ABC Audit Report. This confirms or adjusts the information contained in the two Publisher's Statements.

ABC notes any discrepancies of 2 percent or more in a quarterly variation report. Also reported for newspapers is an analysis of cities and towns that receive 25 or more copies.

Monroe-Mendelsohn

Mendelsohn Media Research annually publishes a "Survey of Adults and Markets of Affluence." Unlike many other syndicated research reports, Mendelsohn limits its reports to include only those people who claim a household income of $60,000 or more. Because of its large sample concentrated among upper-income respondents, Mendelsohn reports on many publications not measured elsewhere.

All of the information obtained is based on self-administered questionnaires mailed to respondents. The reports contain audience data for approximately 100 magazines and six newspapers (four dailies, one Sunday, and one weekly), and television viewing and radio listening patterns by daypart as well as by cable network.

Readership of most publications is measured for four issues. Readership for weekday publications is ascertained for five issues. In each case audience measurement takes place within the time frame of the frequency of issuance: for monthly magazines, for example, it is the number of issues read in the past four months (one month per issue times four issues). This number is then averaged through a weighting process to obtain average-issue audience. Electronic media consumption is based on the past week's activity for cable TV, and the average weekday plus average Saturday and average Sunday for broadcast TV.

MRI (Mediamark Research Inc.)

MRI uses two different questionnaire techniques to collect audience data for adults age 18 and older. Data pertaining to media exposure (magazines, newspapers, radio, and television) are obtained in a personal face-to-face interview. Product and service usage, as well as viewing for specific TV programs, is obtained from a self-administered questionnaire left with the respondent.

The personal interviews involve (among other things) the collection of data as shown below:

1. Newspaper reading. Reported is the reading of both daily and Sunday/weekend newspapers circulated in the area where the respondent lives. The audience measured is based on the number of people who report reading the daily newspaper "yesterday" (or the most recent weekday), or reading the Sunday paper within the past seven days. Place of reading information is also obtained.

2. Newspaper-distributed magazines. Reported data are for the carrier newspapers.

Recent Reading A research technique to determine the average issue audience of print media. Used, for example, by MRI.

3. Magazine reading collected in the reading audiences of some 200 magazines. MRI uses a **recent-reading** technique whose principle is that the number of people reading *any* issue of a magazine during a given circulation period (recently read) is equal to the total number of people reading any particular issue over its total life (average issue audience). The procedure for establishing whether a person is a reader encompasses the use of a sort board and magazine logos printed on a deck of cards.

   Although there are many steps involved in this procedure, the essential process is as follows:

   - The respondent is asked to sort the cards on the sort board into three groups (and eventually two groups) depending on whether or not they were read or looked into within the last six months.

   - For those magazines that the respondent claims to have read or looked into within the last six months, he or she is asked, first, how many issues were read or looked into and, eventually, when that consumption took place, using each magazine's "most recent publication interval," i.e. the last seven days for weeklies, the last month or 30 days for monthlies, etc.

   Upon completion of these steps, a series of qualitative questions is asked for each publication, which refer to place of reading, reading days, reading time, reader's actions, source of copy, percent of pages looked at, etc.

4. Radio listening: This encompasses the listening during any period within an average half-hour, during an average weekday, or an average weekend. The respondent's answers are based on listening "yesterday," "last Saturday," or "last Sunday" to specific stations. From this, estimates are made for listening levels by daypart and by station format.

5. Television viewing (broadcast and cable): To determine daypart viewing levels (something like a Persons Using Television estimate), the respondent is queried about "yesterday" viewing of broadcast TV and the "last seven days" of viewing for cable TV. To estimate viewing for specific TV programs, the respondent is asked to fill out a self-administered questionnaire.

MRI reports are issued twice each year—in the spring and fall. A "Doublebase" report, available via on-line systems, combines the samples (and therefore audience estimates) of two MRI semiannual reports, and is released once per year, each September.

NSI (Nielsen Station Index)

The A.C. Nielsen Company surveys the viewing levels of all TV stations in all markets in the United States and issues reports at least four times a year for each market.

Nielsen uses a combination of self-administered diaries and electronic meters. Both meter and diary information is used to project audience data for 26 markets. All remaining markets rely solely on diary information.

The Nielsen meter system uses automatic instrumentation that electronically stores minute-by-minute records of TV receiver tunings. The tuning records are automatically communicated by phone to a central computer each day. The meter system can monitor up to 12 TV sets in each household.

All households in the survey panel are asked to record their TV viewing for programs viewed for five or more minutes on a printed diary form provided by Nielsen. Respondents are asked to record the station call letters, channel number and person(s) in the household viewing at that time (including visitors, if any). Basic demographic data are obtained for each household member.

Audience estimates are computed separately for each quarter-hour. Household ratings are based on metered reports in meter markets, and on diary information in all other markets. Demographic audience data are based on diary information for all markets. In meter markets, demographic adjustment factors (based on diary data) are applied to the meter household viewing data.

VCR recording of TV programs is credited for the time of recording, but currently not for the time of playback. TV usage for video games, computers, and the like is excluded.

In a multi-set usage situation (households viewing on more than one TV set at any given time), the simultaneous use of more than one TV set does not increase the HUT level—the household is counted only once. Duplicate viewing entries—to the same station at the same time from different TVs in the home—are counted for each station. As a result, the sum of the reported station ratings may equal or exceed the HUT level.

NTI (Nielsen Television Index)

A.C. Nielsen provides estimates of in-home audiences of network television programs. NTI is the only syndicated research supplier that continuously reports on all national television programs.

Nielsen preselects sample households and collects the name, age, and gender of each household member, as well as other demographic data about the household, through personal interviews. Each selected household is equipped with a Nielsen People Meter (NPM)—an electronic device that consists of an on-set unit and a remote control unit—for each operable TV set. Each member of the household is assigned a button on the NPM. When a TV set is turned on, respective buttons are pushed for each audience member viewing TV at that time. As household members come into or leave the room, they are requested to indicate their attendance by pushing their assigned button.

The NPM stores minute-by-minute records of TV receiver tuning activity and of the People Meter audience data entries in the NTI sample households. When a visitor indicates a viewing entry, flashing lights on the set-top unit of the NPM prompt the visitor for data on gender and age. The stored tuning records are automatically transmitted by telephone to a central computer. In addition to recording set-tuning for broadcast programs, the NPM also stores records for cable and pay TV (e.g., HBO). Video games, computer and clock displays, closed-circuit TV, and security appliances are not reflected in the national audience estimates. VCR recordings of broadcast and cable material are considered at the time of taping, while replays of VCR recordings are currently excluded from TV usage.

Among the many reports issued by Nielsen which are based on NPM data are:

- NTI Dailies Plus (Overnights)—Available the day after telecast, this report lists household and persons estimates for primetime programs.

- NTI Dailies Plus (Weeklies)—Audience information is shown for syndicated TV programs and multi-day network programs.

- The Pocketpiece—A listing of audience data for all commercial network TV programs; issued each week.

The data that can be found in each weekly "Pocketpiece" include the average minute audience as reported under various descriptors:

- Household rating and share by program, by quarter-hour, half-hour, and total program duration.

- People ratings (e.g., total persons 2+, working women, men and women 18 and older by age segment, teens 12–17 by gender, children 2–11 and 6–11).

- Viewers per 1000 viewing households by age segment.

- Household rating and share for non-network telecasts, PBS, cable originated programs, and pay services (e.g., HBO).

RADAR® (Radio's All Dimension Audience Research)

Statistical Research conducts daily telephone recall interviews among people age 12 and older to determine their personal radio listening for a one-week period.

Counted as audience are people who reported that they listened to or could hear radio for at least three minutes within a quarter-hour period—whether they were at home or away from home.

In order to prepare network radio audience estimates, quarter-hours of radio usage as reported by respondents are matched with program and commercial clearances for each station carrying such programming.

RADAR   Radio All Dimension Audience Research report issued by Statistical Research, Inc.

Two **RADAR** reports are issued each year: spring and fall. Each report covers the average listening levels during the full year. Network radio estimates are compiled using stations associated with the individual networks in the most recent six-month period.

The Scarborough Report

The Scarborough Report includes media and product consumption data for 56 markets throughout the United States. Reports are issued annually.

Data are collected using two interviewing techniques: telephone and self-administered questionnaire. Telephone interviews are conducted to determine radio listening (by station and time), newspaper readership, and weekly magazine readership. Two telephone interviews are conducted in the top ten markets and selected other markets in order to tabulate cumulative audience data (i.e., read two issues of a magazine). All remaining markets are surveyed via telephone only once.

A self-administered questionnaire is used to collect product consumption data for approximately 450 different products. Additionally, the respondent is asked to list the TV program and station viewed during each half hour of a given week, as well as to indicate which of the monthly magazines listed in the questionnaire were read.

A person qualifies as a member of a radio station's audience if he or she listened for five minutes or more. Qualification for being part of a magazine or newspaper audience, or part of the audience of a television program/station, is based on the respondent's claim of having read (or viewed).

As with many syndicated media research sources, The Scarborough Report is available in hard copy form and via on-line computer systems—the latter allowing the media planner to cross-tabulate any reported data for any of the markets.

Simmons Market Research Bureau

Simmons conducts an annual survey of adults age 18 and older. It uses various mechanisms to collect audience data: personal interviews, self-administered questionnaires, telephone interviews, diaries of TV viewing and listening. Two personal interviews are conducted: the first to obtain print media readership and cable TV viewing data (as well as demographic data); the second to cover the same readership information (to enhance reliability and measure audience turnover) and also to obtain radio listening audiences. The methods for obtaining media consumption habits are as follows:

1. Newspaper reading. Reported is the number of respondents who claimed to have read a daily newspaper circulated in their area "yesterday" (or "since last Saturday" for Sunday editions). In addition to estimates on the average issue audience for daily/Sunday/weekend newspapers, Simmons also obtains information for readership by section (business/finance, classified, etc.),

Sunday comic sections, and nationally distributed Sunday newspaper magazines.

2. Magazine reading. Simmons collects information for more than 100 publications using a **through-the-book** measurement technique. The first step is the administration of a preliminary logo screening. Then, for each publication the respondent claims to have read or looked into in the last six months, he or she is taken through a skeletonized version of the test issue containing nine items—ostensibly to establish which items appeared interesting. This is an aided recognition technique which establishes if a person, indeed, read or looked into the test issue. Once qualified as a reader, the respondent is taken through five qualitative questions regarding where the reading took place, overall rating ("one of my favorites," etc.), time spent reading, number of days spent reading, and how/why read.

3. Radio listening. Listening information is obtained from personal interviews and telephone interviews, or a self-administered diary, depending on the availability of the respondent at the time of the research study. A person is counted as a listener of a specific radio network or station format type, if he/she listened for five or more minutes of an entire daypart averaged across two weekday observations.

4. Television viewing. Reported is the average half-hour audience by daypart and by program for respondents who claimed to have viewed TV for any duration. This information is obtained from self-administered diary keeping by the respondent during a two-week period. Also obtained is "attentiveness of viewing" via the question: "For the most part of the period (that you viewed) were you out of the TV room, in the room paying some attention, in the room paying full attention?"

5. Cable TV viewing. Reported as "viewed last week" by networks for both Basic and Pay. Information is obtained in the first personal interview.

6. Outdoor audiences. Simmons reports on the reach/frequency provided in a one-month (30-day) period by various "showing sizes." These data are obtained by "mapping" the respondents' specific trips made during the past week and overlaying the location of each outdoor panel location (and the direction it is facing). One exposure is counted each time the respondent passed by a marked outdoor panel, on the street or road closest

Through-the-Book   A research technique used to determine the average issue audience of print media. Used, for example, by SMRB.

to the location, moving toward the panel's face. Using a mathematical formula, this information is projected to predict each respondent's long-term average frequency of exposure.

STARS (Simmons Teenage Research Study)

The Simmons Market Research Bureau conducts a biannual survey of media and product/service consumption patterns among teenagers age 12 to 19.

Personal interviews are conducted to determine magazine and newspaper readership using the same techniques used in Simmons' adult survey. This "through-the-book" technique establishes the number of readers of each publication studied. Additional questioning determines where the publication was read, the frequency of reading, the respondent's value rating of the publication, and the actions taken as a result of the advertising in the publication.

A self-administered questionnaire is used to report on radio and television listening/viewing as well as to obtain product/service usage levels.

TAB (Traffic Audit Bureau)

Although the Traffic Audit Bureau of Media Measurement does not issue audience measurement reports, it does audit the estimates produced by member out-of-home plant operators every three years to ensure that the plant operator's and government's traffic counts are a true reflection of the market.

Bus Shelter/Bus Bench Advertising posters positioned as an integral part of a freestanding covered structure or bench, often located at a bus stop.

Audiences for out-of-home media (posters, bulletins, **bus shelters**) are measured in terms of circulation, which consists of movement of people by vehicle (the primary source of circulation) or on foot.

Counting circulation Circulation is obtained by counting the number of vehicles passing any advertising structure. The count includes the number of cars, trucks, or vans, number of pedestrians, and number of bicyclists. The number of vehicles counted is converted to number of people using a conversion factor of 1.75 people per car. Based on updated research, future circulation counts will use a factor of 1.35 to reflect the number of adults 18 years and older. A plant operator may include traffic volume from all four modes of transportation (excluding mass transit). Out-of-home audiences, therefore, primarily reflect the number of people in motor vehicles, and only secondarily the number of pedestrians/ bicyclists. The exception to this rule is for advertising units located in downtown business districts, airports, rail and bus terminals, shopping centers, and malls where pedestrians are dominant.

Circulation of every advertising unit in a market is counted using one of two methods:

1. Machine traffic count—taken by government agencies and recorded over a period of time. Referred to as *average annual daily traffic (AADT)*, these counts are adjusted using an established factoring system to reflect the circulation that should be expected during the exposure time of the advertising unit. An illuminated unit, for example, has a usual exposure of 18 hours per day (6:00 a.m. to midnight) compared to an unilluminated unit, which has a 12-hour exposure period (6:00 a.m. to 6:00 p.m.).

2. Head counts—taken by the plant operator using established techniques for estimating each unit's DEC (Daily Effective Circulation). This technique requires the plant operator to count traffic during any 15-minute segment between 9:00 a.m. and noon or 1:00 p.m. and 4:00 p.m., Monday through Friday, March through Memorial Day or Labor Day through December 1 (but not on atypical days, such as during a snow storm, or on the day of a state fair). These head counts are then converted to DEC using established projection factors.

OVRS (Outdoor Visibility Rating System)

Outdoor Visibility Rating System (OVRS)
A system of grading a poster panel's "visibility."

Developed by the American Association of Advertising Agencies in cooperation with the Outdoor Advertising Association of America, the Outdoor Visibility Rating System (**OVRS**) grades the "visibility" of 30-sheet poster panels. The OVRS replaces a previous system which was based on the same overall concept and was known as the SPV (Space Position Visibility System). The OVRS requires that a panel meet four minimum standards:

1. The panel must not be set back more than 150 feet from the center of the approach lane.

2. The panel must be angled to face traffic.

Facing   In outdoor advertising, the direction a poster faces—e.g., a south facing can be seen by northbound traffic.

Panel   Generally a "poster" panel—one outdoor or transit advertising unit.

3. There must not be more than two **panels** in a **facing**.

4. The panel must have at least five seconds of clear approach at the posted speed limit.

Panels that do not meet these criteria are classified as "non-qualifying" and receive zero points. Panels that do meet these criteria are rated 10 and are eligible for bonus points, which are awarded on various bases (e.g., four points for a single panel facing, two points if a stop sign is in the immediate vicinity of a panel). With bonus points, a panel can receive a maximum rating of 23. As with DEC, the combined OVRS ratings are added for all panels and divided by the total number of panels in market to get a published average.

Chapter 22

Geographic Areas

I n this chapter we will concentrate on describing the various geographic units used by a media planner for analyzing media audience and product/service usage information.

Most source material showing product sales or media delivery presents information on some territorial basis that allows you to make evaluations based on geographical units rather than relying only on national data. This type of investigation leads to more precise media plans—plans that target not only demographic groups, but demographic groups within specific cities, states, etc. Here are the more common geographic units.

Broadcast Coverage Area

Broadcast Coverage Area The geographic area within which a signal from an originating station can be received.

A **broadcast coverage area** is the geographic area within which a signal from an originating television station can be received.

A television signal is broadcast from a point of origin. As shown in Exhibit 22.1, TV stations originating in Syracuse can be viewed in an area extending from Watertown down to Elmira. Exhibit 22.2 shows that people living in Yates County are within the broadcast coverage area of both Syracuse and Rochester stations.

Exhibit 22.1   Broadcast Coverage Area

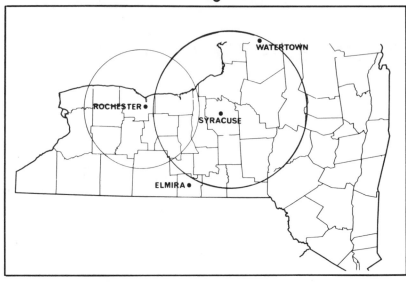

Television Market

TV Market An unduplicated television area to which a U.S. county is assigned based on the highest share of viewing to originating TV stations.

A **TV market** is an *unduplicated* geographic area to which a county is assigned on the basis of the highest share of viewing of originating stations.

Both the A.C. Nielsen and Arbitron companies survey viewing habits in every county in the United States. These data report how much the people in each county view each TV station. With these data, they are able to determine which stations are viewed most and then assign the county to one market or another.

The homes in Yates County view more hours of programs originating from Syracuse than they do programs coming from Rochester stations. Yates County, therefore, is assigned to the Syracuse television market.

It is necessary to place a county in only one TV market to avoid an overlap of information. If a county were assigned to more than one television market, it would make geographic analyses of media delivery impossible.

There are just over 200 TV markets in the United States, encompassing over 3,000 counties. Arbitron's term for a TV market is Area of Dominant Influence (ADI); Nielsen's term is **Designated Market Area (DMA)**. Although the terms differ, and to some extent so do the research techniques establishing viewing habits,

Designated Market Area (DMA) A.C. Nielsen's definition of a TV market.

Exhibit 22.2   Television Market

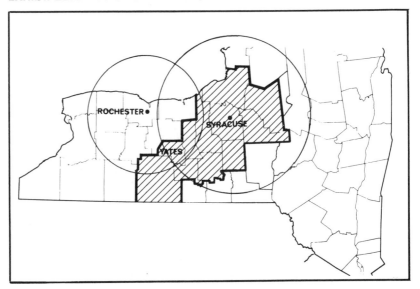

ADI and DMA are quite similar, and both are synonymous with the term *TV Market*.

Various data are often tabulated according to these designations, such as the demographic characteristics of the population (age, sex, income, etc.), purchasing patterns (food expenditures, gasoline consumption, etc.). Media consumption is also tabulated for the same geographic areas (television viewing, radio listening, magazine and newspaper circulation, etc.). Having all these data enables us to conveniently assess how to spend advertising budgets in each medium on a geographic basis.

Cable TV Market

About six out of ten homes in the United States have cable TV through which they receive all television programs. These programs consist of broadcast transmissions that can ordinarily be received over the air (via a TV antenna), cable-originated programs (both nationally telecast shows, like MTV, and locally originated and telecast shows), distant broadcast stations (which beam their signal up to a satellite where it is then bounced down to other markets), and subscriber-paid non-commercialized programming (such as HBO). Although there is an abundance of programs and stations that can be viewed, there is currently no defined and accepted geographic area which can be called a Cable TV Market.

Unlike broadcast TV, where stations transmit their signal and anyone within a reasonable distance from that transmission point can receive the signal, cable TV can be seen only if a household subscribes to the service and is wired to receive the service in their home (or if they have their own satellite dish). Because people must subscribe to the service, cable operators can pinpoint the physical location of each home receiving cable TV. This suggests that a cable TV market could be defined, but various other considerations argue against such a definition.

There are currently about 10,000 cable systems in the United States, contained within the roughly 200 TV markets (ADI or DMA). Each market, therefore, has an average of 50 systems. Of the 50 systems, about 10 offer local commercial availability—via placement in either a national cable program or a locally originated program. These 10 systems per market (about 2,000 in number nationally) have a government-licensed franchise to offer their service to a specific geographic area, which may or may not follow any commonly defined boundaries (such as counties). This lack of commonly defined boundaries inhibits a clear definition of each system—that is, it is difficult at best to "map" all systems in the United States.

An additional inhibitor to defining a cable TV market is the lack of other data needed to properly assess the market. For example, no data exist for the viewing habits of the subscribers in each system—no rating information a la Nielsen or Arbitron to determine the delivery of national or local programs in each system. Therefore, even if you took pains to construct a cable TV market map for the United States, you would have to work in a vacuum in deciding which systems have viewers that would best meet your needs, and therefore which systems should be part of your media plan.

You can work around this geographic area definition deficiency by using ADI and DMA information to analyze each of the 200 TV markets, and then crafting highly localized media efforts within each market using cable TV. For instance, to assess the relative importance of the geographic areas covered by different systems, you can look at the product sales information that you have available, or at geodemographic data that are available from several marketing/ media research suppliers.

Radio Market

A radio market is generally referred to as either a Total Survey Area (TSA) or a Metro Survey Area (MSA). Unlike TV markets, TSAs can overlap: a number of counties can receive originating radio stations from different cities. MSAs, however, do not overlap and are therefore used for buying purposes.

For a county to be part of the TSA, people living in the county must have established certain levels of listening to the radio station(s) broadcasting within their geographic area. These listening levels are tabulated from the survey diaries filled out by those in the survey sample. One listening level, for example, requires that a radio station be mentioned (listed) in at least ten diaries as being listened to for at least five minutes during any quarter hour within a survey week.

Metropolitan Statistical Area

Designated by the federal Office of Management and Budget, a Metropolitan Statistical Area (MSA) always includes a *city* (or cities) of specified population which constitutes the central city, and the *county* (or counties) in which it is located. An MSA also includes contiguous counties when the economic and social relationships between the central and contiguous counties meet specified criteria.

The basic criteria for an MSA are:

- It must include at least one city with 50,000 or more inhabitants, or an urbanized area of at least 50,000 inhabitants and a total metro area population of 100,000.

- It must have one or more central counties. These are the counties in which at least half the population lives in the Census Bureau urbanized area.

Counties that do not meet the above criteria could be included in an MSA if they satisfy other requirements. There must be significant levels of commuting from the outlying county to the central county (ies), and the county (ies) must display a specified degree of "metropolitan character" by meeting any one of the following conditions:

- Counties with a commuting rate of 50 percent or more must have a population density of at least 25 persons per square mile.

- Counties with a commuting rate from 40 to 50 percent must have a population density of at least 35 persons per square mile.

- Those with a commuting rate from 25 to 40 percent must have a population density of at least 50 persons per square mile, or at least 35 percent of their population classified as urban by the Bureau of the Census.

In addition to the designation of MSAs, the government has also defined two other geographic entities based on the 1980 Census:

Consolidated Metropolitan Statistical Area (CMSA). This is the largest designation in terms of geographic area and market size. It is made up of component PMSAs (see below) that together total at least one million in population. These CMSAs, or *mega* areas, are usually of little use to marketers because of their prohibitive size. However, they exert some influence on bordering counties because of the proximity of potential buyers for area goods and services.

Primary Metropolitan Statistical Area (PMSA). These are the component pieces that make up the CMSAs. They are directly associated with other PMSAs, but remain separate entities in terms of the socioeconomic data collected for them and presented in various research reports. To be classified as a PMSA, an area must be comprised of counties that conform to the following standards:
- A total population of at least 100,000.
- A population that is at least 60 percent urban.
- Less than 50 percent of the resident workers commute to jobs outside the county.

Newspaper Areas

Audit Bureau of Circulation (ABC)   An organization formed by media suppliers, advertisers, and advertising agencies to audit the circulation statements of its member newspapers and magazines.

City Zone   The area bounded by the corporate limits of a community.

Retail Trading Zone A geographic area around a central city.

Primary Market Area A geographic area defined by a newspaper in which the publisher believes the newspaper has its greatest strength.

The **Audit Bureau of Circulation (ABC)** verifies member newspapers' total circulation statements and reports circulation on various geographic bases that aid the media planner in assessing precisely where the newspaper is distributed. Three geographic units are generally reported:

- **City Zone** is the area bounded by the corporate limits of the community in which a newspaper is published. Additional contiguous areas are included in the City Zone if these areas have the same characteristics as the community itself.

- **Retail Trading Zone** is the area beyond the City Zone whose residents regularly shop in the City Zone.

- **Primary Market Area** is defined by the newspaper publisher and is that area in which the publisher believes the newspaper has its greatest strength on the basis of readership, editorial coverage of the communities, and advertising.

Based on ABC data, other research syndicators report circulation on a metro area and TV market basis.

Nielsen County Size Groups

County Size Designation of all U.S. counties into one of four categories as defined by A.C. Nielsen based on population density and labor force concentration. Commonly referred to as "A," "B," "C," and "D" counties.

Nielsen **County Size** Groups are composed of counties assigned to one of four designations by A.C. Nielsen, based on population density and labor force concentration.

The specific definition of each county size group is as follows:

A   All counties belonging to the 25 largest MSAs.

B   All counties not included under "A" that either have over 150,000 population or are in metropolitan areas of over 150,000 population.

C   All counties not included under "A" or "B" that either have over 40,000 population or are in metropolitan areas of over 40,000 population.

D   All remaining counties.

County size is used to investigate urban/rural patterns of sales and media delivery. Several syndicated sources show sales as well as media delivery (such as magazine circulation) on a county size basis. Quick assessments can be made about the concentrations in the biggest cities ("A"), big cities ("B"), smaller cities ("C") and rural areas ("D"). If sales of Product X skew to "A" counties and Magazine Y has its highest penetration in "C" and "D" counties, then Magazine Y is probably not a desirable medium.

County size investigations should be made as an adjunct to television market analysis or in lieu of TV market data when the latter are not available. For example, if you are estimating potential sales for TV markets for which there are few or no sales data available, you can assume that counties within the TV market will perform by size as do the national sales by county size.

Geodemographic Areas

Geodemographic areas are quite different from the other types of geographic areas we've discussed. The others are defined on the basis of "who can physically receive a broadcast signal" (TSA), or "what the social and socio-economic relationship is of people who live in and around a central city" (MSA), etc. Geodemography is based on much smaller geographic entities than any of the other definitions—using Census Block Groups, for example, of which there are over 250,000 in the United States, with the average Group containing approximately 350 households.

A mention of geodemographic areas is appropriate here because these areas are, indeed, defined pieces of geography for which media consumption patterns can be obtained—which could therefore lead to recommendations for selecting media types or media vehicles. The primary placement of our discussion on geodemographic areas remains, nevertheless, in Chapter 20, "Media Audience Definitions," inasmuch as the thrust of the definition is primarily on the "demography" portion of the word.

A Note of Caution

Although you can obtain a lot of information for most of the geographic areas we have discussed, not all information is available for all areas. Further, the various types of geographic areas may overlap or otherwise not fit together snugly. For example, a radio Total Survey Area may or may not be wholly contained within a TV market; a newspaper Primary Market Area may or may not jibe with a Metro Area; the counties within a DMA may or may not be the same as the counties within an ADI bearing the same market name.

Whenever you analyze geographic data you must appreciate the geographic boundaries of the designated area with which you are dealing. If you are mixing data from one media research source with another, you have to make sure both sources define the geography in the same way. If they do not, you should be keenly aware of the differences and determine if the differing definitions have any substantial effect on your analysis. For example, if the difference between two sources amounts to the inclusion or exclusion of one county, and this county represents a very small portion of population, there will be no substantial risk in using both sources. Conversely, if the difference between the two sources involves a city or county with a large portion of the population, mixing the data could lead to misinformation.

PART III
HOW TO CONSTRUCT A MEDIA PLAN

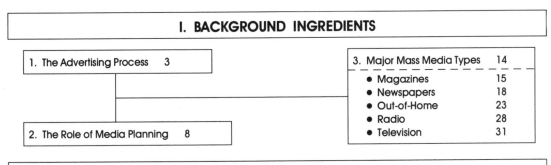
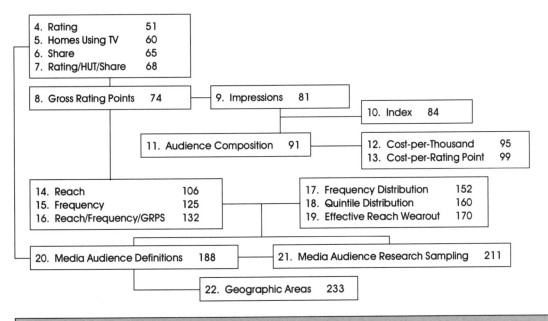

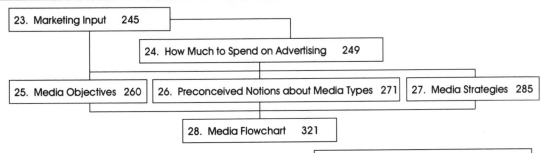

Chapter 23

Marketing Input

I n this chapter we discuss the need for the media planner to fully understand the marketing plan before writing a media plan, and to take from that marketing plan specific direction or information in the areas of:

- Achievement Goals
- Consumer Definitions
- Sales Data
- Competitive Activity
- Promotion Strategy
- Creative Strategy

Considerable study and knowledge are needed *before* you set out to write a media plan for a product or service. You need to dig deep and immerse yourself in the marketing plan, playing the role of both the marketer (the advertiser) and the consumer. You need to be proactive in defining the marketing goals you want to achieve, and reactive in terms of predicting how the consumer will be exposed to the advertising (and all related communication elements) as well as attempting to predict what the consumer stimulus (the advertising message) will elicit—i.e., what action the consumer might take as a result of being exposed to the advertising.

Whether or not a marketing plan, in the classic sense, exists, you must nevertheless hammer out all important ingredients of the plan so all efforts are appreciated, and responded to, by all concerned parties and disciplines: not only advertising, but manufacturing, distribution, sales, public relations, trade relations, promotion, etc. All disciplines must be dancing to the same tune: all communication efforts need to be orchestrated so the consumer hears a symphony, not a collection of different bands each playing its own music.

Six of the more important ingredients in the marketing plan which apply directly to advertising (and therefore to media planning) are discussed below.

Achievement Goals

Regardless of the product or service to be marketed, there is always some kind of goal to be achieved. If there is no goal, there is no need to advertise. Goals may be defined in terms of sales dollars at wholesale or retail, product unit or case volume, share-of-market, advertising awareness and usage levels, or any number of other designations. Having identified these goals, you're in a far better position for getting a handle on what you need to accomplish with the use of media. For example, if you are introducing a new product is a highly competitive arena, you probably will need to have high levels of media delivery to quickly capture consumers' attention. Conversely, a sustained level of advertising support, at somewhat lower levels of advertising intensity, might be more appropriate for an established product with relatively little competition. A goal of sustaining advertising awareness would point you in a different direction than a goal of increasing awareness. Building share-of-market suggests a different media plan than one that requires maintaining an existing share.

Consumer Definitions

In addition to the quantitative information that is available from a wide variety of syndicated market and media research sources, there is often proprietary information known by the advertiser. This could come from the advertiser's own research, or could be based simply on intuition and belief. This kind of information usually transcends what you can find in research books, and often segments consumers in terms other than those found in standard research. Having as complete a dossier on the consumer as possible will prove to be extraordinarily advantageous in designing the best media plan. It will also reinforce the fact that not all consumers conveniently fit into predefined demographic groups. This, in turn, will open your eyes to possibly unique ways to use media to reach these consumers.

Sales Data

For most products and services, sales data are a must. It is the rare brand that has a flat sales picture in all of the United States. There are always areas of high and low development where local factors or competitive forces play on the vitality of a brand. Knowing these pockets of strength or weakness will prove invaluable in guiding your media investments. Likewise, knowing seasonal sales patterns, by market, will also prove very worthwhile.

Competitive Activity

It is also the rare brand that has no competition. A brand might have the lion's share of a category, but there are always other competitive animals hovering to gain a share or increase their share. Knowing the competition, and knowing what they are doing in advertising, is a must. You need to analyze competitive activity to see which media competitors are using, how much they use, in which markets and to what level they are advertising, etc. Such knowledge could reveal opportunities for dominating media not used by the competition, or could suggest increased spending in media used extensively by competition.

Promotion Strategy

You need to be aware of any promotional efforts planned for the product or service, whether or not these are media driven, in order to coordinate media activity appropriately. For example, if a cents-off coupon is to be distributed via direct mail or a free-standing insert, you might want to ensure that consumer advertising is scheduled to heighten awareness of the product at the time the consumer receives the coupon. Certainly, if the cents-off coupon is distributed via consumer media, you need to know how many will be distributed, how often, what kind of redemption is planned, which areas of the country will receive the coupons, etc.

Creative Strategy

Not to minimize the importance of all the other marketing ingredients discussed above, but the creative strategy is one of the more important elements guiding the media plan. Media are the conduit for delivering the creative message. If the media you select and the manner in which you use them do not reflect the creative thrust or specific creative executions, your media plan is dead wrong. If the marketing plan does not contain a creative strategy (or creative positioning statements), it should be contained in your "media objectives."

Chapter 24

How Much to Spend on Advertising

One of the most difficult decisions an advertiser has to make is how much to spend on advertising. The major problem is that no one *knows* the optimal amount to spend. Everybody believes there is a threshold of spending below which advertising has little or no effect on consumers. Many also believe that there is a maximum amount, beyond which additional advertising again has little or no additional effect. But no one knows precisely what the threshold or maximum is. In this chapter we will lay out the thought process you should go through in trying to decide how much to spend on advertising. The process requires you address key issues, such as understanding what the role of advertising is for your brand or service. We will also examine five methods for deciding a media budget with specific discussion on the strengths and weaknesses of each of these methods.

Quite often advertisers rely on historical information to decide future advertising expenditure levels. Also common is the use of some ingrained formula based primarily on establishing a ratio of advertising spending to predicted sales volume—commonly known as an advertising/sales ratio. Although these mathematical devices can help you decide how much to spend, neither is necessarily foolproof or exact. There are innumerable outside factors that influence the appropriation of advertising funds—from the profit margin of the brand, to the financial stability of the corporation, to competitive pressures and changes in the marketplace, to the cost of media and advertising production.

Determining the appropriate amount to spend is especially challenging when your goal is relatively intangible—that is, when there is no sales measurement against which you can assess an advertising expenditure. It's relatively easy, for example, to determine that you will spend 5 percent of your sales revenue for product X because that is what you always spent, and sales are doing just fine. It's quite another matter, however, to determine how much to spend if the task of your advertising is to create a positive image for a corporation among its suppliers, stockholders, and employees. The "softer" the measurement of what advertising is supposed to accomplish, the more difficult the task of deciding how much to spend.

Some argue that the results of direct response advertising can be used to pinpoint optimal spending. In large part, this is true. Direct response *measures* responses. Almost immediately after the advertising effort is executed, an advertiser can know the precise results and assess the cost against those results—such as how many people bought the advertised product and how much it cost to get them to buy. But direct response advertising requires trial and error. Unless repeated advertising efforts are conducted (using alternative creative executions or directing advertising to different geographic or demographic groups), the advertiser never knows if a lower or higher expenditure could have resulted in the same sales, more sales, or a lower cost per product sold. Additionally, direct response operates within the ever-changing environment of competitive marketplace, etc., thereby prohibiting us from using this form of advertising to conclusively establish an optimal level of advertising investment.

Although no one knows how much to spend, an expenditure level must nevertheless be decided before any advertising can take place. There is no such thing as an open-ended budget. Getting at this answer usually requires detailed analyses of the product, its history, the category of products in which it competes, the cost and audience delivery of various media types, etc. Getting at this answer also requires you to make various *strategic* decisions. The strategy you use should reflect the marketing and selling objectives of the brand or company. To have ambitious marketing goals supported by a modest advertising budget is an irreconcilable situation. Conversely, it makes no financial sense to have an ambitious budget if the marketing/selling goals are modest.

The role of advertising must therefore be clearly defined, and its task must be decided before determining how much should be spent. Until the advertising task has been determined, you cannot apply *any* analytical discipline or technique to calculate how much money is required. For example, is the role you have set for advertising to:

- Increase market share?

- Reverse a declining sales trend?

- Introduce a new product?

- Heighten the level of product awareness?

- Stimulate repeat usage of a product?

- Promote a positive image of a company?

- Persuade a constituency to take an action?

Importantly, you also need to decide if advertising *can* accomplish a specific goal.

Depending on the objective to be achieved, the condition of the brand (or service) to be advertised, and the marketing environment as a whole, a decision could be made not to advertise. Advertising cannot be a panacea for all deficiencies. For example, if a product distribution deficiency exists whereby the product cannot reach the consumer or is available in inadequate quantities, any dollar spent in advertising will be wasted. If the product itself is inadequate and cannot match the competition, advertising might promote first-time trials among consumers but probably will not convince consumers to purchase the product again.

After you decide the advertising's role, and before you set out to calculate how much should be spent, you need to consider a number of factors:

1. What market will you compete in?

The competitive environment must be selected to determine how much money you will need to accomplish your goals. For example, if you are advertising lemonade, you might decide to compete against all other lemonades, or all non-carbonated beverages, or all citrus beverages, or all refreshment beverages including soft drinks.

The broader the market you compete in, the larger the advertising budget required. If you decide to compete against all refreshment beverages, versus just lemonade advertisers, you will have to talk to more people because the competitive world is more diverse. Also, the amount of advertising money being spent in each of these categories varies dramatically. Therefore, a given advertising budget for your brand could represent either a major or minor portion of the total spent in the target category.

2. **What is your current market position?**
   When you have decided upon the market in which you will compete, you will know your competitors' and your brand's relative strength. You should bear in mind the following tenets as expressed in various market/advertising research findings:
   - The market leader can usually retain business by spending relatively less than the second, third, or fourth brand.
   - A minor brand must spend proportionately more to stay in business.
   - To increase your competitive position, be prepared to spend proportionately more than the brands you want to overtake.

3. **Who is the target consumer?**
   Inherent in the competitive decision is the choice of demographic target. If you are going to compete only against other lemonades, for example, you might select an adult target, whereas if you choose to compete against all refreshment beverages, you may target adults, teens, and children.
   The greater the number of people in your target audience definition, the more money you will have to spend to reach these people with advertising. Further, the more demographically different these people are, the greater the number of different media vehicles you will have to select to address each of these groups—and the greater the probable cost of production for varying creative executions. For example:
   - Advertising just to children requires fewer funds than advertising directed to both children and their parents.
   - Reaching only women can be done more efficiently than reaching all adults.

4. **Where will you advertise?**
   Invariably, all brands have pockets of strength and weakness across the country. Spending decisions must take these variations into consideration. The same rate of spending in every city

or region will not necessarily produce the same results because of the competitive environment variations from city to city and other environment and media cost factors.

It is not sufficient simply to know the amount of sales in each city or region. You must determine the share of market in each location and the reason that share exists. For example, poor sales in a particular area could be the result of distribution deficiencies, pricing policies, sales force weaknesses, or the strength of a specific local brand. Knowing the reasons will help you judge the contribution that might, or might not, be made by advertising. This in turn can guide you in spending policies.

Systems to Determine Spending

Once these factors are considered, and a decision is made to advertise, there are a number of different techniques that can be used to determine how much to spend and how to allocate those dollars. Five methods are discussed here.

Advertising/Sales Ratio

This is the most commonly used method for determining advertising budgets. Advertising expenditures are considered an integral part of the marketing budget of a product and funds are set aside as a *cost of doing business.*

The mechanics of the A/S method require that you first decide the sales against which you will apply the A/S ratio. This alone could be a tricky process inasmuch as it requires you to predict future sales. The calculation, nevertheless, is simple multiplication:

Product A sales:	$10,000,000
A/S ratio:	× _____ 10%
	= $1,000,000

You may choose to adjust the A/S ratio geographically. You may opt, for example, to spend at a higher A/S ratio in certain markets that appear to you as having greater opportunity for sales growth, or at a lower A/S ratio in mature markets where you are already the brand leader with little or no competitive threat.

There is no standard A/S ratio that applies to all products and services. The ratio will vary widely among corporations, and often among different products within the same corporation. In part, the percentage is a function of the cost of goods and the pricing policy within the corporation and/or within the industry. For example, a drug item, which might cost ten cents to manufacture and distribute and sells for one dollar, has a considerable margin available for advertising, promotion, and profit. A car, which might cost $10,000 to manufacture and distribute and sells for $15,000, has a lower margin available for advertising, etc. This difference in margin generally results in a difference in the A/S ratio. Table 24.1 shows hypothetical margins and A/S ratios for these two distinctly different products. Also notable in this comparison is how the advertising budget compares to the dollars of margin. The drug item, with a higher A/S ratio, has a lower percentage of advertising dollars relative to margin dollars.

TABLE 24.1: A/S Ratio Applications

	Drug Item	Car
Sales dollars per unit:	$1.00	$15,000.00
Cost to manufacture and distribute:	$ .10	$10,000.00
Margin:		
Dollars:	$ .90	$ 5,000.00
Percent of Sales:	90%	33%
A/S Ratio Defined by the Advertiser:	10%	5%
Advertising Budget/Unit:	$ .10	$ 750.00
Advertising Budget as a Percent of		
Margin Dollars:	11%	15%

While the appropriation for advertising is part of the marketing budget, it is nevertheless the most vulnerable cost element. Manufacturing and distribution costs, as well as profit margins, are usually fixed. The only flexible marketing cost is the amount of money to be spent in advertising. Therefore, while budgets could be derived using the advertising/sales ratio method, they are quite often subject to revision.

There are strengths and weaknesses in the A/S approach.

Strengths:
- It is self-correcting in regard to sales performance and maintains a consistent profit margin for the brand.

- The budget allocation is relatively easy to manage.

- The relationship is easily understood and generally suits the interests of both the financial and the marketing groups.

- An implicit incentive system operates: increased sales generate additional funds to support an aggressive advertising program, while poor sales penalize the brand.

Weaknesses:
- The requirements for an advertising program do not always vary directly with sales, particularly when brand sales are declining and increased advertising may not be the cure.

- Considerable historical information is required to determine the correct A/S ratio.

- A/S ratios should vary by area, which requires exhaustive analysis.

- The basic assumption—that there is a direct linear relationship between advertising and sales—might not be true.

Share of Advertising

In this system, the advertising budget is chosen as a *share of total category "pressure."* This pressure can be defined as category *spending* or as the amount of *media delivery* (with the latter sometimes referred to as "share of noise"). As with the A/S method, it is necessary to decide what the right share is. And here again there is no definitive research or magical model to point you in one direction or another. Some of the research that does exist indicates:

- For new products, the share of advertising should be at least double the brand's share objectives during the first year.

- For mature products, share of advertising should be commensurate with share of market.

Mechanically, this system is identical to the A/S ratio: it simply requires multiplication. What is not simple is establishing the precise base. Although there is syndicated media research which compiles competitive advertising expenditure data, the findings are not necessarily totally accurate (i.e., a competitor could have actually spent less or more than reported). If your base is predicated on media audience delivery (e.g., impressions or GRPs) you will find the same deficiencies in syndicated research material.

The strengths and weaknesses of the "share" system can be summarized as follows:

Strengths:

• It positions your advertising budget competitively.

• You can react to competitive changes in advertising, such as new brands entering the market.

• It places expectations for the advertising effort in a realistic perspective. For example, if you spend half as much as your nearest competitor, you cannot expect to exceed that competitor's share of market.

Weaknesses:

• The information you gather might not be accurate, because competitive advertising expenditure data are not easily obtained.

• The basic assumption—that there is a direct relationship between share of advertising and share of market—might not be true.

• Unless the right competitive market is defined, the wrong budget will be calculated.

• Share of *advertising* might be too narrow a view when one considers the influences of point-of-sale material, promotions, etc.

• Competitors could be dictating your budget, leading you into spending at the wrong rate.

Mathematical Models

Different formulas have been developed, mostly proprietary, which are used by some advertisers to define the advertising budget. Some of these formulas, or models, calculate the interrelationships between advertising, share of market, and profits, or various other combinations of marketing ingredients. Others are based on advertising awareness levels—primarily supposing that there is a one-to-one relationship between advertising awareness and sales.

If you have such a formula, and its results have proven to be correct, you are one of the fortunate few.

Available Funds

In the view of some critics this system is not a system at all. This method of determining an advertising budget is based solely on "what's left over" after you subtract total manufacturing expenses and profit goals from predicted revenue. There are a host of non-advertising expenditures that could be more important to the marketing effort than advertising is. A company's sales force, for example, might require the majority of available marketing funds. For another company, promotions or trade shows might be mandatory. Still another company might need to place disproportionate amounts of money in public relations. Therefore, advertising can be afforded only if there is enough money left over.

Clearly, there are no strengths to the "available funds" system. There are, however, several dangers:

- The leftover money might be too little to do a complete, effective job. It might be like buying a cruise ticket halfway to Hawaii and having to get off the ship in the middle of the Pacific.

- The affordable advertising effort could be viewed by customers, suppliers, and employees as insufficient relative to their exposure to competitive efforts.

- If yours is the only product or service in the category conducting any meaningful advertising, it could trigger competitors to follow suit.

Task Method

This method requires you to establish actionable marketing or media objectives, create an advertising plan to deliver the necessary creative and media to the target audiences, and *then* cost-out the plan to see how much you *need* to spend to fulfill the objectives.

There are any number of tasks (objectives) you can set. For example:

- At minimum, reach at least 50 percent of the target audience three or more times during each four-week flight.

- Provide continuous advertising at X level throughout the year.

- Increase advertising awareness from X to Y.

- Spend at least twice the rate of the nearest competitor.

As will be discussed, media objectives require extensive investigation and thought. However, once specific objectives are set forth, you can use simple mathematical procedures to determine the cost of purchasing the required media to accomplish the objectives.

The strength and the weakness of this system are interrelated. If you *know* precisely what advertising levels are required to accomplish a task, the system is very powerful. But if you do not know (and this is usually the case), this approach is highly subjective and therefore questionable, and very risky. Wantonly spending dollars to achieve marketing/media objectives undermines any advertiser's fiduciary responsibility to achieve profits.

Lastly, it is this writer's experience that the Task Method seldom sees the light of day in the real world. In wanting to achieve certain objectives, marketers' hearts and minds are in the right place, but the monetary answer that usually results from the Task Method generally exceeds expectations and affordability.

Additional Food for Thought

As admirable as it is to decide how much to spend on advertising by using one or another analytical method (as opposed to guessing) phenomena about which we know little or nothing at all could still cause our answers to be incorrect.

For example, rarely does one know the precise contribution advertising makes to share of market, or to a brand's profits. It is reasonable to assume that there is a point beyond which additional media investment will not result in greater share of market or increased sales—because there is always a segment of consumers who will not use your brand. Spending more therefore results in profit loss. But what is that share limit? How much must be spent to reach that limit? How long will it take to realize the limit?

Evidence suggests that striving to achieve maximum share of market seldom results in maximum profits. There is never a one-to-one correlation of increased spending to an increased share of market. The law of diminishing returns prevents this. So does the reality that it takes more effort to convince a user of a competitive product to switch to your brand than it does to keep your current user. Therefore, each additional share point commands a disproportionately higher advertising investment. Table 24.2 demonstrates a hypothetical scenario in which an advertising investment of $1 million is needed to achieve a 20 percent share of market. To achieve higher share levels requires a disproportionately larger investment. For example, to go from a 20 to a 21 percent share (a five percent relative increase) requires a 15 percent increase in advertising costs. Advertising expenditures as a percent of sales will, therefore, steadily increase—conceivably to the point of lost profits.

TABLE 24.2: Hypothetical Correlation of Advertising and Share of Market

Share		Advertising Cost to Achieve This Share	
Percent	Index	Cost	Index
20	100	$1,000,000	100
21	105	1,150,000	115
22	110	1,350,000	135
23	115	1,600,000	160
24	120	1,900,000	190
25	125	2,250,000	225

This entire phenomenon is exacerbated with new products. With no specific history, the question of how much to spend on advertising comes down to a guessing game: What is the optimal A/S ratio? Which task should be accomplished at what cost? If expenditures are too low to achieve the unknown threshold, the product is doomed to failure. If expenditures are too high, profitability suffers.

A dollar spent in advertising is a dollar that cannot be invested elsewhere. Advertising must compete with other income-producing alternatives—stocks, bonds, real estate, etc. The level of the advertising budget needs to be viewed as an investment, with the marketer seeking a proper return on that investment.

Chapter 25

Media Objectives

M edia objectives define the *goals* you want to achieve through the use of advertising media. These goals must be explicitly stated so you have a clear and precise idea of exactly what you expect to achieve. The goals cannot be wishy-washy. They must guide you in a specific direction and be action-oriented. You won't know how to get someplace if you don't know where you are going.

In this chapter we discuss a discipline for writing media objectives—one which requires answering various questions. We examine the virtues of advertising in geographic markets where a brand has a strong franchise versus a relatively weak franchise. We also discuss how the need for consumer coupons, or the desire for in-market media testing, can affect the writing of media objectives.

Media objectives must position the media plan relative to the market and to the marketing plan. An objective that states:

"Introduce product X in order to achieve high levels of awareness"

does not provide direction. It merely says: Advertise. To guide you in assessing alternatives, you need a more realistic and actionable objective such as:

"Reach at least 80 percent of the potential market within the first month of advertising, ensuring that the average consumer will be exposed to a minimum of four advertising messages."

Or:

> "Direct advertising to current and potential purchasers of product X by weighing current purchaser characteristics 60 percent and potential purchaser characteristics 40 percent."

The best approach to formulating media objectives is to answer basic questions that encompass the general areas of audience, geography, scheduling requirements, copy needs, reach and frequency, and testing. These questions are: Who? Where? When? How? How much? and What else?

Who?

- Whom does the brand want to reach?
- What is the relative importance of each group?

A thorough objective recognizes the importance, or lack of importance, of each demographic cell. You should analyze audiences on the basis of age, sex, income, education, race, employment status, family size, marital status, possessions, lifestyle characteristics, and any other traits for which data are available.

Quite often you'll discover that there are one or two *key* target audiences which appear to account for most of the sales of a product, or most of the opportunity for sales growth. The temptation is to home in on these groups in all media analysis and consideration, completely disregarding all other groups. By limiting analysis in this manner, you've made the conscious decision that all other groups have zero value—that the media reaching these non-defined groups are providing unwanted or wasted delivery.

No matter what the product or service, you will generally find that nearly all groups, regardless of their demographic description, consume a product to one degree or another. A group is key—of primary importance—to the extent that it accounts for a disproportionately greater level of consumption than average. But other groups, with disproportionately lower levels of consumption, must be viewed as having secondary or tertiary importance, not complete unimportance.

It behooves you to place a "value" on all consumer groups. The value should be expressed as a quantitative "weight"—such as a percentage of the whole, or a ratio to the average. For example, you might define women 18–34 as your key target audience because they account for 30 percent of all product usage. You could decide that 30 percent of all impressions you will generate in the media plan should be directed to this group. Or you can decide that this group should receive three times as many impressions as the average person (a 3:1 ratio). By placing this numerical weight on the target group you have made a decision to specifically address this group, and by definition, to provide some level of advertising to all other groups.

For example, having data as shown below, you could properly write the following objective:

Direct media to demographic groups in accordance with current consumption patterns:

	Percent of Total Consumption
Women 18–34	30%
Women 35–49	20
Women 50+	10
Men 18–34	20
Men 35–49	15
Men 50+	5
Total	100%

Had you written an objective that cited only women 18–34 (because they account for the majority of consumption), you would have dismissed people who account for the remaining 70 percent of consumption.

Where?

- Where should the brand concentrate its advertising efforts?
- Are there markets that have minimal sales? How should these markets be valued?
- Are brand sales changing disproportionately in any market?
- Are there markets with a disproportionately high BDI?
- Are there markets with a low BDI and a high CDI that should receive special recognition?
- Is national advertising mandatory?

In the consumer's eyes, all advertising is local. Seldom does a consumer know if a TV commercial is broadcast nationally or locally, or if an ad in a magazine is running only in one geographic area or in many. The geographic scope of any advertising has nothing to do with *one* consumer in *one* market. You therefore need to think locally and address geographic considerations market by market—and the smaller the geographic universe, the better. If data are available, you should target advertising in the following priority order:

- Census tract

- Neighborhood

- ZIP code area

- County

- Metropolitan area

- TV market

- State

- Region

- County size

At this juncture, it does not matter if you can analyze or select media based on the chosen geographic area. Media selection *follows* the marketing analysis and establishment of media objectives—it should not force the objectives. For example, if you conducted a marketing analysis based on TV markets, you might decide (as shown in Table 25.1) that markets 1 and 2 should receive equal support—they have the same sales level and the same BDI. A

TABLE 25.1:   Marketing Analysis

	% U.S. Population	% U.S. Sales	BDI
TV MARKET #1	10%	10%	100
Metro Area A	6	9	150
Metro Area B	4	1	25
TV MARKET #2	10	10	100
Metro Area C	7	7	100
Metro Area D	3	3	100

more in-depth marketing analysis reveals that metro area A is far and away the most important of all the areas shown. Knowing this and writing a media objective that addresses this *could* lead you to select alternative media to focus on this area.

Sales, brand development, and the like are obviously important in this analysis. Nevertheless, you should also analyze other factors that might prove important, such as income, housing, and mobility. Often, you can use related data as a predictor of product sales or sales growth potential. For example, automobile mileage can be used to predict tire sales; temperature can be used to forecast sales of hot weather soft drinks.

Once you amass all of these geographic data, you then need to decide on one of two basic philosophies for how best to allocate your advertising budget or advertising delivery (impressions, GRPs, etc.)

Advertise Where the Business Is

This is basically a defensive posture. It protects the existing franchise and simultaneously seeks to develop more business on the assumption that increases in brand sales can be achieved most efficiently where the brand is currently strong.

The underlying belief of this allocation philosophy is that it is easier to build on an existing base where product distribution has been established and where there is apparent consumer awareness and acceptance of your product. Further, current non-users in these areas, who ostensibly have similar demographic characteristics, have a greater propensity to become users than non-users in areas where your product sales are low.

Advertise Where the Business Is Not

This philosophy take an offensive posture. It is based on the belief that changing consumer demands, as well as changes in product formulation for your brand or the competitive brands, results in brand-switching. Advertising in areas of low consumption would therefore announce your presence and keep your brand in consumers' minds should they decide to switch brands. To implement this philosophy successfully, you must first ensure that other marketing factors are in place: You must have the right product for the consumers, competitive pricing, widespread distribution, sufficient inventory position to restock for repurchase after initial trial, and good display. Advertising alone will not produce sales, nor will it remedy marketing deficiencies.

You can use either philosophy, or some combination of both, depending on the marketing strategy. In any case, the objective at this stage of the analysis is to assign a "target percentage" to each market in the United States. The target represents the *share* that market should receive of the total advertising effort. The target percentage for all markets combined must equal 100 percent.

When?

- To what degree should the brand recognize seasonal sales patterns?

- Are there any discernible patterns?

- How important is the introductory versus the sustaining period?

- Should scheduling address any planned changes in the creative execution, or additions to the pool of commercials/ advertisements?

- Should competitive efforts be countered?

- Is there need to support planned promotions?

- Are certain periods more important than others—for instance, national or local holidays?

- What is the minimum number of weeks, through the year, that advertising must run?

You need to formulate precise direction for each of these concerns, and conceivably for other timing aspects important to the brand. When possible or appropriate, use the most specific calendar units: time of day, day of week, week of month, month of year. As with all objectives, strive to quantify your decision. Avoid words like "most," "emphasis," "majority," and so forth. None of these is precise. "Emphasis," for example, could mean a five percent increase for a certain period versus the average period, or 10 percent, 20 percent, or more.

Examples of precise objectives are these:

- Spend advertising dollars in accordance with the percentage of sales each month.

- Allocate no more than 60 percent of advertising expenditures during the introductory 13-week period, ensuring sufficient funds to cover the remainder of the year.

- Increase advertising activity by 50 percent during each of the three planned promotion periods. Precede the promotion by one week and run concurrently during the remaining four weeks of the promotion.

- Concentrate all advertising from Wednesday to Saturday in order to reach high potential product X buyers immediately prior to the highest usage day, Sunday.

How?

- What are the basic requirements for color, audio, visual?

- How does the complexity of the message affect copy length? What is the brand's creative experience?

- How many different creative executions will be employed?

- Are there different creative executions for different target audiences?

- Do some creative executions require more advertising pressure than others?

Copy is obviously of extreme importance to any viable advertising effort. Regardless of the impact of the media plan, if it does not properly reflect the copy strategy, the entire campaign suffers. The media planner should not, however, play second fiddle to the copywriter. It is important for both to work together to create the best copy in the best medium, and this should happen in the early stages of planning. The copywriter should be made aware of the media ramifications of certain decisions—just as the media planner should have a complete understanding of the copy needs.

How Much?

This has to do with "communication goals," such as:

- What reach level is needed?

- How much frequency is required?

- What level of effective reach (frequency) is optimum?

- Should reach/frequency vary by geographic area?

- Are delivery objectives different for different target groups (primary, secondary, etc.)?

- Should reach/frequency be addressed for each creative execution, or for all executions combined?

- Should reach/frequency goals vary by advertising message length (e.g. 15-second versus 30-second spots, 1/2 page versus full page ads)?

The number of people you need to reach with advertising, and how often you need to reach them, has the most demonstrable effect on a media plan. If it is possible to have a precise objective that clearly establishes how many people need to be reached and how often, this will significantly influence your choices of which media forms to consider, how much of each medium can be used, the number of weeks that advertising is affordable, or what budget is necessary to achieve this objective.

There is a temptation to write this objective *after* a plan is constructed and the delivery of that plan is determined. While this guarantees the objective will be achieved, it is a pointless exercise. If a predetermined level of advertising intensity is desirable or needed based on past performance, competitive pressure, or judgment, you should state that level in the objectives—*prior* to devising the actual media plan. For example, if you decided to diet to lose weight, it would be silly to first lose a few pounds and then announce that was your goal. Far better to state your goal ("I want to lose ten pounds") and strive to achieve that goal. Having a media goal for reach/frequency will present a challenge and a stimulus for you to overcome any obstacles to achieve the goal. It will force you to be a more creative media thinker.

What Else?

Objectives can be written for anything you wish to accomplish through the use of media. Two examples are discussed here.

Coupons

- Will the media plan require the support of a consumer promotion in the form of a media-distributed coupon?

- How many coupons will be distributed?

- In what geographic areas will the distribution be made? Are there variations by area?

A number of advertising plans contain a promotional effort that can be either trade- or consumer-oriented. Trade promotions could take many forms, such as in-store displays, cost allowances (discounts) for purchasing certain quantities of product or purchasing at certain times of the year, sales contests, etc. These kinds of trade promotions do not generally require a consumer media effort.

A promotion directed to the consumer does require media support. Although this effort is considered *promotion* rather than *advertising*, the two must work in concert. If the marketing objective requires distribution of a cents-off coupon in order to counter competitive efforts or promote consumer trial, then this must be translated into an actionable media objective so the media planner can schedule appropriate media to deliver these coupons into the consumers' hands.

Testing

- Should a media or copy test be conducted?

- Should alternative advertising budgets be tested?

- What information can be garnered with a test?

Throughout our discussion on media dynamics you've noted that there are many unanswered questions: How does advertising work? What is the optimal level of reach/frequency? When does a commercial wear out? . . . and so forth. Although getting at these answers might be difficult or currently impossible for the *average* situation, a media test for a specific product or service *could* provide valuable information that could guide future media efforts. When you consider that many media tests can be implemented for relatively little cost, the obvious conclusion is that testing should be part of most media plans. Regardless of the media plan recommended, there is always room to conduct a test. For example, you could experiment with:

- An unused medium—magazines if you are using TV, or radio if you are using magazines.

- Media mix—magazines and TV versus either alone, or radio plus newspapers.

- Copy length—ten-second commercials if the plan calls for 30-second spots, or half pages instead of full pages.

- Scheduling—flighting advertising with hiatus periods as opposed to continuous advertising, or concentrating in one television daypart rather than dispersing announcements through two or more dayparts.

Test Market   A market (or markets) chosen for the purpose of conducting a media test.

Conducting a test requires you to carve out representative areas of the United States. The **test market** areas should not only be a microcosm of total U.S. demography, but should also be representative of any other marketing variable that affects sales, such as product brand development vis-a-vis the competition, distribution, etc. If no one area represents this "average" microcosm, two or more areas could be chosen that together approximate the average. The purpose of selecting a microcosm is to obtain testing results which are projectable to the entire United States (or to the entire geographic area in which a product is sold). Testing in only high-development areas, for example, would yield results that are projectable only to other high development markets, not necessarily to low development markets—which have other marketing forces affecting their relative sales position.

You should give any test a chance to work. There is no magic timetable for a test that will tell you when you can draw valid conclusions. But it is fair to assume that a media or copy or spending test will take weeks, months, or perhaps a year before its thrust is felt at the consumer level.

Finally, you also need to ensure that appropriate media are available in the chosen test markets. It's senseless, for example, to formulate a test of national magazines and find none which offer local or test market editions in your chosen test markets, or to devise a test of cable TV only to find that penetration levels in the test markets are at below-average levels.

Priorities

In some cases, not all objectives can be realistically met. For example, there may be an objective to reach at least 80 percent of a target group, and a second objective which requires advertising continuously throughout the sales season. Media availability and cost could prohibit you from accomplishing both of these objectives. It is therefore wise to give priorities to the objectives in order to have a clear direction in the decision-making process. If reach is given a greater priority than continuity of advertising, you can then elect to provide the needed levels of reach for as long a period as is affordable without necessarily advertising throughout the sales season.

Chapter 26

Preconceived Notions about Media Types

I n this chapter we suggest that media planners have preconceived notions about how various media perform their task of delivering audiences and, therefore, whether a medium should be used to accomplish a specific media objective. These preconceived notions are usually based on the media planner's individual experience of having used (purchased) the medium, but can also be based on the simple understanding of what a particular medium can or cannot offer. We examine some of the more popularly believed notions and display them, by medium, as either positive or negative attributes.

A popularly held scientific belief is that the left hemisphere of a person's brain primarily handles verbal and mathematical tasks, and the right hemisphere primarily handles spacial and musical skills. Left brain, right brain; science and art. The seasoned media planner approaches the creation of a media plan using both hemispheres. The left brain deals with all the numbers at hand by manipulating data found in current media research reports, determining audience delivery, calculating cost efficiency, etc. The right brain functions at the same time by accessing the accumulated knowledge of media dynamics—based on past involvement with the media, interpretations of ancillary research, personal consumption of the media, thoughts and opinions of fellow workers, etc. Consciously or unconsciously, the planner deals with all this input not only during the planning process, but even before putting pen to paper.

It is rare for a planner to approach a media plan with questions like: "Should I use newspapers or TV?" or "Should I plan for a month-long effort in billboards or select weekly magazines?" Commonly, the planner has preconceived notions about media types and specific media vehicles which have taken shape over time. These notions are believed to be "truths" about each medium —whether or not they actually are true. The notions do change over time as the planner absorbs more knowledge of the media, but the change is a slow evolution. With the exception of entirely new media forms, media do not revolutionize themselves and take on completely new images in the planner's mind. Before the planning process begins, the planner brings these notions to the party and is guided by these personal judgments of how each medium works, how it can accomplish the advertising objectives, and how it might be used in the media plan.

Depending on the advertising objectives for a particular product, you'll find that you will mentally preselect media to be analyzed to fulfill those objectives. You will have a sense of how different media will contribute either positively or negatively to the accomplishment of communication goals. Generally, no one medium can accomplish all the objectives of a media plan. More often than not, several media offer benefits that you should take advantage of if the advertising budget and creative platform permit. Importantly, no one medium is perfect. All have positive and negative attributes. Additionally, what might be a positive attribute in one media plan for product A can conceivably be a negative attribute for product B. Additionally, not all media experts necessarily agree on the positive and negative attributes of each medium—they all have their own opinions based on their personal past experiences.

Following are basic notions about the most commonly used mass media forms—some inarguable, some postulates, but all generally accepted as positive or negative attributes in the average situation. Although the attributes apply to the media category, they may or may not necessarily apply to a specific vehicle within that category. Further, many of the attributes (positive or negative) apply to more than one of the media. Lastly, not all vehicles are contained within these general category descriptors. For purposes of clarity, the categories presented contain these media types:

- Direct Mail: The advertising material a consumer receives in the mail (either directed by name or addressed to "resident") which requests the consumer to take an action, such as calling an 800 number, redeeming a coupon, or mailing back something to the advertiser.

- Magazines:

The average monthly, weekly, quarterly, or annual consumer magazine distributed via reader subscription, on newsstands, or both. Not included, for example, are advertiser-produced magazines or (for the most part) trade magazines.

- Newspapers:

The typical national or metropolitan newspaper issued daily or weekly and/or Sunday. Not included, for example, are Pennysaver-type periodicals.

- Outdoor:

Posters (30-sheet, 8-sheet, etc.) and painted bulletins. Not contained are the many out-of-home vehicles which may perform similarly, but offer their own particular attributes (e.g., kiosks, taxicab tops, commuter rail posters).

- Radio:

Programs produced by broadcast media suppliers which can be purchased either nationally or locally. Not contained are advertiser produced and placed programs (e.g. **infomercials**).

Informercial (Infomercial) A long-form broadcast commercial which provides much more information than can be supplied in a typical, say, 30- or 60-second commercial. Also called *Advertorial*.

- Sunday Magazine Supplements:

Magazines produced by a media supplier and distributed (generally) on Sunday as part of a metropolitan newspaper. The periodical is produced either by a central media supplier who syndicates the product, or by the metropolitan newspaper itself. Not contained are advertiser-produced magazines which can be carried as an FSI (free standing insert) in the newspaper.

- Television:

Programs produced by either broadcast or cable media suppliers, which can be purchased either nationally or locally. Not contained are advertiser-produced and placed programs (e.g., home shopping, half-hour or hour advertiser infomercial).

Direct Mail

Positive Attributes

- Allows extraordinary creative flexibility limited only by postal regulations for size and content (note: if delivered by other methods, there are conceivably no limitations).

- Offers unlimited geographic targeting (from total national to one individual person) not available in any other media form.

- Delivers precise demographic and psychographic groups, with an absolute minimum of waste to non-targeted consumers, via innumerable database and list sources.

- Provides an automatic lead source for people who have responded to the advertiser, which can be productively used for future direct mailings.

- Allows relatively precise timing of delivery of the advertising message, not dependent on normal media consumption habits or mass media delivery timing.

- Gives the advertiser total control over the production quality of the advertising message the consumer will see, unhampered by extraneous forces (e.g., poor television reception).

- Offers total control over the breadth and scope of advertising delivery (e.g., reach and frequency).

- Offers permanence of the advertising message—for repeat exposure during a second reading, for later reference, for exposure to others to whom the recipient might give it, and for response at a later time.

- Can be directed to consumers at their homes or at their places of business.

- Quickly indicates if an advertising message is producing sales.

- Can be constantly changed and tested to determine which specific creative elements produce the highest response.

Negative Attributes
- Is usually cost-inefficient vis-a-vis other mass media forms.

- Generally requires a proportionately high out-of-pocket cost for production and postage.

- If perceived as "junk mail," will not be opened by the consumer.

Magazines

Positive Attributes
- Offer a wide array of editorial formats and different editorial focuses to reach readers while they have a specific state of mind, which can complement a specific advertising message.

- Have high-fidelity color produced on quality paper, allowing for effective product presentation.

- Are capable of reaching specific demographic groups with relatively minimal waste to groups outside the target audience.

- Offer the opportunity for long copy exposition via full-page or multiple-page ads.

- Can bind-in preprinted material supplied by the advertiser.

- Allow distribution of reader-response materials: coupons, sweepstake/contest entry forms, surveys, etc.

- Offer permanence of the advertising message—repeat exposure during a second reading of the magazine, for clipping/saving/reference, and for exposure to others who might read the same copy.

- Are capable of reaching large numbers of people, either as a single entity or when purchased in combination with other titles.

- Can accommodate unique creative executions: microencapsulation, holograms, micro chips, die-cut pop-ups, special inks, unusual space configurations, ink-jet personalizing for each reader of the publication, etc.

- Can be purchased nationally, regionally, or locally.

- Can be purchased to reach specific demographic segments within the total readership of the magazine.

- Allow distribution of the advertisement to possible nonreaders who might be part of an advertiser's secondary target audience (its employees, the trade, etc.) via overprints.

- Depending on the target audience, can be relatively cost-efficient compared to other media forms.

- Produce frequency of exposure—a reader may see the same advertisement more than once in an issue (repeat readership) or may read other magazines on the advertising schedule.

- Reach people who are lightly or not exposed to other media forms, and thereby extend reach and/or frequency.

- Can accommodate listings.

Negative Attributes

- Unlike broadcast media, do not deliver their entire audience instantly. A magazine accumulates its audience over time depending on when a reader decides to read it and when pass-along audiences are exposed to it.

- Charge relatively high cost premiums for purchases that are less than full-run.

- Do not (except via microchip insertion) offer sound.

- Currently do not offer motion, as TV does.

- Do not generally offer the total reach potential of other media forms.

Mechanical A camera-ready pasteup of artwork—includes type, photography, and artwork or line art, all on one piece of artboard. Also known as a *Keyline*.

- Require advertising materials (**mechanical**, keyline) well in advance of issue date—usually a longer lead time than some other media (with the occasional exception of those magazines offering a "fast close").

- Once in the printing process, cannot be cancelled, thus becoming relatively inflexible for acccommodating last-minute changes.

- Do not produce as high a frequency level as other media forms.

- Usually do not expose an advertising message to more than one person at a given moment.

Newspapers

Positive Attributes
- Immediately deliver their reading audience, generally 100 percent within one day.

- Offer wide array of editorial environments (depending on scope of an individual publication) via different sections (international, national, or local news; food; entertainment; etc.) which can complement a specific advertising message.

- Offer the opportunity for long copy exposition via full-page or multiple-page ads.

- Can accommodate preprinted material supplied by the advertiser (e.g., Freestanding Insert).

- Allow distribution of reader-response materials: coupons, sweepstakes/contest entry forms, surveys, etc.

- Offer permanence of the advertising message—for repeat exposure during a second reading of the newspaper, for clipping/saving/reference, and for exposure to others who might read the same copy.

- Are capable of reaching large numbers of people, either as a single entity or when purchased in combination with other newspapers.

- Can be purchased nationally, regionally, or locally.

- Can be purchased to reach specific demographic groups via distribution to predetermined ZIP Code areas.

- Allow distribution of the advertisement to possible nonreaders who might be part of an advertiser's secondary target audience (its employees, the trade, etc.) via overprints.

- Can be relatively cost efficient compared to other media forms, depending on the target audience and the size of the advertisement.

- Require a lower advertising production cost than some other media forms.

- Can produce frequency of exposure by a reader seeing the same advertisement more than once in a copy (repeat readership).

- Reach people who are lightly or not exposed to other media forms, thereby extending reach and/or frequency.

- Offer an audience which often uses the medium for shopping purposes (e.g., what's on sale where, which movie is playing at which theatre).

- Generate a relatively higher local market penetration than magazines.

- Can accommodate unique ad space configurations.

- Allow a relatively faster space and material close than magazines.

- Can accommodate dealer listings.

Negative Attributes
- Charge relatively high cost premiums for less than full-run purchases.

- Do not offer sound or motion in the advertising message.

- Do not offer the total reach potential of other media forms.

- Once in the printing process, cannot be cancelled, thus becoming relatively inflexible for accommodating last-minute changes.

- Do not produce as high a frequency level as other media forms.

- Are relatively cost-inefficient for large-space ads.

- Contain little or no separation between less-than-full-page advertisements, which results in clutter and could lead to reduced advertising readership.

- Are short-lived and do not offer substantial pass-along audiences.

- Generally do not offer high-fidelity color reproduction except in within-newspaper magazines.

- Do not deliver non-adult audiences to the extent other media do.

- Usually do not expose an advertising message to more than one person at a given moment.

Outdoor

Positive Attributes
- Provides for 24-hour exposure of the advertising message.

- Offers creative flexibility for size, shape, coloration, and three-dimensional display.

- Is the second most geographically selective medium (behind direct mail).

- Offers the opportunity for advertising exposure at or near the point of product purchase.

- Is considered the most cost-efficient of all major media forms.

- Has unlimited reach potential.

- Allows delivery to multiple household members simultaneously (e.g., while members are in a car).

- Can be used to direct people to specific locations while they are traveling—commonly called *directional boards*.

- Can produce high levels of frequency.

- Can allow movement to be displayed.

Negative Attributes
- Does not allow for effective presentation of extended advertising copy.

- Has a short duration of message delivery—usually six to eight seconds for motorists to see and read.

- Offers limited demographic flexibility.

- Requires a relatively high out-of-pocket cost for broad coverage.

- Is not available in all geographic areas.

Radio

Positive Attributes
- Offers a wide array of formats (program types) to reach listeners during a specific state of mind, which can complement a specific advertising message.

- Allows delivery to multiple household members simultaneously.

- Provides for relatively immediate delivery.

- Is advertiser driven and does not require the listener to seek the advertising—that is, it is intrusive.

- Can be purchased nationally, regionally, or locally.

- Is capable of producing one of the highest levels of reach of most generalized consumer segments (e.g., teens, men, women, adults 18–34, etc.).

- Can produce high frequency levels.

- Can deliver advertising messages at any time during any 24-hour period.

- Can reach people immediately prior to shopping—for instance, in their cars enroute to a supermarket.

- Offers a proportionately low cost per commercial announcement.

- Is one of the most cost-efficient of the major media forms.

- Can elicit the visual elements of a television commercial based on the phenomenon of *imagery transfer*.

- Allows the commercial message to produce images not physically executable in other media forms by using the listener's imagination.

- Can reach people who are lightly or not exposed to other media forms.

Negative Attributes

- Is often considered a background medium to which audiences are not always and continuously paying full attention.

- Generally requires relatively higher levels of frequency to overcome possible consumer non-attentiveness.

- Does not always allow listener to take physical action as a result of the advertising message (such as calling an 800 telephone number or writing down information), depending on the location of listening.

- Generally requires a high out-of-pocket cost to purchase multiple stations in order to accumulate high levels of reach.

- Does not offer any tangible visual elements.

- Does not offer any tangible motion elements.

Sunday Magazine Supplements

Positive Attributes

- Have high-fidelity color produced on quality paper, allowing for effective product presentation.

- Can bind-in preprinted material supplied by the advertiser or "float" the material within its pages.

- Offer the opportunity for long copy exposition via full-page or multiple-page ads.

- Allow distribution of reader-response materials: coupons, sweepstakes/contest entry forms, surveys, etc.

- Offer permanence of the advertising message—for repeat exposure during a second reading of the magazine, for clipping/saving/reference, and for exposure to others who might read the same copy.

- Are capable of reaching large numbers of people.

- Can accommodate unique creative executions similar to those of magazines and newspapers.

- Allow distribution of the advertisement to possible nonreaders who might be part of an advertiser's secondary target audience (its employees, the trade, etc.) via overprints.

- Can be relatively cost-efficient, depending on the target audience.

- Usually require a lower advertising production cost than some other media forms.

- Produce frequency of exposure —by a reader seeing the same advertisement more than once in an issue (repeat readership).

- Reach people who are lightly or not exposed to other media forms, and thereby extend reach and/or frequency.

- Immediately deliver nearly their entire audience in one day.

- Can be purchased nationally, regionally, or locally.

- Generate a relatively higher local market penetration than typical consumer magazines.

- Can accommodate dealer listings.

Negative Attributes

- Are nonintrusive relative to broadcast, because the reader controls page turnings.

- Do not (except for microchip insertion) offer sound.

- Currently do not offer motion.

- Require advertising materials (mechanical, keyline) well in advance of issue date—usually a longer lead time than some other media.

- Once in the printing process, cannot be cancelled, thus becoming relatively inflexible for accommodating last minute changes.

- Do not produce as high a frequency level as other media forms.

- Require a proportionately high out-of-pocket cost for national coverage.

- Are relatively cost-inefficient for large-space ads.

- Are short lived and do not offer substantial pass-along audiences.

- Do not deliver non-adult audiences to the extent other media do.

- Usually do not expose an advertising message to more than one person in a household at a given moment.

Television

Positive Attributes
- Provides full-color advertising.

- Delivers advertising that can simultaneously be seen and heard and, inherently, allows movement to be displayed: sight, sound and motion.

- Allows delivery to multiple household members simultaneously.

- Provides for relatively immediate delivery.

- Is advertiser driven and does not require the viewer to seek the advertising—that is, it is intrusive.

- Can be purchased nationally, regionally, or locally.

- Can be purchased in fairly concentrated pieces of geography via individualized cable offerings.

- Provides a full array of program types to reach viewers during a specific state of mind, which can complement a specific advertising message.

- Is capable of producing one of the highest levels of reach of most generalized consumer segments (e.g., children, teens, men, women, adults 18–34).

- Can produce high frequency levels.

- Can deliver advertising messages at any time during any 24-hour period.

- Can be negotiated for product category exclusivity.

- Is usually one of the most cost-efficient media forms for most generalized consumer segments.

- Can reach people who are lightly or not exposed to other media forms.

Negative Attributes

- Is considered one of the more "cluttered" advertising media, which could affect viewer retention of the commercial message.

- Has a limited inventory of commercial openings, which could preclude the purchase of specific programs.

- Commands a high out-of-pocket cost for broad coverage.

- Is not as demographically selective as some other media forms (with the possible exception of cable TV).

- Audience size of given programs can fluctuate widely based on changes in counter-programming.

- Is relatively cost-inefficient for narrowly defined target groups.

- Is increasingly being recorded on VCRs for viewing after the original time of broadcast.

- Commercials can be "**zapped**" or **zipped**—fast-forwarded—if viewer watches program after it is recorded on a VCR.

Zapping Deliberate removal by a viewer of nonprogram material (e.g., a commercial) while recording on a VCR so as to play back program(s) without commercial interruption.

Zipping
Fast-forwarding through commercials and/or programs while playing back a VCR recording.

Chapter 27

Media Strategies

In this chapter we discuss the final analytical stage
of how to construct a media plan. We demonstrate
the kinds of analyses which can be conducted and the
thought processes you should undertake in deciding
which media vehicle or combinations of media are best
suited to achieve the media objectives. We focus on
six specific strategic areas: target audience, geography,
scheduling, reach/frequency, couponing, and testing.
Within these strategic areas we delve into methodologies
and systems used to decide how to allocate advertising
dollars or impressions to each geographic area, and how
to execute an in-market test utilizing advertising media.

Media strategies are the solutions to the media objectives.
Strategy statements reflect the specific course of action to be taken
with media:

- Which media will be used

- How often each will be used

- How much of each medium will be used

- During which periods of the year each medium will be used

Devising media strategy requires you have an in-depth knowledge
of media characteristics—how they work, how they are consumed,
how they can be used to generate a desired effect. You must
also have an understanding of the media marketplace—what the
availability and cost structure of each medium is at a given point

in time. If you decide primetime network television should be scheduled for April to achieve a particular objective, you must know if the television networks have unsold inventory for that month and, if so, what the cost of these commercial units might be.

A number of media alternatives are available to achieve media objectives. Your job is to find the medium, or combination of media, that will produce the best overall effect relative to your objectives. This requires extensive analysis.

The following are examples of how you might approach media analysis in order to accomplish several specific objectives. In all cases, the examples are illustrative of a particular situation and should not be construed as the only way to approach media analysis. Additionally, all examples restrict consideration to one or two audience segments and a few hypothetical media alternatives. Actual analysis of media alternatives would require far more extensive tabulating than presented in these examples. The examples shown evaluate each medium—not individual media vehicles (such as magazine B). You could just as easily substitute media *vehicles* in the examples, inasmuch as the concept and the arithmetic are the same.

Target Audience

Let us assume you have established an objective for a $1 million media plan that recognizes the relative importance of men and women in purchasing decisions for Product X:

Select media on the basis of a 40 percent/60 percent weighting for men and women respectively.

For ease of illustration, let us assume you have only one choice of a creative unit for each of the media forms—only 30-second spots for TV, only pages for magazines, etc. Additionally, let us also assume you have determined which of the media vehicles within each media type will be in the considered set, and that you have averaged the cost per advertising unit and the average audience delivery for each of these types, so that you can look at figures for the overall medium, as shown in Table 27.1.

The first step you might take is to analyze audience composition to determine how these media skew to men and women. Table 27.2

shows that A and E are probably not a good fit for the media objective; media B, C, and D are.

TABLE 27.1:   Basic Planning Input

| Medium | Cost/Unit | Average Audience Delivery (000) | | |
		Men	Women	Adults
A	$10,000	1,250	3,750	5,000
B	20,000	1,600	2,400	4,000
C	30,000	1,500	1,500	3,000
D	40,000	3,000	2,000	5,000
E	50,000	7,500	2,500	10,000

TABLE 27.2:   Audience Composition

Medium	Men	Women	Adults
A	25	75	100%
B	40	60	100
C	50	50	100
D	60	40	100
E	75	25	100

The second step might be to calculate total impression delivery within the $1 million budget. This can be done in several ways:

- Determine the number of units affordable and multiply by the audience delivery per unit; or

- Divide the budget by the respective CPMs; or

- Obtain adult impressions in either of the above two fashions, and allocate the total to men and women based on audience composition.

Table 27.3 indicates that medium A produces the most impressions and C the least.

TABLE 27.3:   Impressions—$1 Million Budget

Medium	Affordable # Units	Men	Women	Adults
			Millions of People	
A	100	125	375	500
B	50	80	120	200
C	33	50	50	100
D	25	75	50	125
E	20	150	50	200

Following an impression analysis, the logical next step might be to calculate cost-per-thousand. Table 27.4 shows that medium A has the lowest CPM and C the highest, which jibes with the previous impression analysis. As is always the case, the more impressions per dollar, the lower the CPM.

TABLE 27.4:   Cost-per-Thousand

Medium	Men	Women	Adults
A	$ 8.00	$ 2.67	$ 2.00
B	12.50	8.33	5.00
C	20.00	20.00	10.00
D	13.33	20.00	8.00
E	6.67	20.00	5.00

At this point it makes sense to specifically address the media objective of weighting men 40 percent and women 60 percent. Table 27.5 performs this calculation: men impressions times 40 percent plus women impressions times 60 percent equals adult "weighted" impressions. Media A still comes up the winner; C is still the lowest producer. If you stopped your analysis at this point, you would give preferential consideration to medium A, followed by B, E, D and C in that order. This means you would analyze many alternative plans, each of which would include a proportionately higher amount of medium A.

You might opt, however, to continue the basic analysis by also considering media *values*. These values can be based on anything

TABLE 27.5:   Weighted Impressions

| Medium | Millions of People | | Total |
	Men @ 40%	Women @ 60%	
A	50	225	275
B	32	72	104
C	20	30	50
D	30	30	60
E	60	30	90

you wish and are generally based on qualitative factors (which may or may not be backed by quantitative information), your judgment, or tangential quantitative information at your disposal. For example, you may elect to favor a medium that has these attributes (and thereby disfavor those that do not):

- A programming/editorial environment which is perceived to be compatible with the basic elements of the creative execution with which you are dealing;

- Ability to deliver sight, sound and motion;

- Ability to deliver high fidelity color;

- Ability to be seen/heard by the sales force during their workday;

- A track record of proven performance (relative to product X);

- Timing flexibility to buy late or cancel at the last minute;

- Ability to reach both men and women at the same time.

Suppose, therefore, that you made these judgment calls for each of the media types, giving those that met most or all of your evaluation criteria a value of 100 percent, those that met only a few criteria a value of 25 percent, and those in the middle, values of 50 percent or 75 percent. You could then apply these values to the weighted impressions generated by each media form to yield a "weighted/valued" impression delivery, against which you could calculate a CPM. This math is shown in Table 27.6. Here we see that medium B is top ranked.

TABLE 27.6:   Weighted and Valued Impressions

Medium	Weighted Impressions (millions)		Media Value		Valued Impressions (millions)	CPM
A	275	×	25	=	69	$14.49
B	104	×	75	=	78	12.82
C	50	×	100	=	50	20.00
D	60	×	100	=	60	16.67
E	90	×	50	=	45	22.22

Different analyses can yield different answers and thereby steer you in different directions. For example, shown in Table 27.7 are the priority choices you could have made for each of the previous analytical ingredients.

TABLE 27.7:   Ranking of Media

Analysis Ingredient	Rank				
	1st	2nd	3rd	4th	5th
Audience Composition	B	C	A	D	E
Adult Impressions	A	B	E	D	C
Adult CPM	A	E	B	D	C
Weighted Impressions	A	B	E	D	C
Weight/Valued Impressions	B	A	D	C	E

Clearly, an impression and CPM analysis is not the be-all-and-end-all. It is only one evaluation tool for helping you decide which media (or medium) could be in the considered set.

Geographic Objective

There are usually pronounced differences in a brand's sales, competitive pressures, category development, distribution patterns, and a host of other marketing variables from market to market. If it is assumed that advertising affects sales, the more advertising pressure in a market the greater the opportunity to build sales.

With a finite advertising budget, however, you certainly cannot just spend everywhere at high levels. One of your media objectives, therefore, might be to allocate media delivery to each market in the United States in proportion to sales (or some other marketing criterion). The strategy needed to execute this objective is to create geographic alignment between sales and media delivery.

Local Market Targets

The first step in accomplishing an alignment objective is to establish precise goals in each market. For example, you might decide to spend your advertising budget in direct relationship to sales—that is, have the same advertising/sales ratio in each market. Table 27.8 demonstrates this array for a hypothetical scenario encompassing five markets in the United States, sales of $10 million, and an advertising budget of $1 million. To calculate how much to spend in each market you can either multiply the percent of sales in each market by the total advertising budget, or you can apply the national A/S ratio to the sales in each market.

TABLE 27.8:   Equalizing the A/S Ratio

Market	Sales (000)	% Total	Advertising Budget (000)	A/S Ratio
A	$ 1,100	11%	$ 110	10%
B	1,500	15	150	10
C	1,800	18	180	10
D	3,000	30	300	10
E	2,600	26	260	10
Total	$10,000	100%	$1,000	10%

You might, however, decide to establish local market goals based on additional ingredients, such as category development (CDI) or judgment. Table 27.9 demonstrates the kind of analysis you might undertake. Here we see that market A accounts for 10 percent of the U.S. population and has a BDI of 110 and a CDI of 90. Your brand is therefore performing above average, and better than the category at large. Market E, however, is performing below average, but the category is doing very well—indicating that there is possible opportunity for increased sales. Market E also happens to be the largest of the five markets in terms of population. Your judgment might direct you to have the following spending strategy:

- Support all markets because all are important.

- Spend proportionately more in markets where the BDI is less than the CDI

- Spend proportionately less in markets where the BDI is less than the CDI

As shown in the table, you determined that market A should receive 8 percent of all media spending, market B, 12 percent, etc. The A/S ratio, therefore, varies by market—less than 10 percent in some, more than 10 percent in others.

TABLE 27.9:   Establishing Local Market Targets

Markets	% U.S. Population	% Brand Sales	% Category Sales	BDI	CDI	Target %	A/S Ratio
A	10%	11%	9%	110	90	8%	7.3%
B	15	15	15	100	100	12	8.0
C	20	18	22	90	110	20	11.1
D	25	30	14	120	56	25	8.3
E	30	26	40	87	133	35	13.5
Total	100%	100%	100%	100	100	100%	10.0%

Local Market Media Delivery

The easiest way to align spending with sales by market is to use only local media (spot TV, newspapers, etc.). Local budgets can therefore be translated into local media delivery by dividing the budget by the cost of media.

You might, however, decide to use a national medium in lieu of local media in all markets (for whatever media rationale you've divined). Local delivery of national media will not, however, correspond with your local target goals. All national media exhibit audience variation from market to market. For example, a national magazine might be more popular in some markets than in others, resulting in varying levels of circulation coverage by market. A network TV program, which might get a 10 national rating, will have ratings higher or lower than 10 by market, depending on the local viewing patterns. Therefore, if you purchase, for example, ten network TV programs and produce 200 GRPs nationally, you might get 180 GRPs in one market, 210 in another, and so forth. The chance that any national medium will distribute its audience delivery in direct proportion to the local market targets you establish is nil.

Table 27.10 displays this variation phenomenon for a hypothetical national media schedule encompassing 200 GRPs against a U.S. population base of 100 million people. This schedule will produce 200 million impressions overall. Market A will generate 18 million impressions based on the delivery of 180 GRPs against a population of 10 million. These 18 million impressions represent 9 percent of total U.S. impressions. If you intend to spend $1 million on this national schedule, you have proportionately invested 9 percent into market A—$90,000. If your national CPM is $5 ($1 million divided by 200 million impressions) you must assume that you are spending $5 against each 1000 people regardless of their geographic location —thus the $5 can be applied to the local market impressions to yield the same local market budget—that is, $90,000 in market A.

TABLE 27.10:   **National Media Impressions and Dollars by Local Market**

Market	U.S. Population (MM)	GRPs	Impressions (MM)	% Total	CPM	Equivalent Dollars (000)
A	10	180	18	9%	$5.00	$ 90
B	15	200	30	15	5.00	150
C	20	210	42	21	5.00	210
D	25	200	50	25	5.00	250
E	30	200	60	30	5.00	300
Total	100	200	200	100%	$5.00	$1,000

Dollar Allocation System

Once you have established local market targets, such as those presented in Table 27.9, you can use one of two methods to allocate national or local media to each market. One method is the *dollar allocation system*. This method apportions the total *dollar* spending of all media combined to each market relative to the target percentage. If market A is targeted to receive 8 percent of your national investment, then 8 percent of your total media budget should be spent in market A.

Table 27.11 continues the above example by comparing the local market spending equivalents of the national medium you have chosen to the local market spending targets. Market A is to receive 8 percent of your advertising budget—a total of $80,000. The selected national medium delivers the equivalent of $90,000 in market A, thereby producing an over-delivery of $10,000. Conversely, market E is receiving $50,000 less than targeted.

TABLE 27.11: Media Dollar Allocation—Only National Media

Market	Target %	Target (000)	National Media (000)	Difference (000)	Index
A	8	$ 80	$ 90	$10	113
B	12	120	150	30	125
C	20	200	210	10	105
D	25	250	250	—	100
E	35	350	300	(50)	86
	100%				
Total		$1,000	$1,000	—	100

If the goal is to align spending with established targets, you need to reduce the level of spending in national media and reinvest the difference into local media. Determining the proper balance between national and local can be done by a simple mathematical procedure:

Procedure	*Results*
1. Find the market with the greatest relative over-expenditure:	Market B—125 spending index
2. Determine the maximum budget for this market—i.e., the spending goal:	$120,000

3. Find the percent of national impressions accounted for by this market (from Table 27.10):   15%
4. Divide the budget ($120,000) by the impression percentage (15%) to yield the national budget: $800,000

With a total budget of $1 million and a national budget of $800,000, you now have $200,000 to invest (market by market) via local media. Table 27.12 demonstrates the procedures for establishing how much should be spent in local media in each market. For example, with a budget goal of $80,000 in market A and a prorated national budget of $72,000, you need to spend $8,000 locally so the total national plus local spending equals the goal. You'll note that market B, which was overspent when the entire budget was invested in national media, is allocated no money for use via local media.

TABLE 27.12: Media Dollar Allocation—National and Local Media

	Target		National	Local	Total	
Market	%	(000)	(000)	(000)	(000)	Index
A	8	80	$ 72	$ 8	$ 80	100
B	12	120	120	—	120	100
C	20	200	168	32	200	100
D	25	250	200	50	250	100
E	35	350	240	110	350	100
Total	100%	$1,000	$800	$200	$1,000	100

Once you've defined local media budgets you can proceed with determining which media will be used and how much of each can be used within the budget. For example, if you are using spot TV, all you need is the anticipated CPP (cost-per-point) for each local market to calculate total affordable GRPs. Let us assume that the four markets that are slated for local media in our example above will all receive spot TV. Let us also assume the following CPPs:

Market	CPP
A	$ 650
C	1,300
D	1,500
E	1,200

Table 27.13 compares the two plans we have discussed: Plan I, using all national media, and Plan II, using a combination of national and local media. Also shown is the spending target percentage by market. You'll see substantial differences between the plans from one market to another. Plan II, which incorporates "controllable" local media, allows you to produce more GRPs in the relatively important E market, albeit at the reduction of GRPs in other markets. Plan I produces GRPs by market relative to local viewing levels, not relative to the target percentage. You will also note that Plan II produces slightly more GRPs overall—202 versus 200. This is only a function of the local media chosen, which happen to have an average CPM slightly less than national media *in this example*. You will find in your actual real-world analyses that total national average GRPs (or impressions) will be less or more or the same for local media compared to national media based on which local or national media you choose.

TABLE 27.13:   Comparison of Plans—Local GRPs

		Plan I	Plan II		
	Spending	All National			
	Target	Media	National	Local	Total
Market	%	GRPs	GRPs	GRPs	GRPs
A	8%	180	144	12	156
B	12	200	160	—	160
C	30	210	168	25	193
D	25	200	160	33	193
E	35	200	160	92	252
Total/Average	100%	200	160	42	202
Budget (000)		$1,000	$800	$200	$1,000

Also in real-world analyses you should judge the numbers you've produced—don't be a slave to the findings. In the above table you'll note, for example, that market A is to receive 12 GRPs via spot TV. As we've seen from our discussions on average ratings and reach/frequency, 12 GRPs is not very much and will probably have only a minor effect on total advertising delivery—that is, on top of the 144 GRPs produced by national media in market A. If your analysis yields local market budgets or local market media delivery which you judge to be too small or ineffective, you would be wise to capture those funds and redistribute them into other markets.

Dollar Allocation/Impression Allocation

All of the above was based on allocating *dollars* to each local market. An alternative to a dollar allocation system is an impression allocation system. In this system, you calculate the estimated total impressions you believe you can purchase via a combination of national and local media, and allocate these to each local market based on your target goals. For example (as shown in Table 27.14), market A is to receive 8 percent of the total U.S. impressions of 200 million—16 million in total. National media deliver 14.4 million impressions (based on the GRP pattern displayed in an earlier table). Your goal, therefore, is to purchase 1.6 million impressions via local media to yield a total of 16 million impressions in the market. Market A has a local media CPM of $6.50. By multiplication (impressions × CPM) you can determine the local media budget—$10,400 for market A.

TABLE 27.14:   Media Impressions Allocation

Market	%	Target Impressions (000)	Impressions National (000)	Impressions Local (000)	Local CPM	Local Cost (000)
A	8%	160,000	14,400	1,600	$6.50	$ 10,400
B	12	24,000	24,000	—	—	—
C	20	40,000	33,600	6,400	6.50	41,600
D	25	50,000	40,000	10,000	6.00	60,000
E	35	70,000	48,000	22,000	4.00	88,000
Total	100%	200,000	160,000	40,000	—	$200,000

For demonstrative purposes, this example has been structured to yield the same total U.S. target impressions as shown in the previous Plan I (dollar allocation system). You will often find that the combined cost of the local media you need to purchase to fulfill your impression goals will exceed your local media budget. This results from lack of spending "control" by market. Spending in the impression allocation system is a result of multiplying the amount of media you need by the cost of media, without regard, per se, to the absolute CPP or CPM. In real-world analysis you will often have to adjust impression goals by market to afford the total number of impressions.

Dollar versus Impressions

The major differences between these two allocation systems can be summarized as follows:

Dollars

- Presupposes that *dollars* should be controlled without regard, per se, to media audience delivery

- Determines ad budgets in proportion to target percentages

- Produces a controlled A/S by market.

- Produces more impressions overall than the alternative system

Impressions

- Presupposes that consumers react to advertising delivery, not to dollars, per se

- Produces local impressions in proportion to target percentages

- A/S is a function of the cost of local media.

- Produces fewer impressions overall than the alternative system.

Table 27.15 demonstrates the difference between the two allocation systems using the same national/local media Plan II discussed above. You'll see some notable differences:

- Market E is allocated fewer GRPs in the impression allocation system—because of the need to purchase GRPs in other, higher CPM markets.

- National average GRPs are less for the impression allocation system than the dollar system.

TABLE 27.15:   Dollar versus Impression Allocation—Local Market GRP Delivery

	Dollar Allocation			Impression Allocation		
Market	National Media	Local Media	Total Media	National Media	Local Media	Total Media
A	144	12	156	144	16	160
B	160	—	160	160	—	160
C	168	25	193	168	32	200
D	160	33	193	150	40	200
E	160	92	252	160	63	223
Average	160	42	202	160	37	197
Budget (000)	$800	$200	$1,000	$800	$200	$1,000

Either of these allocation systems can be manually calculated, but they are obviously easier to effect using a computer. When these systems were first devised by the author and labeled *NASTEA* (Network And Spot TV Equalizing Allocator), all calculations were done on a desk calculator. Today, the same kind of system can be accessed from on-line media information suppliers.

Scheduling Objective

Every media plan should have a scheduling objective to guide the planner in allocating media across the year, even, conceivably, by day of the week and time of day. *When* advertising is delivered is often a critical issue. Advertising for suntan lotion should obviously be concentrated in those months when people need suntan lotion. Advertising for a product consumed to varying degrees throughout the year, however, presents a less obvious scheduling requirement. As stated earlier, you must conduct a complete investigation of the brand's needs vis-a-vis its competitive position and historical sales trends, and consider other important marketing input as well, so you can translate these considerations into actionable media objectives that will address the requirement for timing.

There are very few products or services that have a flat seasonal sales pattern—that is, where there is no discernible difference in sales from week to week. Because different products serve different consumer needs, and because consumer needs vary throughout the year, you generally find seasonal sales variations. Additionally, people exhibit different lifestyle patterns from one season to another, such as staying home more in the cold months and going out more in the warmer months. There are also different sales patterns exhibited by day of the week, again depending on consumer behavior. Table 27.16 shows the percentage of homemakers who do grocery shopping each day of the week. Not only do you see that many people shop more than one day a week (as evidenced by the fact that the percents sum to more than 100 percent), but also that they tend to shop more on the weekend than on weekdays. The pattern for male homemakers, however, is somewhat different. Recognizing these kinds of differences can lead you to define scheduling objectives that will allow you to deliver advertising when you believe it will have its greatest impact to stimulate consumers to take action.

TABLE 27.16: Days Shopped for Groceries

	Female	Male
Monday	21.5%	31.6%
Tuesday	25.5	21.4
Wednesday	20.8	19.9
Thursday	26.4	25.5
Friday	25.1	22.9
Saturday	32.2	29.0
Sunday	33.6	31.5

Source: Mediamark Research, Inc.

Hiatus A period of non-activity—the period between advertising flights.

Flighting The scheduling of advertising for a period of time, followed by a hiatus, then another "flight" of advertising.

Pulsing A flighting technique that calls for either a continuous base of support augmented by intermittent bursts of heavy pressure, or an on-again-off-again pattern (e.g., one week on, one week off).

Beyond the general timing consideration, you also need to think about the *pattern* of weekly audience delivery. You may have an objective, for example, that requires you to advertise at least to some extent during each calendar quarter. Thus you must decide whether to schedule *continuous* advertising covering every week, or, alternatively, to schedule bursts of advertising for selected weeks, each burst followed by a **hiatus**. This pattern is known as **flighting**. You might decide that some combination of continuous and flighting be effected via a pattern known as **pulsing**. Exhibit 27.1 illustrates these three techniques using a hypothetical schedule encompassing a total of 1,200 GRPs during the course of a 12-week period.

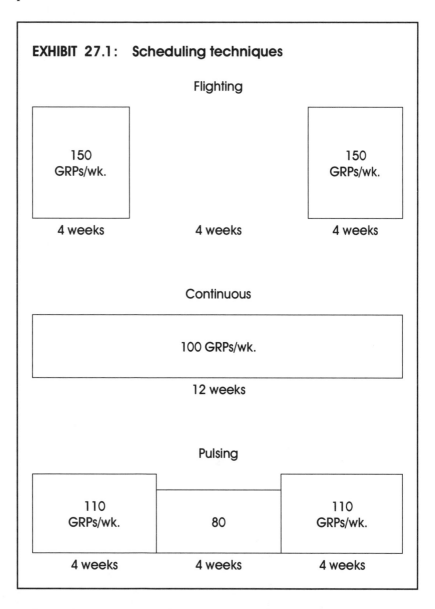

EXHIBIT 27.1: **Scheduling techniques**

Flighting

150 GRPs/wk.

4 weeks   4 weeks   4 weeks

Continuous

100 GRPs/wk.

12 weeks

Pulsing

110 GRPs/wk.   80   110 GRPs/wk.

4 weeks   4 weeks   4 weeks

Over the *long run*, audience accumulation of flighted and continuous schedules at equal rating levels is identical. All three schedules will accumulate the same number of GRPs; all three will reach the same number of people with equivalent average frequency; all three will distribute impressions among the different audience segments in about the same manner.

Over the short run, however, audience accumulation of flighted and continuous schedules will vary considerably. As shown in the frequency distribution in Table 27.17 (based on the first four weeks of the flighted and continuous schedules in Exhibit 27.1), the flighted schedule produces slightly higher total reach over a four-week period than the continuous schedule at the "1 or more" frequency level, but substantially more reach at the higher frequency levels. If you have established an "effective reach" level of at least four exposures, for example, then the flighted schedule has a distinct advantage in the short run: a reach of 66 versus 50.

Although much research has been conducted to answer the question of how much frequency is required to communicate the advertising message effectively, no study provides a definitive answer applicable to every situation. The hypotheses of all these studies (as we have somewhat reviewed in a previous section) are:

- There is a direct relationship between frequency of exposure during a given period of time and advertising effectiveness.

- There is a minimum rate of exposure (frequency) below which the sales motivation value is either unproductive or marginal.

TABLE 27.17:   Frequency distribution (four-week schedule).

Number of Exposures	Percent Reach		Reach Difference
	Continuous Schedule	Flighted Schedule	
1 or more	91%	95%	4
2 or more	78	86	8
3 or more	64	76	12
4 or more	50	66	16
5 or more	38	56	18
6 or more	28	47	19
7 or more	20	39	19
8 or more	14	31	17
9 or more	10	25	15
10 or more	6	20	14
Schedule:	100 GRPs/week	150 GRPs/week	

- There is a ceiling of frequency above which additional exposure is either unproductive or produces diminishing returns.

- There is decay in recall levels and established attitudes during hiatuses.

- Advertising effectiveness does *not* immediately cease when advertising is discontinued.

The dimensions of these factors may vary in accordance with the product's purchase cycle, stage of product maturity in the market, product category competitive environment as it relates to advertising pressure, creative execution, media selection, and media weights. If you believe the hypotheses to be correct and have considered these factors as they apply to the product for which you are writing a media plan, you can then be decisive in selecting a scheduling pattern.

Within any basic scheduling pattern you can also use several alternative methods for scheduling specific media that can produce any effect you wish. For example, if your media plan is composed of

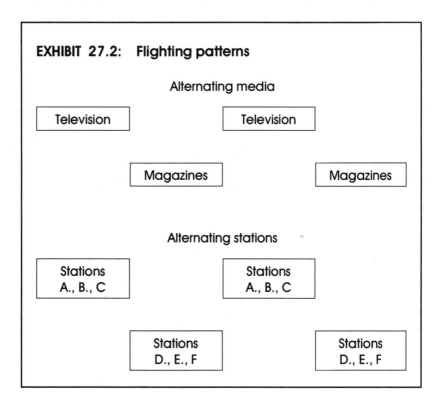

EXHIBIT 27.2: Flighting patterns

Alternating media

| Television | | Television |

| | Magazines | | Magazines |

Alternating stations

| Stations A., B., C | | Stations A., B., C |

| | Stations D., E., F | | Stations D., E., F |

two television dayparts, or both national and local media, or two different media forms, each of the components can be flighted in an alternating pattern. Additionally, different broadcast stations or different magazines or newspapers can be scheduled at different times to produce a flighted effect for a specific vehicle, while maintaining a continuous effect across the media form. See Exhibit 27.2.

Regardless of which scheduling pattern you use, keep in mind that the average consumer will not be aware of *how* you are producing advertising impressions, only that he or she is exposed to what you are doing. No consumer will say, for example: "Product X must be alternating newspaper advertising with TV advertising because I see one or the other in any given week, but never both together." Further, average consumers are not aware of *how much* advertising you are producing, only that they tend to hear or see or read more or less about your product depending on how much media you are scheduling. Lastly, keep in mind that advertising generally produces a cumulative effect, regardless of how you schedule it. The pattern of this accumulation will of course vary based on your scheduling pattern, but this is what media scheduling is all about—producing a cumulative effect over some defined period of time.

Reach/Frequency Objective

Assume an objective has been established to maximize reach of women with a minimum of four advertising exposures per month (once per week). For demonstration ease, let us assume that network television has been chosen as the only medium to be used. You are now faced with deciding between network TV dayparts, and if a combination of dayparts is to be used, what proportion of each should be used.

You could start the analysis by devising as many alternative schedules as are affordable within the given budget. Shown in Table 27.18 are six alternatives (though numerous alternatives are possible). The six plans are different in many ways, as the comparison in Table 27.19 shows. They produce different numbers of announcements, different women GRP levels, different cost efficiencies, and different total women reach and average frequency. The only thing in common among the plans is that they are all national in scope (network television), and each costs the same amount of money ($1 million).

TABLE 27.18: Alternative media plan considerations

	Percent of $1,000,000 Budget			
Plan	Primetime	Daytime	Late Evening	Early News
A	100	—	—	—
B	—	100	—	—
C	—	—	100	—
D	—	—	—	100
E	50	50	—	—
F	50	—	50	—

None of the above information, however, is useful in making a decision if the objective is *effective* reach (maximize reach of women with a minimum of four advertising exposures per month). The number of announcements is a function of the budget and the cost per commercial unit—it does not reveal anything about reach. Total women GRPs is informational and offers an indication of the gross delivery, but does not reveal facts about reach. Cost-per-thousand is useful for assessing the efficiency of one alternative versus another, but again, provides no information about reach. Total women reach/frequency, at first blush, might be used as the criterion for selecting one plan over another, but *average* frequency does

---

TABLE 27.19: Media plan comparison

Plan	Number of :30 Announcements	Total Women GRPs	CPM	Total Women Reach/Frequency
A	8	90	$9.41	60/1.5
B	50	250	3.42	55/4.6
C	38	114	7.52	30/3.8
D	15	121	7.05	51/2.4
E	28	170	5.02	59/2.9
F	23	102	8.36	53/1.9

---

not indicate the percentage of women who will be exposed to at least four advertising messages.

You have to take the analysis a step further by calculating a frequency distribution for each plan. Table 27.20, based on a frequency distribution for each plan, exhibits the percentage of women who will be exposed to at least four advertising messages.

TABLE 27.20:   Effective reach comparisons

Plan	Women Reach at 4.0+ Frequency Level
A	5
B	24
C	9
D	12
E	15
F	11

Based on the above, you would opt for plan B, composed of all daytime TV. This plan reaches more women who will be exposed to at least four advertising messages. If you had not done a frequency distribution you might choose plan A because it generates more total reach than the other plans.

Although this analysis seems very straightforward, you will seldom have the flexibility to select media vehicles on the basis of just one objective. In addition, all analyses are complicated by a number of other factors which have an effect on how the planner addresses each medium at any given time.

Costs, for example, fluctuate among network TV dayparts throughout the year based on supply and demand. For example, primetime network might be less cost efficient than late night network in one calendar quarter, and more cost efficient in another. The lower the cost-per-thousand, the more GRPs can be purchased within a set budget. The more GRPs that can be purchased, generally the higher the reach and/or frequency that can be produced.

Let us take the above exercise one step further and assume that "communication values" are part of the media analysis. If we assume, for example, that daytime's communication value is 75 percent that of primetime, we could make a totally different strategy decision based on an analysis of effective reach. If primetime GRPs are valued at 100 percent, and daytime GRPs at 75 percent, then the effective GRPs for Plan E are 139 (as opposed to 170 when each daypart is given full value). This calculation is shown in Table 27.21.

TABLE 27.21: Weighting Media by Communication Values

	Women GRPs	×	Value	=	Weighted Women GRPs
Primetime	45		100%		45
Daytime	125		75%		94
Total	170				139

If you calculate a frequency distribution based on the above weighted GRPs, the reach of women at the 4+ frequency level is 11. This is the same effective reach as generated by Plan F (50 percent prime and 50 percent late evening). If an evaluation of effective reach does not reveal major differences among plan alternatives, or if other objectives bear importantly on media usage, then you must use other criteria to decide which media are most appropriate for accomplishing the objectives of the plan.

Coupon Objective

If you have defined an objective to distribute a coupon via media, you will need to analyze alternatives in a somewhat different fashion than we previously discussed. Reach and frequency, for example, are not necessarily important; primary audience data become much more important than total audience.

There are different kinds of coupons (cents-off, free trial offer, premium offer, sweepstakes entry, etc.) which can be configured in different ways (on-page, tip-in, FSI). The type of coupon generally has little to do with how you will select media. The configuration, however, directly affects media selection:

- FSI (Free Standing Insert). One method of distributing a coupon is via an FSI, which can be preprinted in a variety of creative formats and inserted (but not bound) into newspapers, supps, and some magazines, or distributed via direct mail. If direct mail is used, you have choices between a co-op effort with other advertisers or a solo venture—the latter costing substantially more. As we discussed, direct mail efforts require a specialized understanding of this specific communication form, and analytical tools which are apart from those used for mass media. If you choose to use mass media, however, you will need to use the basic tools of circulation, audience delivery, cost, etc., to determine the best media vehicles.

Tip-in Card   An insert card in a magazine that is bound in with, or glued onto, the printed pages. Also called a *B*

- **Tip-in card**. This card-stock type of coupon, also referred to as a "pop-up coupon," is bound into a magazine or partially glued onto a magazine page. Magazines will generally limit the number of coupons accepted to one per signature break (consisting of 16 to 24 folded pages bound together to form a section). Some publications restrict the face value of a single coupon to the cost of their cover price, while some place a limit on the total cumulative value of insert coupons within a single issue. In nearly all cases, a tip-in requires the purchase of a back-up page on which the card will lie. Selecting magazines for a tip-in coupon (plus back-up) therefore requires that basic media evaluation be used.

- On-page. This refers to any coupon or offer that is literally printed on the page as part of the advertisement you place in selected print media. All print media accept on-page coupons. The evaluation process for selecting specific media vehicles for an on-page coupon includes many of the analysis tools used for any print advertising effort.

Whenever you conduct a media analysis to decide which vehicle(s) to select for coupon distribution, you need to look at circulation or primary audience data rather than total audience information. The reason is that the passalong reader may not have an opportunity to receive the coupon because the previous reader tore out or cut out the coupon. This is especially important for an on-page coupon, inasmuch as its extraction also mutilates the page and therefore the advertisement. Table 27.22 shows, for example, that primary readers have a proportionately higher incidence of cutting-out and using coupons in magazines; the incidence for secondary audiences is approximately half that of primary audiences.

TABLE 27.22: Cut-out/Used Coupons by Type of Magazine Audience

	Total Women Audience	Cut-out/Used Coupons	Index
Total Audience	100%	18%	100
Primary Audience	100	25	144
Secondary Audience	100	14	78

A tip-in coupon does not present this mutilation problem unless the entire advertisement is directing the reader to tear out the tip-in. If this is the case, then the backup ad is virtually useless without the tip-in card. The nature of the advertising message will help you decide if the ad lives for the coupon, or if it can remain an effective advertising communication after the coupon is removed.

The specific ingredients you choose for your print media analysis of a coupon effort are very much a result of your overall objectives, pertinent data at hand, and your judgment. If, for example, you need to cover a relatively small area, you will have to rely more on circulation data for magazines than on readership data—inasmuch as readership data within small geographic areas are generally not available for most magazines. If you have useful and pertinent data —such as coupon response rates for past efforts—this certainly should be part of your equation. You should also exercise judgment in deciding which kinds of information you will use and how you might value (or weight) each piece of information.

Table 27.23 demonstrates one possible analysis you might undertake.

TABLE 27.23: Magazine Analysis for Coupon Distribution

	Magazine A	Magazine B	Magazine C
Circulation (000)	8,000	5,000	4,000
Audience			
Total women (000)	24,000	21,000	20,000
Primary (000)	10,900	6,600	6,400
Secondary (000)	13,100	14,400	13,600
Cut/Used Coupons			
Total Audience (000)	3,700	3,700	4,800
Primary Audience (000)	2,350	1,525	2,000
Secondary Audience (000)	1,350	2,175	2,800
Weighted Audience* (000)	3,025	2,613	3,400

Cut/Used Coupons—Weighted Audience* Estimated Reach (000)

Magazine A + B	––––––––– 4,800 –––––––––
Magazine A + C	––––––––––––––– 5,600 –––––––––––––––
Magazine B + C	––––––––– 5,400 –––––––––

Cost/Unit	$120,000	$115,000	$100,000

CPM-Cut/Used Coupons

	Magazine A	Magazine B	Magazine C
Total Audience	$ 32.43	$ 31.08	$ 20.83
Primary Audience	$ 51.06	$ 75.41	$ 50.00
Weighted Audience*	$ 39.67	$ 44.01	$ 29.41
Magazine A + B	––––––––– $48.96 –––––––––
Magazine A + C	––––––––––––––– $39.29 –––––––––––––––
Magazine B + C	––––––––– $39.81 –––––––––

*100% of Primary plus 50% of Secondary

Let us assume you can afford to purchase only two of three magazines within your considered set. Your selection will vary depending on the evaluation criteria you use. The following lists the kinds of choices you might make:

Choice	Explanation/Rationale for Choice
A + B	You're concerned mostly with absolute distribution of coupons. These two magazines have the highest circulation.

A + B or C	You are also concerned with total women audience delivery. A has the most; B and C are very close.
C + A or B	You have data showing the number of readers who have cut out or used coupons, and you believe that your coupon will have an average chance of being cut out. Magazine C is the clear winner; A and B are tied.
A + C	You also have data showing how many *primary* readers have cut/used coupons. Believing that secondary readers will not have a significant opportunity to retrieve the coupon (because primary readers already cut it out), you decide A and C appear to offer the most audience.
C + A	You believe your advertisement will have some positive effect on readers even if the coupon has already been extracted. You therefore place a value on secondary audiences—half that of primary audiences. By adding 100 percent of the primary audience to 50 percent of the secondary audience you obtain a "weighted" audience.
A + C	You've calculated the estimated reach of pairs of magazines for women who cut/used coupons (using proprietary research of formulas, syndicated research, or an extrapolation of related reach estimates). Combination A + C delivers the greatest audience amount.
A + C or B + C	You are concerned with cost efficiency and your cost-per-thousand analysis indicates either of these combinations has a lower CPM than the A+B combination. The minor difference in CPM between these two combinations should be disregarded, given that the CPM is based on an estimated weighted audience, not necessarily on the absolute number of women who will see your ad and cut out the coupon.
A + B or A + C or B + C	These alternative choices are presented only to reinforce that all of the above choices were made solely on the basis of quantitative considerations.

Qualitative factors should also be included in your rationale: editorial environment of the publication and its relevancy to your advertising message, possible positioning advantages in one publication versus another, reproduction quality, advertising/editorial ratio, and so on.

Testing Objective

If you have read all preceding pages in this book you will have concluded not only that there is a great deal of information to help guide you in the media planning process, but also that there are very few, if any, definitive answers on which media are best for advertising your product, how much reach/frequency is optimal, how much should be spent on advertising, and so forth. With a relative paucity of the kind of information needed to make critical media decisions, you would be wise to incorporate some form of media testing into every media plan you create. Media/marketing tests should be conducted to gain knowledge so better decisions can be made in the future. All tests have two things in common:

- They help minimize the risk of incorrectly spending media funds.

- They are learning experiences from which we can extrapolate results for future use.

Among the more common types of tests are those for a new product prior to its national launch. Many advertisers hedge their bet before they embark on a broadscale national introduction of a new product or new version of an old product. A great deal of money is needed to properly launch a new product nationally—money for manufacturing, distribution, and advertising. To spend these funds without knowing the consumer reaction to the product—how much of it they will buy—is at best a financially unwise decision.

Additionally, there are a number of other tests that can be conducted, all of which can provide useful information. For example, you can test:

- Spending levels. Increasing or decreasing ad spending relative to the current level.

- Allocation strategy. Spending where the business *is* or where the business *is not*.

- Scheduling. Testing the effects of continuous advertising versus flighting, etc.

- Media mix. Using different media than currently used, either exclusively or in combination with current media.

- Creative configurations. Using 60-second spots versus 10-second or full pages versus half pages, etc.

- New media. Experimenting with any number of new media which have entered the scene.

Regardless of the test conducted, you need to concern yourself with a variety of factors such as devising the plan that will be tested, timing implications, selection of test markets and controls, and the methodology you will use to implement the test.

Devising the plan

You must keep in mind that whatever you are testing has implications for broader implementation. For example, if you are testing a 100 percent budget increase on a $5 million media plan, the *test* might cost $100,000, but the implication (assuming the test is successful) is to spend an additional $5 million nationally. It is therefore important that you first construct a national plan, and then test the proposition in one or more local markets. The geography of the national plan must reflect the geographic parameters of your product, that is, if the product is sold nationally, the geography will encompass the entire United States; if the product is sold only in certain regions or markets, then these regions or markets become your national universe.

Constructing a national test plan requires that you approach it as if it is the only plan, not an extension of your base plan. Some advertisers refer to this as *zero base*—starting from ground zero. The purpose of zero base thinking is to allow you to dismiss solutions to a previous problem in order to devise the best solutions for new problems. You might, for example, have used only one national medium in your base plan because you could not afford to purchase a meaningful level of activity in a second medium. At an increased budget level, however, you might be able to afford a second medium. Had you not used a zero base approach, you might have concluded that increased spending will automatically result in increased pressure within the first medium.

Timing

There are two aspects to timing that could have a substantial effect on your test implementation. The first deals with the length of time you will allow a test to run. If you are testing a direct response mechanism, you could obtain test results relatively quickly, so your test period need not be extended. If you are testing the effect of increased media or a different media mix on advertising awareness levels, you will need to run the test for an extended period of time. As we've discussed, people learn over time, with the learning curve accelerating as people are exposed to more and more advertising messages. Although the length of time needed for advertising awareness to peak is not known, there is a general consensus that the period is longer rather than shorter. Likewise, if you are testing for a product with an infrequent purchase cycle, you'd best run the test for a long enough time to cover several purchase decisions.

The second aspect of timing is to consider when the test, if successful, will be implemented nationally. You need to construct a national test plan for the period in which it will run, rather than for the period in which it will be tested. If a national plan is constructed for 1995 and tested in 1995, it might not be affordable in 1996 due to media price increases from one year to the next.

Test Markets and Controls

Selecting the proper test markets is critical. You need to concern yourself not only with how well they represent your national plan universe, but also with any potential aberrations that might affect test results.

First you must select test markets that are representative of the universe to which results will be projected. This representation includes demography, marketing phenomena, and media.

The test market(s) must reflect the general demographic characteristics of your national universe. If the test market displays an atypical skew to one or another demographic group, test results might not be indicative of what will happen in the entire universe.

Marketing phenomena, such as BDI and CDI, must also be assessed in your market selection. It stands to reason that if you test in a very high development market, test results will not be applicable to low development markets.

Because media vehicle availabilities vary by market, as do media consumption patterns, it makes sense to select markets that not only contain the media forms being used in your national plan but reflect the average national consumption pattern for those media. If you are testing a national plan that uses a high level of cable TV, for example, you need to select test markets that have an approximately average level of cable penetration.

Table 27.24 on the following page displays some basic data for three TV markets to demonstrate the differences you might find among various markets during your selection process. These three markets happen to be approximately the same size, each representing about 0.5 percent of U.S. TV households.

Conceivably, you could find one market that meets all of your criteria and therefore select it as the only test market. This is, however, a potentially risky proposition; any number of noncontrollable factors could adversely affect your test result. There could be an economic downturn in the market resulting from the closing of a major factory, or a natural disaster (such as an earthquake) that substantially alters buying patterns. If affordable, it is best to select two or more test markets. If one of these markets becomes "unreadable," results in the other(s) can still be read.

In addition to deciding how many markets, you need to consider the absolute population and/or business base in the test markets. Statistically, the larger the population base the more reliable will be your test results. If you are testing in markets that encompass far less than one percent of your national universe, test results could have a substantial margin of error (*sampling error*). Conversely, although more and bigger markets are best, you need to judge the out-of-pocket test cost relative to absolute reliability. Selecting test markets that represent ten percent of your national universe appears to be a safe bet, but such a large test would probably be inordinately expensive.

As test market selection is important, so too is deciding how you will *read* test results. This reading could be based on historical data on the performance of one or more "control" markets. If you assume that point A is your current national media plan, and point B your test plan, you need to evaluate what happens between points A and B—how much sales have increased, how high advertising

TABLE 27.24: Basic Data on Three Possible Test Markets

	Index to Average U.S.		
	Albuquerque – Santa Fe	Dayton	Albany – Schenectady – Troy
Population Composition:			
White	102	105	113
Hispanic	465	9	14
Black	13	83	26
Household Size:			
1 member	98	103	104
2 members	91	98	100
3 members	102	103	96
Education:			
High School Graduate	98	120	107
College Graduate	109	83	102
	Income and Sales per Household		
Effective Buying Income	$27,069	$32,508	$35,361
Food Store Sales	3,460	3,153	3,964
Retail Sales	15,851	16,787	21,149
	Television Dynamics		
% Cable Penetration	54	65	68
% Spill-in	9	17	12
% Spill-out	3	15	7
AQR Household Reach by Local			
Stations:	69	112	70
Daytime	66	54	40
Late Fringe			

Source: Nielsen-DMA Test Market Profiles

awareness levels have climbed, etc. To judge these differences you need to define point A and establish it as your *base* measurement. For example, if you currently have a 10 percent share of market, point A is a ten share. At the conclusion of the test period you will read your share of market and compare it to the base. If you are defining point A in terms of the current or historical situation in the test market, you do not necessarily need to monitor share trends in other test markets.

You may elect to define point A as the marketing situation in other markets. Then you will evaluate performance in the test markets compared to performance in other markets that received representative advertising as part of your base national plan. You might select these control markets because historical data are unavailable in the test markets, or because you believe that any market in the United States can increase its performance (sales, etc.) with or without any changes in media implementation. The selection of the control markets, therefore, must be based on the same rigorous analysis conducted for the selection of the test markets.

Translation Methodology

Once test markets have been decided you need to "translate" the national test plan into these markets, again being cognizant of their representation of media pressure as delineated in your national plan. There are two basic translation methods and several specific translation tactics that can be used.

Little America A method for simulating a test media plan in a test market.

Little America.   The **Little America** method simulates in test markets the advertising pressure that is generated by the national test plan in the *average* U.S. market. The goal of this simulation is to replicate as closely as possible the national test plan weight levels—GRPs or impressions or reach/frequency, etc. For example, if your test plan has 100 GRPs of network TV, you will ensure that the test market receives 100 GRPs regardless of the average viewing level of network TV in the test market (although if you have properly selected the test market the viewing level should be approximately average).

Determining national media pressure is simple: it's whatever the average national effort is—100 GRPs in network TV, or six advertisements in five magazines, or 100 announcements in network radio, etc. Simulating local media in your national test plan into a test market, however, requires some calculation. Shown in Table 27.25 are the GRPs of a national test plan, and the level of GRPs to be executed in the test market. National media, at a total of 500 GRPs, are purchased to the same level in the test market. Spot TV, which in the national test plan is scheduled in three markets, is *averaged for the average U.S. market*. Although the average spot TV market (60 percent of U.S. population) is receiving an average of 100 GRPs, the remaining 40 percent of the United States is receiving zero. The average U.S. market, which represents a "Little America," is therefore receiving an average of 60 GRPs (100 × 60% + 0 × 40% divided by 100% = 60). The test market therefore receives a total of 560 GRPs—500 to simulate national media and 60 to replicate spot TV.

TABLE 27.25: Test Translation Using "Little America" Method.

	% U.S. Population	GRPs National Test Plan	GRPs Little America Test Market
Network TV	100%	400	400
National Magazines	100	100	100
Spot TV:			
Market A	20	150	
Market B	20	100	
Market C	20	50	
Total	60		
Average Spot Market		100	
Average U.S. Market		60	60
Total—All Media:			
Within Spot Markets	60	600	
Remainder of U.S.	40	500	
Average U.S. Market	100	560	560

The Little America method is most commonly used for testing new products where there is no established history for performance, either nationally or in any particular market. It is also used for "soft" measurements which do not encompass absolute sales data, such as measuring recall of varying creative executions.

As It Falls A method for simulating a national test media plan in test markets.

As It Falls. In the **As It Falls** method, the test market receives the advertising pressure it normally would receive under the national test plan. As such, test market goals are unique for each market.

The first step in this translation method is to determine the local market delivery of all national media. A schedule of 100 network

TV GRPs might, for example, deliver 90 GRPs in test market A, 100 in test market B, etc.

The second step is to directly purchase in the test market the local weight it would receive if the national plan was implemented. Referring back to Table 27.25, if you choose Market A as a test market, you would purchase 150 spot TV rating points; Market B, 100; Market C, 50. If your test market is a part of the "remainder of United States," you would not purchase any spot TV to simulate spot TV in the national test plan.

The As It Falls method is commonly used for established products in established product categories where there is a track record of sales performance. However, because there are wide variations in media delivery by market for national media, and because national media plans do not always schedule local media in every U.S. market, selecting several test markets instead of one is the better course of action.

Within either testing method it is desirable to schedule local activity that closely resembles the national media being used. Following are some guidelines you should use whenever you purchase local media in test markets to simulate the media in your national test plan:

Translation Tactics

Television.   Use cut-ins whenever possible for network TV. You can use cut-ins to place the test commercial in the test market within the network program. The nationally scheduled commercial is cut-over (replaced) by the test commercial. This technique requires your brand, or another brand owned by the same advertiser, have network TV scheduled for the test period because you cannot take away (cut-over) advertising paid for by another advertiser. With this method, the viewer in the test market sees what she or he normally would see if the test plan were implemented nationally.

If cut-ins are not available, spot TV can be used to simulate the network TV weight. However, there are differences between spot TV and network TV in terms of audience composition, program type, placement of announcements (in-program in network versus between-program in some spot TV), and reach/frequency accumulation. It is therefore general practice to compensate for the differences by purchasing more GRPs in spot TV than would normally be scheduled via network TV.

Radio   Unlike the differences between network TV and spot TV, network radio and spot radio are virtually identical in terms of environment, commercial positioning, and reach/frequency accumulation. Therefore, network radio can be directly translated into spot radio. Further, there are no adjustments necessary for translating spot radio in the national plan to spot radio in the test market.

Print.   If local editions of the magazines used in the national plan are not available in the selected test markets, other magazines with similar editorial formats should be used. If magazines are not available in the test markets, newspaper supplements can be used as the first alternative, and newspapers as the second alternative.

Although neither supplements nor newspapers have the same editorial environment or readership pattern as magazines, it is best to use these media rather than using totally unrelated media or not using any print media at all. It is important, however, to analyze the delivery of the local print vehicles relative to the national print media to ensure that there are not wide variations in coverage.

Outdoor/Transit   As both are local media forms, both can be translated directly.

Overall Generalities

Regardless of what you are testing—which media, how much of each, budget levels, etc.—your test plan must have a great deal of integrity. You should avoid compromise if at all possible; translate every component of your national test plan, no matter how small. Keep in mind that you are attempting to anticipate in a local test market what will actually happen when the national plan is implemented. This requires you to carefully and precisely simulate the national test plan activity, using the same number and kinds of television programs, the same number and kinds of radio stations and formats, the same number and kinds of print vehicles, etc.

Chapter 28

Media Flow Chart

I n this chapter we provide several examples of how
media activity is shown within a media plan.

Flow chart A
summary of
recommended media
showing their usage
throughout an
advertising period; e.g.,
an annual flow chart.

When all calculations, evaluations, analyses, considerations, and
judgments are completed—when you come to the point of having
selected specific media and having defined how much of each you
want to use and when you want to use them, you can produce the
fruits of your labor on one piece of paper: the media **flow chart**.

This piece of paper is appropriately named because it illustrates
the flow of how you intend to schedule the chosen media. The
following pages (Exhibits 28.1, 28.2, and 28.3) show some examples
of what flow charts can look like. They can be exceedingly brief and
highlight only the most important information (as in an "executive
summary"), or they can contain lots of pertinent data. Their creation
and look are totally a function of what you *need* to display. The idea
in creating a flow chart is to show information clearly so any reader
can quickly and correctly understand which media are going to be
used, how they might be used, and when they are being used.

EXHIBIT 28.1 : Product X Magazine Activity

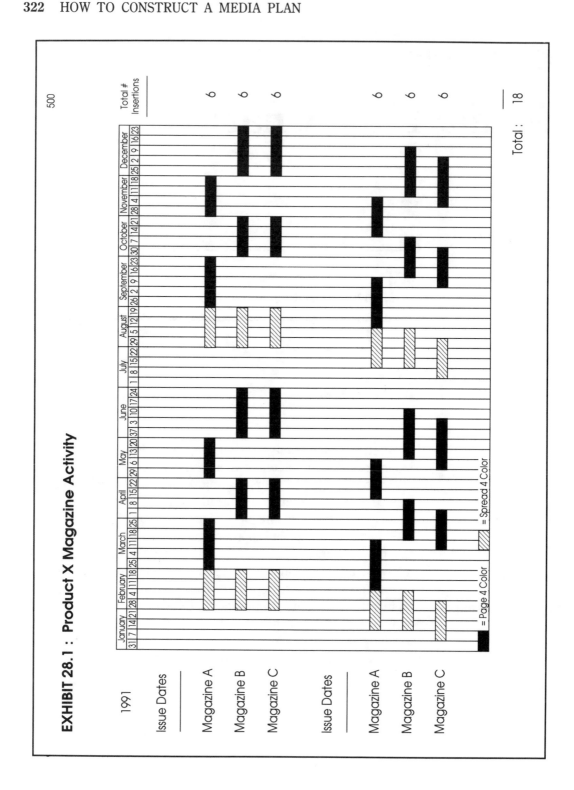

EXHIBIT 28.2 : Product X Television Activity

1991	January 31 7 14 21	February 28 4 11 18 25	March 4 11 18 25	April 1 8 15 22 29	May 6 13 20 27	June 3 10 17 24	July 1 8 15 22 29	August 5 12 19 26	September 2 9 16 23	October 30 7 14 21 28	November 4 11 18 25	December 2 9 16 23	W18-34 TRPS	Budget
Network TV														
(National Activities)														
Prime		100 100 100						100 100 100					800	$
Day		50 50	50 50	50 50	50 50	50 50		50 50	50 50	50 50	50 50	50 50	2,100	$
Late Evening			25 25	25 25	25 25	25 25		25 25	25 25	25 25	25 25	25 25	850	$
Sport TV														
Top 3 Brand Markets		100 100 100 100	100 100 100 100	100 100 100 100	100 100 100 100	100 100 100 100		100 100 100 100	100 100 100 100	100 100 100 100	100 100 100 100	100 100 100 100	4,200	$
Markets 4-10		50 50 50	50 50	50 50	50 50	50 50		50 50	50 50	50 50	50 50	50 50	2,100	$
Budget		$	$	$	$	$	$	$	$	$	$			$

EXHIBIT 28.3 : Product X Market A

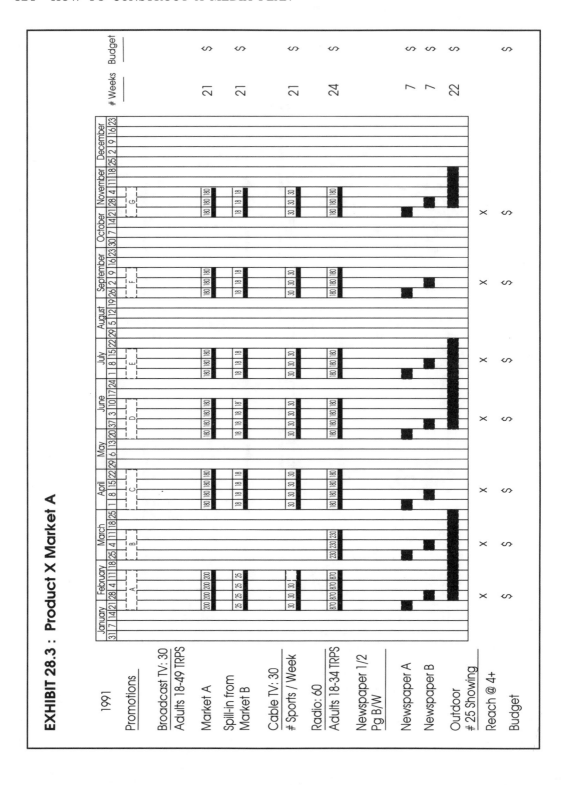

Chapter 29

Principles of Media Management

I n this chapter we punctuate that media planning requires much more than manipulating numbers. We also set forth 10 principles of media management.

It should be apparent that media planning requires much more than simple decisions to select one or another medium. A complete understanding of how media deliver their audiences and thorough analyses of media selection alternatives, combined with a sprinkling of intelligence, logic, judgment, and creativity, are mandatory before astute media decisions can be made. Although much of this "input" is based on numbers, you should always be mindful that numbers don't think . . . *you* do.

Too often numbers are used as a crutch—as the primary rationale for selecting one medium over another or one television spot rather than another. Be wary of myopic reliance on numbers. Know all that goes into generating the numbers, all the varying research techniques used, and all the pitfalls and dangers surrounding the numbers. Know this and you will appreciate why numbers are no more than a guide—not the rule—in the decision-making process.

By all means use computer technology to help you deal with the storehouse of marketing and media information, and to help you analyze multiple alternatives across multiple evaluation criteria. But don't get trapped into thinking that what the computer spits out is gospel. Don't run your fingers down the columns of data on a printout and shout "Eureka!" Realize the computer is no more than a sophisticated calculator. Had you indeed used a simple calculator for your analyses, you would come to appreciate where the input came from, how it was conjured, and how you generated the answers you obtained.

There are now more media outlets than ever. While new ones are ever emerging, old ones are reshaping. Marketing and media research is also changing and becoming more complete and more complex. Media costs will continue to be volatile. There's an ocean of information with which you need to deal to select media, and this ocean is constantly churning. Not only do you need to get your sea legs by becoming expert at media, you also will need to become the captain and navigator of media selection. You should never settle for being a swabbie.

Here are ten principles* you should keep in mind whether you are setting out to write a full media plan, or just deciding if you should place a commercial in program A or program B.

1. You are in partnership with all others who are deciding the advertising plan. A media plan is an extension of the marketing plan and must reflect the overall marketing and creative strategy. Your plan cannot exist in a vacuum and be effective.

2. Media management is money management. Media recommendations are an investment in an advertiser's business. By making the savviest media decisions, you gain the greatest return on that investment.

3. Involvement with all media is a primary requisite. Specializing in one medium, to the exclusion of others, breeds narrow thinking. Try to consider all the options. Never look for the expeditious solution simply to save time.

4. Numbers don't think—people do. Numbers are a big part of a media planner's day-to-day activities. But don't rely solely on them to make your decisions or argue your case. Use your emotions, your gut, your instinct.

5. Cost efficiency is important, but not at the cost of advertising effectiveness. You must make sure your customers *see* and *hear* the advertising you are placing—even if it costs a few pennies more in one medium than in another.

---

* The above ten principles were originally written by the author as a Media Department Credo while he was employed by J. Walter Thompson.

6. Maintenance is as important as building. It is not enough simply to create a media plan. All plans must be monitored after they are implemented to ensure that broadcast schedules are followed, positioning in print media is optimal, and reproduction is acceptable.

7. Everyone should be kept informed. Endeavor to keep your partners informed about media issues and changing dynamics. The more everyone knows, the better their understanding and appreciation of your media recommendations.

8. Keep your door open to media suppliers. Media salespeople often know more about their specific medium than you, as a media planner, will ever know. They can be a storehouse of pertinent information that will help you make better media decisions. Be candid with them and keep them abreast of your needs.

9. Contribute beyond media planning. As a media planner, your greatest contribution will be in media planning and buying. But you should not be inhibited about recommending marketing, creative, promotional, or new product ideas that can build an advertiser's business.

10. Have some fun. Work hard and get ahead. Do superb work. But don't forget that you are doing media planning, not brain surgery.

Glossary

A.A.A.A. American Association of Advertising Agencies, commonly called the "4–A's."

Ad/edit ratio The ratio of advertising to editorial pages in a print medium. E.g., 60/40 indicates 60 percent of all pages are advertising.

ADI (Area of Dominant Influence) Arbitron Company's definition of a TV market.

Adjacency A commercial time period that is scheduled immediately preceding or following a scheduled program on the same station in which a spot TV commercial can be placed. Opposite of an in-program placement. Also called a *break position*.

Advertorial A print advertisement which is styled to resemble the editorial format and type face of the publication in which it runs. Most publishers require advertorials to be labeled "advertisement" at the top. Also refers to *Infomercial*.

Affidavit A notarized statement from a broadcast station that confirms the commercial actually ran at the time shown on the station's invoice.

Affiliate A broadcast station bound to a contractual relationship with one or more networks to carry network-originated programs and commercial announcements. See also *O & O*.

Afternoon Drive A radio daypart—usually 3:00–7:00 p.m.

Agate Line A newspaper space measurement that is one column wide by 1/14 inch high (14 agate lines to the inch). Replaced as an advertising measurement tool by S.A.U.

Agency-of-record (AOR) An advertising agency or independent media buying company that purchases media on behalf of another agency or group of agencies serving the same advertiser. Sometimes also refers to a full-service advertising agency that performs all the services for a particular advertiser.

Allotments The number of outdoor panels in a showing; varies by market.

AM (Amplitude Modulation) The transmission of sound in radio broadcasting in which the amplitude (power) of a transmitting wave is modulated (changed) to simulate the original sound.

ANA Association of National Advertisers.

Announcement An advertising message in broadcast media, commonly 10, 15, 30, or 60 seconds in length. Synonymous with "commercial" and usually referred to as a "spot."

AQH The average quarter-hour rating for broadcast programs as reported by several media research suppliers (e.g., A.C. Nielsen).

Arbitron Company A media research supplier.

Area of Dominant Influence See ADI.

Arrears   As reported by the ABC, these are magazine copies sent to subscribers up to three months after subscription expiration. Also known as "post-expiration copies."

As It Falls   A method for simulating a national test media plan into test markets.

Audience Accumulation   The total net number of people (or homes) exposed to a medium during its duration; e.g., a half-hour broadcast program, a magazine issue.

Audience Composition   The demographic profile of media audiences.

Audience Turnover   The average ratio of cumulative audience listening/viewing to the average audience listening/viewing.

Audit Bureau of Circulation (ABC)   An organization formed by media suppliers, advertisers, and advertising agencies to audit the circulation statements of its member newspapers and magazines.

Availability   The commercial position in a program or between programs on a given station or network that is available for purchase by an advertiser. "Avails" for short.

Average Audience (AA)   In broadcast, the number of homes (or individuals) tuned to the average minute of a program. In print media, the number of individuals who looked into an average issue of a publication and are considered "readers."

Backlit   Describes an out-of-home display where the advertising message is printed on translucent plastic and backlit with fluorescent bulbs.

BAR (Broadcast Advertiser Reports)   A media research supplier concentrating on the reporting of television commercial purchases.

Barter   The exchange of goods and services without the use of cash. Usually the acquisition of media time or space in exchange for merchandise.

Basic Cable   The offering to subscribers of broadcast and cable TV originated programs as part of a "basic" service agreement in which a subscriber pays a cable TV operator or system a monthly fee. Does not include "pay" services which might be offered by the cable operator.

Billboard   In broadcast, free airtime given to an advertiser, usually to one that purchases multiple commercials within a program (i.e., a "sponsor" of the program). In outdoor media, an advertising structure —see *Painted Bulletin*.

Bind-in Card   An insert card in a magazine that is bound in with the printed pages. Also called a *Tip-in*.

Birch   A media research supplier.

Black & White Page   An advertising page that is printed with black on white paper, or in reverse type (white on black paper). Abbreviated as P B/W.

Bleed   In print media, to extend the illustration or copy to the edge of a page so there is no white border. In outdoor media, a poster panel that uses the entire available space.

Blow-in Card   A loose insert in a magazine, used primarily by the publication to sell subscriptions.

BPA   Business Publications Audit of circulation.

Brand Development Index (BDI) A numerical display showing the geographic or demographic areas of a brand's relative strength or weakness. See *Index*.

Break Position A commercial aired between programs as opposed to in-program. Also called *Adjacency*.

Broadcast Coverage Area The geographic area within which a signal from an originating station can be received.

Broadsheet Synonymous with a "standard" size newspaper, as compared to a "tabloid" size.

Bulk Discount The discount offered to advertisers who place large orders in magazines.

Bus Shelter/Bus Bench Advertising posters positioned as an integral part of a freestanding covered structure or bench, often located at a bus stop.

CAB Cable Advertising Bureau.

Cable TV Reception of TV signals via cable (wires) rather than over the air (i.e., via a TV antenna).

Car Card An advertising unit within a transit vehicle, such as a bus.

Cash Discount A discount granted by the media supplier to an advertiser for payment within a certain period of time—e.g., a 2 percent discount if payment is made within ten days of invoice.

Category Development Index (CDI) A numerical display showing the geographic or demographic areas of a product/service category's relative strength or weakness. See *Index*.

Centerspread The facing pages in the exact center of a magazine.

Chain Break The time between network programs when a network-affiliated station identifies itself to viewers and during which commercial announcements air. Also see *Break*.

Circulation In print media, the number of copies sold or distributed by a publication. In broadcast, the number of homes owning a TV/radio set within a station's coverage area. Or, in cable TV, the number of households that subscribe to the cable services that carry a given network. In out-of-home media, the number of people passing an advertisement who have an opportunity to see it.

City Zone The area bounded by the corporate limits of a community.

Clearance The broadcast stations carrying a network or syndicated program. This list is usually accompanied by a "coverage" percentage indicating the percent of U.S. TV homes in markets in which the program airs.

Closing Date The deadline set by a publication for the receipt of material (*keyline* or *mechanical*) for an advertisement to appear in a forthcoming issue.

ClusterPLUS A geodemographic clustering system.

Combination Rate A special rate for advertisers using both morning and evening editions of a newspaper which has two editions, or for an advertiser using more than one vehicle in a group of publications. Related to, but different from, "multimedia" buys.

Competitive (Report) The compilation of figures on media spending and/or media usage by products/services competitive to the advertised brand/service.

Consolidated Metro Area As defined by the U.S. Government's Office of Management and Budget, a grouping of closely related metro areas.

Continuity Discount A rate discount allowed an advertiser who purchases a specific schedule within a series of a publication's issues. Also called *Frequency Discount*.

Controlled Circulation The circulation of a publication that is sent free and addressed to specified individuals.

Conversion Factor A percentage applied to a number (e.g., a household rating) to obtain a different number (e.g., a women 18–34 rating).

Cost-per-Rating-Point (CPP) The cost of an advertising unit (e.g., a 30-second commercial) divided by the average rating of a specific demographic group (e.g., women 18–49).

Cost-per-Thousand (CPM) The cost per 1,000 people (or homes) delivered by a medium or media schedule.

County Size Designation of all U.S. counties into one of four categories as defined by A. C. Nielsen based on population density and labor force concentration. Commonly referred to as "A," "B," "C" and "D" counties.

Coverage The percentage of a population group covered by a medium. Commonly used with print media to describe their average issue audience within defined demographic or purchasing groups. Akin to a *rating*.

Cover Position The usually premium-priced cover space in a magazine. The second cover is the inside front; the third cover is the inside back; the fourth cover is the outside back.

Cume (Cumulative) Rating The reach of a radio or TV program or station, as opposed to the "average" rating.

Cut-in The insertion of a commercial, at the local level, which replaces the nationally purchased (and airing) commercial originally placed in a network broadcast program. Generally used to test media and/or alternative commercial executions.

Daily Effective Circulation (DEC) The gross number of people (without regard to duplication) exposed to an out-of-home advertising display in one day.

Dayparts Broadcast time periods (segments), e.g., daytime: 10:00 a.m. to 4:00 p.m. EST.

Delayed Broadcast (DB) The term given to a network TV program that is delayed for airing in a given market at a different time than the time it airs nationally.

Demographic Editions Special editions of magazines directed to specific audience types.

Demography The study of the characteristics of population groups in terms of size, distribution, and vital statistics.

Designated Market Area (DMA) A. C. Nielsen's definition of a TV market.

Diorama A backlit display often located in airports, bus terminals, and sports arenas.

Double Truck The facing pages in the exact center of a newspaper section where the copy runs across the margin without interruption.

Downlink Part of a satellite transmission in which signals are sent from the satellite to earth.

Drive Time The morning and afternoon hours of radio broadcasting—morning drive: 6:00–10:00 a.m.; afternoon drive: 3:00–7:00 p.m.

Dub (Dupe) Making one or more copies of an audio or video recording.

Duplication The number or percentage of a medium's audience, or of those reached with a media schedule, who are exposed to more than one media vehicle or to more than one advertising message.

Early Fringe The TV daypart between Daytime and Prime Access: generally 4:00–7:30 p.m. EST.

Early Morning A television daypart—usually 6:00–10:00 a.m. EST. Also sometimes referred to as "Breakfast."

Effective Frequency The level of exposure frequency at which reach is deemed "effectively" delivered. See *Effective Reach*.

Effective Reach The number of percentage or a population group reached by a media schedule at a given level of frequency.

Efficiency Generally refers to the relative costs of delivering media audiences. See *Cost-per-rating-point* and *Cost-per-thousand*.

8-Sheet Poster A 5' by 11' poster panel, also known as a *Junior Panel* because it has the same proportions as, but is smaller than, a 30-sheet poster.

Exclusive Cume Listeners The number of different people who listen to a given radio station and to no other radio station during a specific daypart.

Exposure A person's physical contact (visual and/or audio) with an advertising medium or message.

Facing In outdoor advertising, the direction a poster faces. E.g., a south facing can be seen by northbound traffic.

Fiber Optics Thin glass fibers used for transmitting information—e.g. audio/video from a central source to a person's TV set.

Fixed Position In broadcast, a commercial unit purchased with non-preemption guarantees. In print, a position guaranteed to the advertiser within a specific section and/or adjacent to specific editorial.

Flagging In outdoor posters, a tear in the paper causing the advertisement to hang loose and "flag" in the wind.

Flat Rate The nondiscountable rate charged by a newspaper for advertising.

Flighting The scheduling of advertising for a period of time, followed by a hiatus, then another "flight" of advertising.

Flow chart A summary of recommended media showing their usage throughout an advertising period, e.g., an annual flow chart.

FM (Frequency Modulation) A clear radio signal, without static or fading, that results from the adjustment of the frequency of the transmitting wave to the originating sound.

Four-Color Page An advertising page that utilizes three colors (and/or combinations of these colors) plus black and white. Abbreviated as P4–C.

Frequency The number of times people (or homes) are exposed to an advertising message, an advertising campaign, or a specific media vehicle. Also, the period of issuance of a publication, e.g., daily, monthly.

Frequency Discount A rate discount allowed an advertiser who purchases a specific schedule within a specific period of time, e.g., six ads within one year.

Frequency Distribution The array of reach according to the level of frequency delivered to each group.

Free Standing Insert (FSI) A preprinted advertising message which is inserted into, but not bound into, print media (generally into newspapers).

Fringe Time See *Early Fringe, Late Fringe*.

Gatefold A folded advertising page which, when unfolded, is bigger in dimension than the regular page.

Geodemography The demographic description of people living in specific geographic areas.

Gross Impressions See *Impressions*.

Gross Rating Points (GRPs) The sum of all ratings delivered by a given list of media vehicles. Although synonymous with *TRPs*, GRPs generally refer to a "house-hold" base. In out-of-home media, GRPs are synonymous with a *Showing*.

Hiatus A period of non-activity—the period between advertising flights.

Hi-Fi (High Fidelity) Advertising on a continuous roll of paper that is fed into and becomes a preprinted insert in a newspaper. The completed advertisement, usually run on a heavier-than-newspaper stock and in full color, resembles a wallpaper pattern.

Homes Using TV (HUT) The percentage of homes using (tuned in to) TV at a particular time.

Identification (ID) A 10-second TV commercial (10 seconds visual and 8 seconds audio).

Impressions The gross sum of all media exposures (numbers of people or homes) without regard to duplication.

Independent Station A broadcast station not affiliated with a network.

Index A number indicating change in magnitude relative to the magnitude of some other number (the base) taken as representing 100. A 110 index indicates a 10 percent positive change in magnitude; a 90 index a 10 percent negative change.

Infomercial (Informercial) A long-form broadcast commercial which provides much more information than can be supplied in a typical, say, 30- or 60-second commercial. Also called *Advertorial*.

In-Home Readers People who read a magazine or newspaper in their own home.

Insertion Order The form or document sent to a publication that contains information relating to an ad's placement—i.e., its size, rate, frequency, date, etc.

Integration Cost The payment charged by a broadcast network to "integrate" a commercial announcement into a program.

Interactive Cable A two-way communications system which allows the cable TV viewer to respond (interact) to what is being telecast via an electronic device (e.g., a remote control).

Interconnect Two or more cable systems which are linked together to air commercials simultaneously (if possible). A "hard" or "true" interconnect is linked by cable or microwave. A "soft" interconnect is a group of systems with an agreement to insert commercials into programs or time periods.

IOA Institute of Outdoor Advertising.

Issue Life The length of time it takes a magazine to be read by the maximum measurable audience.

Junior Panel A scaled-down version of a 30-sheet poster.

Keyline See *Mechanical*.

Late Fringe A TV daypart that follows Primetime, usually 11:00 p.m.–1:00 a.m. EST. (or later).

Lead-in/Lead-out A program preceding/following the time period of the program being analyzed.

Lifestyle Pertains to the nondemographic characteristics of people in describing their behavior (e.g., recreational habits). See *Psychographics*.

Line Network Now called TV network; was based on transmission of TV signals over telephone lines from one station to the next.

Line-up The listing of stations carrying a radio or TV program.

Little America A method for simulating a test media plan in a test market.

LNA (Leading National Advertisers) A media research supplier reporting on advertising volume by medium by advertiser brand or service.

Makegood In broadcast, a commercial position offered in lieu of an announcement which was (or will be) missed due to either station error, preemption by another advertiser, or movement of the program purchased from one time slot to another. In print, the free repeat of an advertisement to compensate for the publication's error in the original insertion.

Mean The sum of all items divided by the number of items. Commonly called "average." See also *Median, Mode*.

Median The middle number in a sequence of numbers. See also *Mean, Mode*.

Mechanical A camera-ready pasteup of artwork—includes type, photography, and artwork or line art, all on one piece of artboard. Also known as a *Keyline*.

Mediamark Research, Inc. (MRI) A media research supplier.

Media Mix The use of two or more media forms, e.g., TV and magazines or radio, outdoor, and newspapers.

Merchandising Promotional activities that complement advertising and which are provided free or at a nominal charge by media purchased for advertising.

Metro Area   A geographic area defined by the U.S. Government's Office of Management and Budget. Also called a Standard Metropolitan Statistical Area (SMSA).

Mode   The number occurring most frequently in a sequence of numbers. See *Mean, Median.*

Monroe Mendelsohn   A media research supplier.

Morning Drive   A radio daypart, generally 6:00–10:00 a.m.

MPA   Magazine Publishers Association.

Multimedia Buys   The purchase of advertising in more than one medium owned by a media supplier, or by media suppliers who have a cooperative agreement. Multimedia buys can encompass multiple media vehicles within a media form (e.g., several magazines) or different media forms (e.g., magazines and TV).

Multiple System Operator (MSO)   A company that owns more than one cable system.

NAB   National Association of Broadcasters. Also, Newspaper Advertising Bureau.

Newsstand Circulation   Copies of a publication which are sold and purchased at outlets (such as newsstands) selling single copies.

Network   A broadcast entity that provides programming and sells commercial time in programs aired nationally via affiliated and/or licensed local stations—e.g., ABC television network, ESPN cable network, Mutual radio network.

Nielsen, A. C.   A media research supplier.

OAAA   Outdoor Advertising Association of America.

Objectives, Media   The statement(s) of action required of media to fulfill marketing needs.

O & O   A station Owned and Operated by a broadcast network.

Open Rate   The maximum rate charged by a magazine or newspaper; its rate for one insertion.

Outdoor Visibility Rating System (OVRS)   A system of grading a poster panel's "visibility."

Out-of-Home Media   Those media meant to be consumed only outside of one's home, e.g., outdoor, transit, in-store media.

Out-of-Home Readers   People who read a magazine someplace other than in their own home.

OTS (Opportunity To See)   A term commonly used in Europe indicating the amount of "frequency" a media audience receives in a media schedule.

Paid Circulation   Reported by the ABC, a classification of subscriptions or purchases of a magazine or newspaper, based upon payment in accordance with standards set by the ABC.

Painted Bulletin (Paint)   An outdoor advertising structure on which advertising is either painted directly or preprinted on special vinyl and affixed.

Panel   Generally a "poster" panel—one outdoor or transit advertising unit.

Participation A commercial that appears in-program, as opposed to between programs during a "break."

Passalong Readers Readers of a publication who are not primary readers. Also called *Secondary Readers*.

Pay Cable Programs and/or services provided to basic cable subscribers for an additional fee (e.g., HBO).

Pay-per-View A telecast, usually of a special event, for which subscribers pay a one-time fee to view.

Penetration The percentage of people (or homes) within a defined universe that are physically able to be exposed to a medium.

Perfect Binding The process of binding that uses glue rather than staples or stitching and results in a square spine.

Permanent (Display or Bulletin) An outdoor bulletin at a specific location—that is, the bulletin is not rotated to other locations. See *Rotary Display*.

PIB (Publishers Information Bureau) A media research supplier reporting on print advertising volume (vehicle, space, cost) by advertiser brand or service.

Plant The total number of outdoor structures under a single ownership in a city.

Plant Operator The owner of an outdoor advertising company in a certain city or area.

Pod A grouping of commercials and nonprogram material in which (usually) more than one advertiser's commercials air. Also referred to as a "commercial interruption" or "commercial break," but airing in-program.

Point-of-Purchase Display (POP) An advertising display at the place where consumers purchase goods or services (e.g., counter card at a retail outlet).

Porta-Panel A mobile poster panel that is wheeled to a given location (e.g., a supermarket parking lot).

Post Analysis An analysis of a media schedule after it runs—generally based on physical evidence of its running (broadcast station affidavit of performance, magazine tearsheets, etc.) and incorporating audience delivery estimates in effect at the time the schedule ran.

Poster Panel An outdoor advertising structure on which a preprinted advertisement is displayed.

Post-Expiration Copies See *Arrears*.

Preemption The displacement of a regularly scheduled program or commercial announcement, on a broadcast facility, by the station or network.

Preferred Position The opposite of ROP, these print advertisements are scheduled in specific positions as agreed by the advertiser and the publication. They sometimes command a premium price.

Primary Market Area A geographic area defined by a newspaper in which the publisher believes the newspaper has its greatest strength.

Primary Readers Readers who purchased a magazine or who are members of a household where the publication is purchased.

Prime Access A TV daypart immediately preceding primetime in which local stations were originally charged by the FCC to broadcast programs in the interest of the local community, but which now contains various local or syndicated programs. Generally, the half hour from 7:00 to 7:30 p.m. or 7:30 to 8:00 p.m. EST.

Primetime   In broadcast, the general reference is to that time period which attracts the most viewers or listeners. Specifically, in TV, generally 8:00–11:00 p.m. EST. Monday through Saturday and 7:30–11:00 p.m. EST. Sunday; in radio, generally 6:00–10:00 a.m. (a.k.a. Morning Drive) and 3:00–7:00 p.m. (a.k.a. Afternoon Drive).

PRIZM   A geodemographic clustering system.

PSA   A Public Service Announcement on TV or radio.

Psychographics   Pertains to the identification of personality characteristics and attitudes that affect a person's lifestyle and purchasing behavior.

Pulsing   A flighting technique that calls for either a continuous base of support augmented by intermittent bursts of heavy pressure, or an on-off-on-off pattern (e.g., one week on, one week off).

PUR   The percentage of people using radio at a particular time.

PUT   The percentage of People Using TV at a particular time. Identical to *PVT*, People Viewing TV.

Quintile Distribution   A display of frequency (or related data) among audiences grouped into equal fifths of reach.

RAB   Radio Advertising Bureau.

RADAR   Radio All Dimension Audience Research report issued by Statistical Research, Inc.

Random Combination   A mathematical formula for estimating the reach of two or more media.

Rate Base   The circulation of a print vehicle upon which advertising space rates are based; it may or may not be guaranteed by the publisher.

Rate Holder   A unit of space or time, usually small, that is used to maintain or establish a contractual agreement over a period of time.

Rating   The percentage of a given population group consuming a medium at a particular moment. Generally used for broadcast media, but can be used for any medium. One rating point equals one percent.

Reach   The number or percentage of a population group exposed to a media schedule within a given period of time.

Readers-per-Copy (RPC)   The number of individuals who read a given copy of a publication.

Rebate   A payment to the advertiser by a medium when the advertising schedule exceeds the contractual commitments originally agreed to and the advertising schedule earns a lower rate.

Recent Reading   A research technique to determine the average issue audience of print media. Used, for example, by MRI.

Repaint   Executing of an advertiser's painted bulletin copy subsequent to the original painting.

Retail Trading Zone A geographic area around a central city.

Riding the Boards A physical inspection in the field of the poster panel or bulletins that comprise a showing.

Roadblock A scheduling device used with broadcast media to increase reach at a given point in time (e.g., scheduling a commercial on all local market stations at 9:00 p.m.).

ROI (Return On Investment) Generally refers to the advertiser's desire to have a return on the advertising funds invested in media.

Roll-Out A marketing procedure where advertising is progressively expanded into more geographic areas over time.

ROP Run-of-Press or Run-of-Paper. A position request to run an advertisement anywhere (unspecified) in the publication. Also commonly used to describe any form of newspaper advertising.

ROS Run-of-Station. A tactic used in broadcast media whereby commercials are scheduled throughout the day and night at the discretion of the station or network, as opposed to time periods designated by the advertiser.

Rotary Display An option for purchasing painted bulletins whereby the display face is periodically rotated to new locations, as opposed to a *Permanent Bulletin*.

Saddle Stitched The binding process whereby a publication is held together by staples through the middle of the fold—like *Time* or *Newsweek*.

Sampling Error The possible deviation in the reported finding of media audience research based on a sample from what might be the actual finding had a complete census been done. Usually reported as "±" the reported number.

Satellite Station A broadcast station that rebroadcasts the transmission of another station (generally operating in a nearby market) to an area that cannot otherwise be serviced by that station.

S.A.U. (Standard Advertising Unit) A measurement system for selecting and placing ad sizes in newspapers.

Scarborough A media research supplier.

Scatter Purchasing commercial time in broadcast media in many different programs. Also refers to the purchasing of network TV time which is not purchased during an "upfront" media buy.

Secondary Readers See *Passalong* readers.

Sets in Use Antiquated and replaced by *HUT*. Referred to the number of TV sets in use (turned on) at a given time.

Share "Share of audience" is the percentage of HUT (or PUT, PUR, PVT) tuned to a particular program or station. "Share of market" is the percentage of total category volume (dollars, units, etc.) accounted for by a brand. "Share of voice" is the percentage of advertising impressions generated by all brands in a category accounted for by a particular brand, but often also refers to share of media spending.

Sheets A way of designating poster panel size based on number of pieces of paper originally needed to cover a poster panel area—it used to take 30 sheets to cover the average panel.

Short Rate In print media, the dollar penalty an advertiser pays for not fulfilling space requirements that were contracted for at the beginning of a given period, usually one year. The penalty is the difference in rate between the contracted rate and the actual earned rate.

Showing Gross rating points within out-of-home media, or number of posters displayed in transit media.

Signature The name given to a printed sheet of a magazine after it comes off the press and has been folded into eight, sixteen, or thirty-two pages.

Simmons Market Research Bureau (SMRB) A media research supplier.

Simulcast To broadcast simultaneously by AM and FM radio or by radio and television.

Single-copy Sales Denotes newsstand sales of a publication.

Single Source Data The reporting of data based on the product/service purchase patterns and media consumption habits from a single source (i.e., an individual or family).

SMSA Standard Metropolitan Statistical Area. See *Metro Area*.

Spectacolor An advertising insert in newspaper, similar to Hi-Fi, but trimmed at the correct place.

Spill-In/Spill-Out Spill-in is viewing of television broadcast from a different market (e.g., people in San Diego viewing Los Angeles stations). Spill-out is viewing outside the originating TV market (e.g., Los Angeles stations delivering audiences in San Diego).

Split Run A scheduling technique whereby two different pieces of copy are run in the circulation of a publication with no one reader receiving both advertisements. This can be accomplished via a geographic split, a demographic split (if the publication offers demographic editions), a subscription/ newsstand sales split, or an every-other-copy split (commonly called an "A/B" split).

Sponsorship The purchase of more than one commercial within a program, allowing advertisers to receive bonus time via billboards, or exclusivity of advertising within the brand's product category, or both.

Spot Refers to the purchase of TV or radio commercial time on a market-by-market basis as opposed to network (national) purchases. Also commonly used in lieu of "commercial announcement."

SRC (Strategy Research Corporation) A media research supplier concentrating on the Hispanic market.

SRDS Standard Rate & Data Service—publications which list data (e.g. costs, circulation) for all media vehicles that accept advertising.

Standard Error See *Sampling Error*.

Starch Inra Hooper A media research supplier.

Starch Scores Print media measurement showing the performance of individual magazine advertisements among readers. Three scores are reported: *Noted*—the percentage that remember having previously seen the ad in the issue being studied; *Associated*—the percentage that saw any part of the ad that clearly indicates the brand or advertiser; *Read Most*—the percentage that read at least half of the written material in the advertisement.

Strategies, Media   The media solution(s) used to fulfill the media objective(s).

Superstation   An independent TV station whose signal is transmitted throughout the United States via satellite. Technically refers only to WTBS, but is also used for other stations.

Sweep   The period when local market TV ratings are studied. Originally coined to represent the time when Nielsen would "sweep" the country to obtain ratings in all markets. Sweeps are now issued four times a year in all markets and more frequently in top markets.

Syndication   In broadcast, a program carried on selected stations which may or may not air at the same time in all markets. In newspapers, an independently written column or feature carried by many newspapers (e.g., Dear Abby). In magazines, a centrally written/published section carried by newspapers, generally in the Sunday edition (e.g., *Parade*).

Tabloid   A newspaper with pages smaller than the size of a standard "broadsheet" newspaper.

Tertile Distribution   A display of frequency (or related data) among audiences grouped into equal thirds of reach.

Test Market   A market (or markets) chosen for the purpose of conducting a media test.

30-Sheet Poster   A 10' by 22' poster panel.

Through-the-Book   A research technique used to determine the average issue audi-

ence of print media. Used, for example, by SMRB.

'Til Forbid   Instructions by an advertiser to run a purchased schedule or advertisement(s) until notified to stop.

Tip-in Card   An insert card in a magazine that is bound in with, or glued on to, the printed pages. Also called a Bind-in.

Tolerance   See *Sampling Error*.

Total Survey Area (TSA)   The geographic area in which radio signals from an originating market can be received.

Traffic Audit Bureau of Media Measurement   A nonprofit organization that audits outdoor advertising structures, as well as other out-of-home media, for circulation and number of people reached.

TRPs (Target Rating Points)   Essentially synonymous with GRPs.

TVB   Television Bureau of Advertising.

TV Market   An unduplicated television area to which a U.S. county is assigned based on the highest share of viewing to originating TV stations.

24-Sheet Poster   A 12' by 25' poster panel. A 24-sheet poster has the same structure size as a 30-sheet poster panel, but with less printed area.

UHF (Ultra High Frequency)   The band added to the VHF band for television transmission—channels 14–83 on a TV set.

Unwired Network   Applicable to either radio or TV, the purchase of preselected local stations not connected by wire or satellite, through a sales organization representing the stations.

Uplink Part of a satellite transmission in which signals are sent from earth to a satellite.

Upfront A method for purchasing TV commercial time well in advance of the telecast time of the programs and generally for a protracted period, such as for a one-year schedule. A relatively common practice among many advertisers for the purchase of primetime TV as well as other TV dayparts and entities (e.g., daytime network, cable TV, syndication).

Universe The total population within a defined demographic, psychographic, or product consumption segment against which media audiences are calculated to determine ratings, coverage, reach, etc.

VALS 2 A research study developed by SRI International which describes eight distinct population groups according to their Values and Lifestyles.

Verified Verified Audit of Circulation Corporation. Also, to prove the truth of something by the presentation of evidence.

VHF (Very High Frequency) TV channels 2–13.

Viewers per 1,000 Households The number of people within a specific population group tuned to a TV program in each 1,000 viewing households.

Volume Discount The price discount offered advertisers who purchase a certain amount of volume from the medium—e.g., pages or dollar amount in magazines.

Wearout A level of frequency, or a point in time, when an advertising message loses its ability to effectively communicate. See other definitions within chapter of book on "Effective Reach."

Weighted Average Generally refers to the arithmetic average obtained by adding the products of numbers "weighted" by a predetermined value.

Zapping Deliberate removal by a viewer of nonprogram material (e.g., a commercial) while recording on a VCR so as to play back program(s) without commercial interruptions.

Zipping Fast-forwarding through commercials and/or programs while playing back a VCR recording.

Formulas

AUDIENCE COMPOSITION (Pg. 91)

$$\frac{\text{Aud. of Demo Cell (e.g. 18–49)}}{\text{Total Aud. (e.g. 2+)}} = \text{Comp.}$$

BDI (Pg. 88)

$$\frac{\text{Market} \times \text{\% Brand Sales}}{\text{Market} \times \text{\% Population}} = \text{BDI}$$

$$\frac{\text{Market} \times \text{Share of Market}}{\text{U.S. Avg. Share of Market}} = \text{BDI}$$

CDI (Pg. 88)

$$\frac{\text{Market} \times \text{\% Category Sales}}{\text{Market} \times \text{\% Population}} = \text{CDI}$$

COST-PER-POINT (Pg. 99)

$$\frac{\text{Cost per Unit (e.g. :30)}}{\text{Rating Per Unit}} = \text{CPP}$$

COST-PER-THOUSAND (Pg. 95)

$$\frac{\text{Cost}}{\text{Audience}} \times 1000 = \text{CPM}$$

$$\frac{\text{Cost}}{\text{Audience (in thousands)}} = \text{CPM}$$

CONVERTING CPP TO CPM (Pg. 104)

$$\frac{\text{CPP} \times 100}{\text{Market Pop. (in thousands)}} = \text{CPM}$$

CONVERTING CPM TO CPP (Pg. 104)

$$\frac{\text{Market Pop. (in thousands)} \times \text{CPM}}{100} = \text{CPP}$$

Example

$$\frac{1,000}{10,000} = 10\%$$

$$\frac{60\%}{50\%} = 120 \text{ (decimal deleted)}$$

$$\frac{12}{10} = 120 \text{ (decimal deleted)}$$

$$\frac{40\%}{60\%} = 67 \text{ (decimal deleted)}$$

$$\frac{\$1,000}{10} = \$100$$

$$\frac{\$1,000}{200,000} \times 1,000 = \$5.00$$

$$\frac{\$1,000}{200} = \$5.00$$

$$\frac{\$100 \times 100}{2,000} = \$5.00$$

$$\frac{2,000 \times \$5.00}{100} = \$100$$

CONVERTING NET COST TO GROSS COST

$$\frac{1}{\text{Net \% Cost} \div 100} = \text{Gross \% cost}$$

$$\frac{1}{85\% \div 100} = 1.1765$$

COVERAGE/RATING (Pg. 51)

$$\frac{\text{Aud. of Demo Cell (e.g. 18–49)}}{\text{Pop. Universe of same demo cell}} = \text{Cov.}$$

$$\frac{1,000,000}{10,000,000} = 10.0\%$$

GRPs/TRPs (Pg. 133)

Reach × Frequency = GRPs

\# Anncts (or ads) × Avg. Rtg. = GRPs

Example

$80 \times 5.0 = 400$

$10 \times 5.0 = 50$

IMPRESSIONS (Pg. 91)

$$\frac{\text{GRPs}}{100} \times \text{Pop. Base} = \text{Imp.}$$

\# Occasions × Audience = Imp

$$\frac{500}{100} \times 100,000 = 500,000$$

$5 \times 10,000 = 50,000$

INDEX (Pg. 85)

$$\frac{\text{Variable}}{\text{Base}} = \text{Index}$$

$$\frac{60\%}{40\%} = 150 \text{ (decimal deleted)}$$

MEAN, MEDIAN, MODE (Pg. 130)

Series: 50
       25
       15
        5
        5

Mean: $\dfrac{100}{5} = 20$

Median: 15 (middle number)
Mode: 5 (most often number)

ONLY-ONLY-BOTH REACH (Pg. 120)

To Solve for Only A:
Reach A + B – Reach of B

$80 - 60 = 20$

To Solve for Only B:
Reach A + B – Reach of A

$80 - 50 = 30$

To Solve for Both A + B:
    Reach A + B
– Only Reach A + Only Reach B
    Reach of Both A + B

    80
– (20 + 30)
    30

CONVERTING FRACTIONS, DECIMALS TO PERCENTAGES

$$\frac{\text{Numerator}}{\text{Denominator}} = \text{Decimal}$$

$$\frac{1}{8} = .125$$

$$\text{Decimal} \times 100 = \text{Percentage}$$

$$.125 \times 100 = 12.5\%$$

RANDOMLY COMBINING REACH OF TWO MEDIA (Pg. 117)

$$\begin{aligned}&100 \\ &\underline{- (100 - \text{Reach A}) \, (100 - \text{Reach B}) \, (.01)} \\ &= \text{Reach A} + \text{B}\end{aligned}$$

$$\begin{aligned}&100 \\ &\underline{- (100 - 60) \, (100 - 50) \, (.01)} \\ &= \qquad 80\end{aligned}$$

RATING-HUT-SHARE (Pg. 68)

Example

Solve for Rating:
Hut × Share = Rating

$$80 \times 50 = 40$$

Solve for Share:

$$\frac{\text{Rating}}{\text{HUT}} = \text{Share}$$

$$\frac{40}{80} = .50$$

Solve for HUT:

$$\frac{\text{Rating}}{\text{Share}} = \text{HUT}$$

$$\frac{40}{50} = .80$$

Solve for non-reported audience segment
(e.g. 35–49)

$$\frac{\text{Aud. } 18\text{–}49 - \text{Aud. } 18\text{–}34}{\text{Pop. } 18\text{–}49 - \text{Pop. } 18\text{–}34} = \text{Rtg } 35\text{–}49$$

$$\frac{600 - 200}{3000 - 2000} = .40$$

REACH-FREQUENCY-GRPs (Pg. 148)

Reach × Frequency = GRPs

$$80 \times 5.0 = 400$$

Solve for Reach:

$$\frac{\text{GRPs}}{\text{Frequency}} = \text{Reach}$$

$$\frac{400}{5.0} = 80$$

Solve for Frequency:

$$\frac{\text{GRPs}}{\text{Reach}} = \text{Frequency}$$

$$\frac{400}{80} = 5.0$$

READERS-PER-COPY (Pg. 204)

$$\frac{\text{Total Audience}}{\text{Circulation}} = \text{RPC}$$

$$\frac{20,000,000}{5,000,000} = 4$$

Circ. × RPC = Total Audience

$5,000,000 \times 4 = 20,000,000$

WEIGHTED AVERAGE (Pg. 307)

$$\frac{(A \times \#) + (B \times \#)}{A + B} = \text{Average}$$

Mkt A 20% U.S. HH × 100 GRPs
+   Mkt B 10% U.S. HH × 400 GRPs
÷   30% U.S. HH
=   200 GRPs

Index

About the Author

In his career Jim Surmanek has worked for a major magazine and some of the world's largest advertising agencies.

Upon graduation from high school he got a job in the mailroom at *Parade*. Adept at organizing mail, he was given the opportunity to organize research facts and figures. This tenure in the research department laid the groundwork for his eventual entry into an ad agency.

He has worked in various cities and in multiple capacities for a wide range of advertisers. He had the great fortune of first joining an agency run by David Ogilvy in the days when Mr. Ogilvy was actively teaching his staff about advertising. That was in New York, where the author worked in media research, media buying, media planning, and account management.

He later ventured to Chicago, where he concentrated on media, and after that to Mexico City, where he became involved in marketing, market research, and creative development.

Returning to the United States in the early 1980s, he took up residence in Los Angeles and expanded his knowledge of the advertising process through his direct involvement in all things media as well as direct marketing, finance, new business development, and general agency management.

He has lectured extensively at *Advertising Age* media workshops, *Marketing & Media Decisions* media workshops, American Association of Advertising Agencies seminars, colleges, universities, and various advertising clubs and trade associations. He has published a number of articles in trade media and has written two previous books and coauthored a college textbook on the subject of advertising media.

Mr. Surmanek is currently on the Board of Governors of Verified Audit Circulation and the Editorial Board of *The Journal of Media Planning*, and is a Certified Radio Marketing Consultant and a member of American Mensa.

TITLES OF INTEREST IN
ADVERTISING, SALES PROMOTION, AND PUBLIC RELATIONS

For further information or a current catalog, write:
NTC Business Books
a division of *NTC Publishing Group*
4255 West Touhy Avenue
Lincolnwood, Illinois 60646-1975 U.S.A.

✓